PUBLIKATIONEN
DER BAYERISCHEN AMERIKA-AKADEMIE
Band 19

PUBLICATIONS
OF THE BAVARIAN AMERICAN ACADEMY
Volume 19

SERIES EDITORS
Bavarian American Academy

NOTE ON THE EDITORS

Barbara Hahn is Professor and Chair of Economic Geography
at the University of Wuerzburg
and a member of the Bavarian American Academy.

Kerstin Schmidt is Professor and Chair of American Studies
at the Catholic University of Eichstaett-Ingolstadt
and a board member of the Bavarian American Academy.

Inequality in America

Interdisciplinary Perspectives

Edited by
BARBARA HAHN
KERSTIN SCHMIDT

in collaboration with
JASMIN FALK

Universitätsverlag
WINTER
Heidelberg

Bibliografische Information der Deutschen Nationalbibliothek

Die Deutsche Nationalbibliothek verzeichnet diese Publikation in der Deutschen Nationalbibliografie; detaillierte bibliografische Daten sind im Internet über *http://dnb.d-nb.de* abrufbar.

COVER PICTURE

© www.wordle.net / Jasmin Falk

ISBN 978-3-8253-6789-3

Imprimé en Allemagne · Printed in Germany
Druck: Memminger MedienCentrum, 87700 Memmingen

Gedruckt auf umweltfreundlichem, chlorfrei gebleichtem und alterungsbeständigem Papier.

Den Verlag erreichen Sie im Internet unter:
www.winter-verlag.de

Table of Contents

Inequality in America: An Introduction

Barbara Hahn and Kerstin Schmidt

Inequality has become a burning issue in contemporary culture and society, especially with regard to political and economic considerations. In a notable speech on inequality, the French lawyer Christine Lagarde, managing director of the International Monetary Fund (IMF), matter-of-factly stated that "reducing excessive inequality is not just morally and politically correct, but it is good economics" (226). To some, this statement may have a tinge of the unexpected, but Lagarde focuses firmly on global concerns, especially those of the poorer countries, regardless of frequently raised criticism that the IMF allegedly favors more well-off states. Lagarde starts off her high-profile lecture with a joke, often told by Wall Street bankers: A visitor to New York City admires the beautiful yachts owned by bankers and brokers, and after gazing on them for a while, he wonders where the customers' yachts might be? They, of course, couldn't afford the gorgeous high-end vessels, even if they had followed the financial advice by their bankers (see 227). The IMF director takes the metaphor of the boat as her point of departure and discusses in her speech why what she calls the 'small boats' of society have not been kept afloat. What she means by this is that poor and middle-class households, the 'small boats,' have painfully realized that no matter how hard they work, they do not fare well in today's economy. By bringing up a plethora of examples from all over the world, Lagarde strongly advocates more equitable growth which, she argues, would prove to be both more durable, more sustainable, and more inclusive (227). Apart from economic and political measures to help the 'small boats,' "education, education, education" is her prime structural tool to reduce excessive income inequality, and equal access to education may also prove to be a most effective strategy to create a more equal society in all respects, not just with regard to income (231).

While the IMF director discusses her ideas and assumptions with regard to case studies from Brazil, Peru, the Netherlands, South-East Asian shores, North Africa, or the Mediterranean, she is convinced that inequality needs to be addressed above all else on the state-level, i.e. within individual nations. And yet, due to outsourcing and off-shore economic practices, among others, it is mandatory to take a global perspective on inequality at the same time as social debates cannot be limited to national borders. Worldwide, inequality between individual countries as well as within countries has been rising, especially economic inequality, while the United States may well be among the most unequal countries in the Western hemisphere. The reason for as well as the development and the implications of inequality have been discussed widely over the last decades. Two of the most prominent economists analyzing inequality are the Nobel laureates Joseph E.

Stiglitz and Paul Krugman. In his book *The Price of Inequality: How Today's Divided Society Endangers Our Future*, Stiglitz, professor at the Business School of Columbia University and former chair of the Council of Economic Advisers during Bill Clinton's presidency, contends that inequality is not only the result of economic forces but mainly of government policies. Krugman, professor of Economics at the Graduate Center of the City University of New York, argues along similar lines. In addition to having written more than 20 academic books and over 200 scholarly articles, Krugman is a *New York Times* columnist and a regular contributor to the newspaper's opinion page. He has added crucial articles to the debate on inequality, such as "Is Vast Inequality Necessary?" or "Inequality and the City;" his *New York Times* blog called "The Conscience of a Liberal" also offers perceptive views on "Explaining US Inequality Exceptionalism" (4 May 2015) or "Pure Class Warfare, With Extra Contempt" (23 June 2017). Needless to say, not all Americans agree with Paul Krugman's or Joseph E. Stiglitz' more liberal positions on the reasons for a rapidly growing, and hence troublesome degree of inequality (cf. Cochrane).

Income distribution is the most common indicator for measuring inequality. In the United States, income inequality declined during the 1930s and 1940s (Koechlin 453). From 1945 to the 1970s, the United States and Western Europe experienced solid economic and wage growth for most of their citizens (Irvin 156). From the 1970s onwards, wages of the working population in the United States decreased as an effect of deindustrialization and weakening trade unions whereas income in many service industries grew disproportionally. Due to the rise of neoliberalism, this trend accelerated in the 1980s during the presidencies of Ronald Reagan in the United States and Margaret Thatcher in Great Britain. The policy of privatization, deregulation of the financial sector, the introduction of flexible labor markets, and the reduction of social services aggravated the situation for common workers and reduced their chances of upward mobility, while the income of well-educated university graduates skyrocketed. This gap has widened since the 1990s as a consequence of the outsourcing of industries and the growing segmentation of the value chain. At the same time, jobs in the service industry were increasingly divided into well-paid financial and judicial services on the one hand and low-paid jobs on the other hand. Globalization seriously hampered job security for many Americans; concomitantly, the distribution of wealth and power became more unequal (Irvin 155-59). However, globalization did effect all countries, not just the United States, and most countries also experienced profound technological changes, but not all countries display the same high degree of inequality. Thus, one may conclude that American politicians have made wrong choices, and that inequality may even have been created purposefully, as Colin Gordon shows in his contribution to this volume.

In the United States, real wages did hardly rise for low-paid service workers over the last few decades, and even though many Americans work three jobs to make ends meet, they still belong to the working poor. On the other end of the spectrum, salaries in the so-called new economy and in the financial sector grew tremendously. It is hence no surprise that the rich became much richer, according to the list of the 400 richest Americans that *Forbes Magazine* publishes annually. In 2016, the richest American (Bill Gates) had a net worth of $81 billion and even the 'poorest' of the 400 still had a net worth of $1.7 billion. Thirty years ago, in 1986, only 26 Americans owned over $1 billion in assets and the richest individual owned 'only' $4.5 billion (Bonavich 81; *Forbes Magazine*). In this volume, Colin Gordon points out that inequality has grown more in the United States than elsewhere because wage growth has been flat for generations. If one takes into account non-wage income like returns on investment or capital gains as well as the gender gap and regional differences in wages, the gap in income and wealth is even more staggering. Gordon refers to this phenomenon as "exceptional inequality."

Economic inequality is exacerbated by racial considerations. Historically, African Americans were at the bottom of society, and the presidency of Barack Obama did not fundamentally change this fact. Even though the situation for African Americans is similar to those of, e.g., Hispanic immigrants in many respects, blacks have hardly been able to move up the socio-economic ladder. Upward mobility in the United States seems very constrained in the first place, as the American Dream has been fading and its large mythic proportions unveiled. 50 years ago, children had a 90% chance to earn more than their parents, today the chance is only 50%. The high costs for education are among the prime reasons for this limited upward mobility (Aguirre and Baker; Chetty et al.).

Inequality also has a notable spatial dimension. As in most countries, poor and rich people in the United States do not live in the same area or neighborhood. In 2014, only 9.5% of New Hampshire's population lived in poverty, but 27.6% of Michigan's population, as the state of Michigan has suffered severely from deindustrialization. Paradoxically, in 2016, Americans living in rural regions of the country had a lower median household income, but lower poverty rates than urban households (Bureau of the Census). But, no doubt, inequality also affects cities and urban areas. For decades, cities have suffered from deindustrialization, high crime rates, racial uprisings, and suburbanization. The upper and middle classes moved to the suburbs, while the poor and working classes stayed in often run-down city centers (Koechlin). Today, many cities are experiencing a revival. Global investors build expensive high-rises in city centers for wealthy buyers while the upper middle class is moving to former poor or working-class areas. As a consequence, the poor population, no longer able to afford living in gentrified neighborhoods, is displaced (Chapple 84). Chicago would be a case in point: As one of the most segregated cities in North America, the wealthy live on the North Side, while the poor are concentrated on the South and West Side of the city. Under the influence of global money and market-driven competition, some areas of Chicago's South Side are undergoing change as well. David Wilson (in this volume) argues that a government-led redevelopment is in the process of destroying the rich cultural history of the South Side, or, to be more precise, its blues clubs that are being commodified. In his empirical study, Wilson describes in great detail the reaction of long-established clubs such as Beebe's and several others.

In South American cities, the ramifications of inequality are even bigger than in US-American cities. In Brazil, for example, the poor are concentrated in favelas. As Eberhard Rothfuß shows in his contribution to our collection, favelas are, on the one hand, blatantly visible and can hardly be overlooked, while they are, on the other hand, denied and kept invisible in social terms. Rothfuß calls this phenomenon the 'paradox of urban inequality.' By resorting to a large corpus of interviews, he unveils the rich culture of favelas – a view that clashes with the dominant narrative constructing favelas as spaces of the abnormal, the violent, and the precarious. As favela inhabitants feel excluded from mainstream society, some are presented as having developed strategies of actively fighting against the derogatory stereotype, whereas others blame themselves for their low social status and purported failure.

And yet, inequality is an issue that not only concerns the poor as they are forced to get by on low wages, with little or no health insurance and a lack of financial resources to afford decent education for their children. Inequality is also a determining factor to indicate the condition of a country's overall political and social system. While Gordon (in this volume) discusses this issue for the United States, political scientist Susanne Pickel adopts a transatlantic perspective and focuses on European countries by comparison. Pickel sets an interesting contrast to inequality in the United States by looking at social inequality, the system of political equality, and political participation in the EU-28 countries as well as Iceland, Switzerland, Norway, and Serbia. Her argument is that the wealthy, at the top of the social pyramid, have a much more gripping influence on political decision-making than the poor at the pyramid's bottom, whose interests are far less represented in politics. By the same token, poor people tend to remain at the bottom of the pyramid as social inequality also compromises equal opportunity, and age and level of education are significant predictors for voting behavior. Additionally, Pickel locates notable differences between individual countries, as, for instance, West Europeans are more likely to participate in elections, petitions, and demonstrations than East Europeans. Among others, this assessment leaves one to wonder about the degree to which people care about inequality in their respective country. Why Americans arguably care so little about inequality is the topic of Lisa Keister's sociological analysis, while historian Axel R. Schäfer looks at historical roots of inequality as he thoroughly analyzes US social welfare policies and health care reform during World War I.

In its October 2016 issue, *Harper's Magazine* featured a photo essay titled "Division Street" with photographs by Robert Gumpert and a short introduction by Rebecca Solnit. The piece was advertised as "Photographs from San Francisco's Inequality Boom." Gumpert's pictures show homelessness in terms of the gradual exclusion and chasing away of the poor by exclusionary city policies and hence give *Harper's* readership an impressive, and thoroughly depressing idea of the shapes and forms of inequality in the Silicon valley – a region where not only digital entrepreneurship booms, but, as the title so pointedly expresses, inequality 'booms' just as well. Julia Faisst's essay in this collection focuses on the subprime housing crisis by looking at twenty-first-century American plays that deal with property relations and real estate distribution as a consequence of the housing crisis. Bruce Norris's *Clybourne Park* and Lisa D'Amour's *Detroit*, both of which premiered in 2010, blatantly establish inequalities in property and homeownership as central predicaments along the lines of both race as well as class. That class is a strong determining factor in the experience of inequality is apparent both in Faisst's essay and the plays under consideration as well as in the photo essay on San Francisco's "Division Street." Rebecca Solnit's accompanying text attributes poverty, homelessness, and eviction to unequal policy-making in the city, as the poor and homeless are constantly driven away from their temporary, make-shift abodes; home-ownership is presented almost as precarious as homelessness, as those on the 'wrong side' of "Division Street" are driven away, being left with no other option than to take to the streets. Perceived as a threat to society, the forced and precarious life on the streets collides with the middle-class idea of a home as a safe haven and sanctuary. This condition is not without historical antecedents. In her book *The Syntax of Class*, Amy Schrager-Lang discusses literary expressions of a crisis of social class in the second half of the nineteenth century, resorting to fiction by Maria Cummins, Nathaniel Hawthorne, Frank Webb, Elizabeth Stuart Phelps, or Horatio Alger, Jr. And in *American Hungers*, Gavin Jones studies literary and cultural negotiations of poverty that, as he argues, has been denied its importance as a critical factor in American lives. While poverty is material and real, the author holds, it is also culturally and ideologically significant. Jones analyzes works giving tramps, sharecroppers, and factory workers a voice as they constitute a significant segment of American society that should be at the center of debates on national justice – and not be pushed to the margin, or altogether ignored. Seen this way, cultural artifacts and productions such as novels, poetry, photographs, and many more can be helpful in understanding a condition that, as Jones writes, is both "urgent" and "elusive" (16).

Historically speaking, the so-called "dangerous classes" (Schrager-Lang 4) have been given an impressive literary voice by Jack London. His 1907 novel *The Road* chronicles the novelist's own experiences as a hobo in the 1890s, i.e. during the worst economic depressions that the country had faced until that time. London relates tales of hopping freight trains and escaping the police, but he also speaks about being forced to beg for food and basic supplies or about the "unprintable horrors" (60) of incarceration at a penitentiary. As the eponymous title suggests, the road is, then and now, the place in which inequality plays out most outspokenly. London himself, by the way, joined Kelly's army and became part of the Western section of this protest movement by unemployed workers spurned by severe economic hardship. An advocate of socialism and the rights of workers, London chronicles his own hobo experience 'on the road' as a difficult route to refuge. Until this day, the road has hence remained a paramount place for the poor and for precarious existence and serves as a strong, if not blatant measuring stick for the degree of inequality in a given society.

In a short contribution to the issue of the reparations argument titled "So That's Just One of My Losses," the African-American writer Ta-Nehisi Coates writes about his trip to see a certain Clyde Ross, who had, on his 90th birthday, moved his home from Clarksdale, Mississippi, to Chicago. Asked about his reasons for moving, Mr. Ross replied that he was seeking "the protection of the law." He was convinced that if he had stayed in Clarksdale he would not be save and not enjoy the same protection under the law as elsewhere. For Coates, this experience marks the "branding of black people as outside" of American law and society. Hence, in this case, inequality is directly linked to exclusionary practices based on race. Put differently, a fundamentally unequal past makes an unequal present, as, for example, the powerful Black Lives Matter-movement has demonstrated in the recent past. That exclusionary, unequal practices are strongly intertwined with monetary and economic interests becomes apparent in Rinaldo Walcott's contribution. In his essay, he discusses contemporary Black activism and racial inequality in the Canadian cultural and literary economy, while Shirley Thompson takes a historical perspective and reminds us of Charles Chesnutt's legacy for Black activism in the new millennium. Both essays on activism against racial inequality, from a historical as well as contemporary perspective, underscore the blatant truth of Ta-Nehisi Coates's stance on racist inequality: with Clyde Ross's example, he hopes to shake to the bone the belief that "a society can spend three-and-a-half centuries attempting to cripple man, 50 years offering half-hearted aid, and then wonder why he walks away with a limp." Coates's assessment of the historical roots of inequality, in many ways, echoes economist Thomas Piketty's proposition in *Capital in the Twenty-First Century* when he writes: "the past devours the future" (571).

The essays in this book approach inequality from an interdisciplinary perspective, as contributions come from political science/economics, history, geography, sociology, literary and cultural studies, with a particular emphasis to African-American and gender studies. In addition to being interdisciplinary, the selection of articles portrays a transnational orientation, as we have purposefully invited transatlantic and inter-American considerations. Most of the essays collected in this volume are based on talks presented at the annual conference of the Bavarian American Academy (BAA) on the topic of inequality that was held at the Amerikahaus in Munich/Germany July 9-11, 2015. In the planning stages of this event, we realized how strongly inequalities along the lines of, e.g., race, class, and gender are determined by inequalities in the distribution and granting of basic human rights. Shortly before our conference, the Canadian Museum for Human Rights had opened its doors in Winnipeg, Manitoba. While being exuberantly praised by many as the first and long overdue museum of this kind, the project was also met with critical, at times intense discussions during the planning and implementation processes as well as after its opening. In this collection, Jodi Giesbrecht, manager of research at the museum, gives us a curatorial tour of the museum, pointing out the general ideas and aims as well as the controversies that had accompanied the process of its institution.

Works Cited

Aguirre, Adalberto, and David V. Baker. *Structured Inequality in the United States: Discussions on the Continuing Significance of the Race, Ethnicity and Gender*. 2nd ed. London: Pearson, 2007.

Bonavich, Edna. "Inequality in America: The Failure of the American System for People of Colour." *Sociological Spectrum* 9.1 (1989): 77-101.

Bureau of the Census. <www.census.gov>.

Chapple, Karen. "Income Inequality and Urban Displacement: The New York Gentrification." *New Labour Forum* 26.1 (2017): 84-93.

Chetty, Ray, et al. "The Fading American Dream: Trends in Absolute Income Mobility since 1940." National Bureau of Economic Research, Working Paper 22910. Cambridge, MA: 2016.

Coates, Ta-Nehisi. "So That's Just One of my Losses." *The Atlantic* 21 May 2014. <www.theatlantic.com/business/archive/2014/05/so-thats-just-one-of-my-losses /371396/>.

Cochrane, John H. "How Did Paul Krugman Get It So Wrong?" *Economic Affairs* 31.2 (2011): 36-40.

Forbes Magazine. "Forbes 400: The Full List of the Richest People in America 2016." 4 October 2016. <www.forbes.com>.

Gumpert, Robert. "Division Street: A Photo Essay." Introduction by Rebecca Solnit. *Harper's Magazine* 333.1997 (October 2016): 42-53.

Irvin, George. "Inequality and Recession in Britain and the USA." *Development and Change* 42.1 (2011): 154-82.

Jones, Gavin. *American Hungers: The Problem of Poverty in U.S. Literature, 1840-1945*. Princeton, NJ: Princeton Unversity Press, 2009.

Koechlin, Tim. "Urban Inequality, Neoliberalism, and the Case for a Multidisciplinary Economics." *Review of Radical Political Economics* 46.4 (2014): 451-60.

Krugman, Paul. "New York Times Blog: The Conscience of a Liberal." <https://krugman.blogs.nytimes.com/>.

---. "Is Vast Inequality Necessary?" *New York Times* 15 January 2016.

---. "Inequality and the City." *New York Times* 30 November 2015.

Lagarde, Christine. "Reducing Excessive Inequality Is Not Just Morally and Politically Correct, But It Is Good Economics" (17 June 2015). *50 Speeches that Made the World.* Ed. Andrew Burnet. London: Chambers, 2016. 226-32.

London, Jack. *The Road* (1907). N.p.: Seven Treasures Publication, 2008.

Piketty, Thomas. *Capital in the Twenty-First Century*. 2013. Trans. Arthur Goldhammer. Cambridge, MA: Belknap Press, 2017.

Schrager-Lang, Amy. *Syntax of Class: Writing Inequality in Nineteenth-Century America*. Ann Arbor: University of Michigan Press, 2006.

Stiglitz, Joseph E. *The Price of Inequality: How Today's Divided Society Endangers Our Future*. New York/London: Profile Books, 2013.

American Inequality: A Primer[1]

Colin Gordon

When we talk about inequality, we are talking about nothing less than the basic structure and history of modern society, i.e. the ways in which markets distribute rewards and resources, the ways in which policy corrects or compensates for market failures, and the ways in which both markets and politics shape the experiences and prospects of individuals and of families. Understanding inequality, in this respect, is not just about grasping the dimensions, or the change over time, in the metrics of inequality; it is about the trajectory of modern American political history, and the policies and policy retreats that brought us to this point.[2]

The full meaning and importance of American inequality rests on three observations. The first is that contemporary American inequality is **exceptional**. By any measure, we are more unequal now than we have ever been, and we are more unequal – by a long shot – than our peers among developed and democratic nations. The second is that contemporary American inequality is **purposeful**. American inequality is not an unhappy consequence of unrelenting market and historical forces; it is a direct and tangible result of public policies whose very design and intent was to redistribute income and wealth upwards. And the third is that contemporary American inequality is **consequential**. American inequality hurts not only those that it leaves behind, but does great damage to our more general economic and democratic prospects.

Exceptional Inequality

Let's start with the exceptional, with the basic – and familiar and depressing – dimensions of American inequality. A smaller share of national income is flowing to wages and earnings, and – more importantly – inequality within that labor share is widening. As a result, wage growth has flatlined for a generation. Middle-income workers make no more now than they did in the late 1970s; those in the

1 This essay draws on the web-project "Growing Apart: A Political History of American Inequality" hosted by the Institute for Policy Studies at <www.inequaltiy.org>, and the series "Our Inequality" published by *Dissent* in 2014. Earlier versions were presented to workshops at University of California-Santa Barbara (January 2016); the Bavarian American Academy (July 2015); the Labor and Working Class History Association (May 2015); the Cambridge Forum (March 2015); and the Hall Center for the Humanities at the University of Kansas (March 2014). Thanks to Sam Pizzigati, Colin Kinniburgh, Sarah Bruch, John Schmitt, Larry Mishel, Lisa Levenstein, Nelson Lichtenstein, Mary Furner, and Alice O'Connor for comments.

2 I owe a debt, in framing these issues, to Schmitt (2009).

lower wage cohort have lost ground over that span. And over the long postwar era, the wages of working Americans have come uncoupled from economic growth. Through the early 1970s, wages for all Americans grew with productivity; since then, productivity has continued apace while real wages have stagnated (Kristal; Mishel and Gee; C. Gordon 2014b). The current inequality of labor income in the United States, as Thomas Piketty concludes, "is probably higher than in any other society at any time in the past, anywhere in the world" (2014: 265).

The growing gap in income (including non-wage income like returns on investment or capital gains) is even starker. Between 1979 and 2007, the real incomes of the richest 1% almost tripled, while the real incomes of the median household inched up only about 25% – and that almost all due to an increase in labor force participation (especially by women) and hours worked. The inequality suggested by these numbers is jarring: since 1979, the income of the poorest 20% has fallen by 12% while the income share of the richest 1% – as the research of Thomas Piketty and colleagues has underscored – has more than doubled (Congressional Budget Office 2011b; Stone et al.; Piketty et al.). And inequality in wealth (the sum total of household savings, home equity, investments, and debts) is starker still. The richest 1% claims about a third of the nation's wealth; the top 5% claim over 60%. These shares have grown steadily over the last generation. The recession took a big bite out of middle-class wealth (much of which is vested in home equity). And the gains of the recovery have flowed almost exclusively to the richest Americans (Saez and Piketty).

On each of these fronts, inequality has grown more in the United States than it has elsewhere. Nowhere in the industrialized world is there a bigger gap between wage growth and productivity growth over the last two business cycles. Over the last twenty years, the richest Americans started with a bigger share of income than any of their well-heeled peers and gained more than any of them. Among the world's wealthy countries (those with an average adult wealth of $100,000 or more), the United States ranks dead last on the relevant inequality measures (International Labor Office; OECD; C. Gordon 2013).

To make matters worse, demography and geography widen those gaps for many Americans. The gender gap in wages, income, and wealth has closed very slowly, and much of that progress is driven by the collapse of male wages rather than real gains by working women. The racial gap in wages, incomes, and wealth has closed little, and it has widened for those caught up in the startling (and racialized) spike in incarceration in the United States. While racial segregation in our cities has abated somewhat over the last generation, economic segregation – the likelihood that Americans live in enclaves of wealth or poverty – has hardened. Economic mobility, by any measure, remains weak; the recent spike in inequality has simply underscored that dismal American admonition "choose your parents wisely."[3]

Purposeful Inequality

This brings us to our second observation: why and how did it come to this? How do we explain these jaw-dropping gaps – between rich and poor, between the United States and its peers, between our current circumstances and our own history? Conventional explanations generally posit one or both of two plotlines. The first: somebody took the money. This version stresses Wall Street greed and the Bush-era tax cuts and features a plutocracy determined to claim more than its share of private wealth and shoulder less than its share of public goods. The second: something happened to the economy. This version has a backstory in the inexorable march of globalization and technological change, and a more recent plot twist: the recession that began in 2007 and – for most of us – has not yet ended.

These accounts are not so much wrong as they are misleadingly incomplete, inattentive to longer-term historical trends and to the political choices made across that history. On trade, the ease and speed with which goods and services, money, information, production, and labor can move across national borders – combined with the collapse of American leadership in the world economy – has yielded a form of globalization that is both more intense and more heterogeneous than what came before. Its rewards flow to emerging or resource-rich economies, and to private interests rather than nations. The impact has been starkest on American manufacturing, where we have seen sustained competitive pressures from labor-intensive imports, a diversion of domestic investment, unrelenting pressure on wages, and devastating local impacts in manufacturing cities and regions (Atkinson et al.). But, as explanation for economy-wide wage weakness, the footloose mobility of capital is overdrawn. Much of the economy is rooted in place by labor markets, supply chains, or consumers. Sectors of the economy untouched by liberalized trade shed workers and dampened wages at about the same rate as the rest of the economy in the twenty-five years after 1970. While globalization has accelerated since 1990, wage inequality at the bottom (between low-wage and median-wage workers) has actually slowed over that span. Most of the growth in inequality during this era has been driven by gains made by very high earners – a pattern unlikely to be shaped much by trade.

More to the point, all countries face the forces and consequences of globalization, and yet wage and income inequality is starker in the United States than in most other settings. Indeed, the United States is less exposed to trade than any of its OECD peers, and yet more unequal than almost all of them. It is not

[3] On the racial wealth gap, see Conley; Shapiro; Oliver and Shapiro; Petit and Western. On local and regional inequalities, see Reardon et al. On mobility, see Chetty et al.

globalization (as an abstract and inevitable force) that generates or explains inequality, but the political response to globalization in particular countries. The demands globalization places on the labor market can lead to a race to the bottom, but they need not. Indeed, globalization widens the wage gap (within and across countries) not universally, but when and where labor protections are weak. It is not trade that generates inequality, but its political terms (Machin and Van Reenen; McCann; Burtless; Lawrence; Massey).

Others have argued that shared prosperity has been undone by technological change. In this view, skill-biased technological change displaces 'routine' manual tasks such as working on a production line and creates new tasks and occupations for which skilled workers are better adapted. But it does not displace non-routine, low-wage service jobs. As a result, those with skills and advanced degrees hoard any economic gains and everyone else falls farther and farther behind. As a consequence, we see losses in the middle of the labor market and growth at the edges – in low-wage, low-skill jobs at one end and in high-wage, high-skill jobs at the other (Autor). If nothing else, this is a politically attractive kind of explanation for inequality. Technological innovation or change (like globalization) is not something you can control, so there seems little political recourse but to occasionally lament the quality of American education. But, on closer examination, it is not that compelling.

Despite all the handwringing about our underprepared workforce, the returns on education are not that clear. While those with some college education or better pulled away from the pack in the 1980s and 1990s, that advantage has slowed dramatically. Workers with some college education or a college degree are much more likely now to remain mired in low-wage work than workers with the same educational background a generation ago. The last fifteen years have seen significantly slower growth in high-skill, high-wage jobs than in the economy at large. In turn, the evidence linking technological change and inequality is weak with respect to the timing and the nature of that inequality. Over the long haul, technological change has tended to push job growth to the margins, but this has occurred monotonously, across eras of relative equality and inequality. The modern trajectory of wage inequality, by contrast, is sharply discontinuous, widening between low and median wage workers in the 1980s, and between median and high-wage workers in the last decade. Since 1969 labor's share of income has fallen most rapidly in those sectors where union presence withered, not where computers displaced labor. Indeed, most of the growth in wage inequality across the last generation can be found within occupations and not in their relative share of the labor market (C. Gordon 2014a). And, whatever causal importance we assign to technological change, it is hard to see it as a credible account of the different trajectories of inequality across countries. Like globalization, technological change is a challenge faced by all economies. And yet differences across national settings (and especially the outlying status of the United States) remain profound.

While globalization and technological change undoubtedly contribute to inequality, they can't be convincingly deployed to explain it, or to explain the intensity and timing of its American variant. A fuller explanation starts to come into focus when we consider the political and economic conditions that prevailed right after the Second World War. At that historical moment, the United States displayed much narrower gaps between the rich and poor than they do now. The gains of economic growth back then were much more broadly distributed. And working families (at least white working families) enjoyed much greater economic security.

This was no accident or lucky combination of circumstances. It was the outcome of political struggle and policy choices that erected a foundation and a structure for shared prosperity. The inequality of the twentieth century's early years actually began closing before economic growth took off in the 1940s, as a consequence of the political response to the Great Depression. Thanks to this response, federal support for collective bargaining rights sustained a surge in labor organization that dramatically improved the bargaining power of America's workers. Other political innovations of the New Deal – ranging from Social Security to the minimum wage – secured a floor for working-class incomes. Postwar social movements, especially civil rights and second-wave feminism, then girded that floor by closing off avenues for discrimination. The nation's tax system, meanwhile, and new regulatory obstacles to speculative finance erected something of a ceiling for higher incomes. And substantial public investments – the GI Bill support for access to higher education, mortgage subsidies for veterans, housing projects, the interstate highway system, and the Cold War – kept the rest of the structure in good repair.

Over the last generation, to put it bluntly, we've burned that house down. This conflagration is often recounted as an unfortunate but necessary response to changing economic conditions: the world has become a leaner, meaner, more competitive place. As a result, the policies of the New Deal – and the costs they imposed on business – had to go. But there is little evidence to actually support this account. The retreat from the New Deal order was purposeful and deeply political. The goal was not to sustain the struggling competitiveness of the American economy; it was to dramatically change the distribution of its rewards.

This 'right turn' rested on five key political and policy developments. The first was the precipitous collapse in private sector union membership, from over a third of the workforce in the early 1950s to barely 6% today. Indeed the arc of union membership, rising in the 1930s and 1940s and falling off steadily after the early 1970s is an eerie mirror image of the "suspension bridge" tracing the income share of the top 10% (Gordon and Eisenberry). The postwar attack on organized labor – its bargaining power and its political power – is as long as the postwar era itself, launched in 1947 by the passage of the "right to work" Taft-Hartley Act.[4] In the 1970s and after, political support withered and managerial attacks – virtually unchecked by defanged National Labor Relations Board – stemmed new gains and eroded old ones (Bronfenbenner). Declining union strength destroyed bargaining power, drawing down wages (especially male wages) for union and non-union workers alike (Rosenfeld and Western). The impact of these losses were exaggerating in a setting where workers also relied on private bargaining for access to basic health and retirement coverage – both of which eroded alongside union coverage. In all of this, the United States was a clear outlier, its labor movement peaking earlier (and lower) and declining more dramatically than that of its peers (Warner).

Second, union decline was accompanied by a parallel collapse in basic labor standards and in the 'safety net' policies that protect those on the margins of the labor market. In the United States, the real (inflation-adjusted) minimum wage is worth far less than it was in the late 1960s, and – measured as a share of the median or of the average wage – falls near the bottom of labor standards across our peer countries (Schmitt and Gordon; Schmitt 2012). Raising the minimum wage 'floor' has clear implications for inequality – promising (and demonstrating) higher incomes, lower poverty rates, and economic gains for those workers who need it the most (Dube). The importance of the minimum wage (and other labor standards such as overtime) is magnified by the erosion of job quality and security, and the increased prevalence of temporary or contingent employment relationships.[5] In turn, the reach and adequacy of the policies we rely upon to pick up the pieces (family assistance, unemployment insurance, disability benefits and the like) are categorically and regionally uneven, and poorly-targeted. At its origins, the American welfare state was cut to fit prevailing assumptions (and anxieties) about race, gender, and private employment – sharply limiting its ability to compensate for market failures.[6] And that welfare state is now much weaker than it used to be, and much weaker than that of our international peers. Simply put, market inequalities (uneven rewards from work) are steeper in the United States than in most other settings and American policies do less about this (the rate of redistribution is about half that of the OECD average) than almost any other developed country (Ben-Shalom et al.; Greenstein).[7]

Third, alongside the collapse of bargaining power and labor standards, we have seen the virtual disappearance of market or regulatory restraint on incomes at the

[4] On the labor movement since 1970, see Rogers; Moody; Cowie; Lichtenstein chapter 6; McCartin; Stein.

[5] On job precarity, see Kalleberg.

[6] On the racial limits of the social security act, see Poole; Katznelson; Lieberman; Fox; and the early chapters of Brown. On the gendered limits see L. Gordon; Kessler-Harris; Mink; Mettler. On private benefits, see Hacker; Klein; Gottschalk; L. Gordon and Fraser; C. Gordon 2003; Hoffman.

[7] On the US welfare state in comparative perspective, see also Brady; Zuberi; Rainwater et al.

top (Sherman; Lardner). In part, this is a consequence of the growth of speculative finance (and the dizzying incomes that accompany it). This feeds inequality from both ends: as the poor and middle class borrow to get by, they inevitably borrow from the rich – whose assets, in turn, are increasingly backed by loans that paper over inequality in the short term but exaggerate it in the long term. And in part, it marks a collapse in corporate governance, which has allowed executive salaries – irrespective of firm performance – to balloon from about 25 times the income of the average worker to almost 300 times (Frydman and Sakes; DiPrete at al.; Mishel and Davis). Both trends – financialization and the spike in executive compensation – are political in origin. They have occurred in the space afforded by the deregulation of banking and securities (Appelbaum and Batt; Appelbaum et al.; Fligstein and Shin; Kedrosky and Stangler; Assa). And that deregulation, quite openly and candidly, was accomplished by the political muscle of those who stood to benefit. The dizzyingly high incomes of the 1% are not compensation for exceptional talent or risk; they are simply economic rents.[8]

Fourth, the unfettering of top incomes has been abetted by the transformation of the tax system. These changes have shifted the burden onto the backs of ordinary Americans, both by slashing rates on high incomes (the top marginal rate stood at 90% in the 1950s, it is now 35%), and by paring back corporate tax rates (Thiess; Hungerford). Historically rates are compounded by the leakiness of the American tax code, which invites systemic manipulation and dodges (Anderson et al; Keightley; Congressional Budget Office 2011a; Department of Homeland Security). This means not only windfalls for the rich, i.e., an effective redistribution of incomes and wealth upwards, but a reshaping of incentives and bargaining power and social norms across the economy (Saez and Piketty). And, importantly, it means that the public sector is starved of the resources it might need to solve problems or to mop up after market failures, with runaway inequality foremost among them.

Fifth, and finally, the last generation has seen a fundamental shift in macroeconomic policy which, since the late 1970s, has consistently chosen controlling inflation over maintaining full employment. This preoccupation with inflation serves, first and foremost, the nation's financial powers for whom inflation has always been a particular and overriding concern. And, by accepting higher levels of unemployment, policymakers effectively dampen inflation by dampening wages, through both sustained joblessness and a wider range of policies (deregulation, trade liberalization, attacks on collective bargaining, cuts to social programs) designed to erode bargaining power.

Political choices, not economic necessity, dismantled the New Deal. Future Supreme Court Justice Lewis Powell would first sketch out the organizational and ideological dimensions of these choices in a now infamous 1971 memorandum to the US Chamber of Commerce. The conservative ascendance in state and national

[8] On rent seeking, see Baker; Galbraith; Lind; Hudson; Mishel and Bivens.

politics affirmed these choices across the political landscape, with dramatic consequences: steep cuts in social spending, the political abandonment of organized labor, deregulation and privatization, tax cuts, punitive cycles of unemployment – all justified in the name of lowering business costs, capturing economic efficiencies, and unleashing markets (Phillips-Fein). Such arguments, of course, camouflaged the real goal of the pushback against the New Deal: a redistribution of income upward via the erosion of the hard-earned bargaining power of ordinary Americans. Rising inequality was not a lamentable side effect of America's new policy framework; it was its intent.

Consequential Inequality

These policy choices, taken together, have had real and sustained consequences. Inequality matters to society at large and to the health and prosperity of all who live within it. The evidence on this point is overwhelming. Citizens in unequal societies, researchers have shown, are more likely end up sick, obese, unhappy, unsafe, or in jail. These social outcomes, bad in themselves, also undercut the productivity and efficiency of the economy, as the high costs of poor public health, heavy policing, and mass incarceration siphon off our resources and leave our human capital underprepared and underutilized.[9]

Inequality clearly matters to those who are left behind. Much of the economics profession, of course, has dedicated itself to the idea that this is a good thing; that inequality is an essential incentive within a market economy. People work hard to avoid poverty and even harder to get rich. Any pursuit of 'equal outcomes' would stifle this initiative and, with it, the economic growth on which we all depend. The poor, as they like to say, will find themselves much better off with a thin slice of a growing pie than with a thicker slice of a small one. There is little evidence – historical or economic – to substantiate such silliness. The 'market incentives' argument holds water only as long as hard work is reliably rewarded in the short term (with wages) and in the long term (with economic mobility) – a prospect that has unraveled in the last decade. Stark and sustained inequality discourages those at the bottom of the income distribution ladder (whose hard work goes unrewarded), and encourages those at the top to engage in short-sighted speculation, much of which (think predatory lending and usurious credit card rates) exploits the poor and widens the gap.

Inequality matters to the health of the economy. Stark income gaps hollow out consumption. "A millionaire cannot wear 10,000 pairs of $10 shoes," as one advertiser warned on the eve of the Great Depression in 1929, "but a hundred

[9] This is the point made exhaustively by Wilkinson and Pickett 2009; see also Collins; Center for Disease Control; Wilkinson and Pickett 2006; Kondo et al; Smith et al.; Devaux and Sassi; Kim et al., Offer et al.; Alesina et al.; Choe; Thompson; Western; Western and Pettit; Stiglitz.

thousand others can if they've got the $10 to pay for them, and the leisure to show them off" (Cohen and Gordon). Rising inequality in the last generation has created the same tension, eased only temporarily by the availability of consumer credit and home equity. Such efforts to patch together substitutes for aggregate demand create their own inefficiencies, including a bloated and parasitic financial services sector fed by both the desperate demand for credit from those falling behind and the frantic search for speculative returns by those leaping ahead. In our own recent history, sustained economic growth is closely associated with a relatively equitable distribution of economic rewards. Even the International Monetary Fund has conceded on this point, concluding recently that "lower net inequality is robustly correlated with faster and more durable growth" (Ostry et al.).

And inequality matters to the health of our democracy. Democratic institutions, at their best, provide a basic physical, legal, and fiscal infrastructure in which markets can thrive. These institutions can ameliorate or regulate the excesses of market competition and provide the public goods and services that markets are unable or unwilling to generate on their own. Under conditions of stark economic and political inequality, all of this begins to unravel. Inequality tips the playing field in favor of those with the resources to shape political outcomes, tilts our attention and resources away from collective goods (good schools, infrastructure) essential to future growth and prosperity, and undermines our very faith in democratic institutions in such a way that growing inequality – rather than leaping to the fore of the political agenda – is likely to erode the willingness or ability to do anything about it (Hacker and Pierson; Bartels; Gillens 2012; Gillens and Page). Economic inequality breeds inequality in politics, whose highest goal, in turn, becomes policies that make economic inequality even worse.

Works Cited

Alesina, Alberto, Rafael Di Tella, and Robert MacCulloch. "Inequality and Happiness: Are Europeans and Americans Different?" *Journal of Public Economics* 88 (2004): 2009-42.

Anderson, Sarah, Scott Klinger, and Javier Rojo. "Corporate Pirates of the Caribbean." Institute for Policy Studies, 12 June 2013. <www.ips-dc.org/reports/corporate_pirates>.

---. "Corporate Tax Dodgers: 10 Companies and Their Loopholes." Institute for Policy Studies, 15 April 2013. <www.ips-dc.org/reports/corporate_tax_dodgers>.

Appelbaum, Eileen, and Rosemary Batt. "A Primer on Private Equity at Work: Management, Employment, and Sustainability." CEPR – Center for Economic and Policy Research, February 2012.

---, Rosemary Batt, and Jae Eun Lee. "Financial Intermediaries in the United States: Development and Impact on Firms and Employment Relations." CEPR – Center for Economic and Policy Research, August 2012.

Assa, Jacob. "Financialization and its Consequences: The OECD Experience." *Finance Research* 1.1 (2012): 35-39.

Atkinson, Robert, Luke A. Stewart, Scott M. Andes, and Stephen J. Ezell. "Worse than the Great Depression: What Experts Are Missing About American Manufacturing Decline." ITIF – Information Technology & Innovation Foundation, March 2012.

Austin, Algernon. "The Unfinished March." Economic Policy Institute, 18 June 2013.

Autor, David. "The Polarization of Job Opportunities in the U.S. Labor Market: Implications for Employment and Earnings." Center for American Progress, April 2010.

Baker, Dean. *Taking Economics Seriously.* Cambridge: MIT Press, 2010.

---. *The Conservative Nanny State*. Lulu.com, 2006.

Bartels, Larry. *Unequal Democracy.* Princeton: Princeton University Press, 2010.

Ben-Shalom, Yonatan, Robert A. Moffitt, and John Karl Scholz. "An Assessment of the Effectiveness of Anti-Poverty Programs in the United States." NBER Working Paper 17042, May 2011.

Brady, David. *Rich Democracies, Poor People.* New York: Oxford University Press, 2009.

Bronfenbenner, Kate. "No Holds Barred: The Intensification of Employer Opposition to Organizing." Economic Policy Institute, 2009. <www.epi.org/publication/bp235/>.

Brown, Michael. *Race, Money, and the American Welfare State.* Ithaca: Cornell University Press, 1999.

Burtless, Gary. "Worsening Income Inequality: Is World Trade to Blame?" *The Brookings Review* (1996): 27-31.

Center for Disease Control and Prevention. *Health Disparities and Inequalities Report: United States, 2011.* U.S. Department of Health and Human Services, 14 January 2011.

Chetty, Raj, Nathaniel Hendren, Patrick Kline, Emmanuel Saez, and Nicholas Turner. "Is the United States Still a Land of Opportunity? Recent Trends in Intergenerational Mobility." NBER Working Paper 19844, January 2014.

Choe, Jongmook. "Income Inequality and Crime in the United States." *Economics Letters* 101.1 (2008): 31-33.

Cohen, Donald, and Colin Gordon. "Do America's Corporations Care How Much American Workers Earn?" *Dissent* online, 30 August 2012. <www.dissentmagazine.org/online_articles/do-americas-corporations-care-how-much-american-workers-earn>.

Collins, Chuck. *99 to 1: How Wealth Inequality Is Wrecking the World and What We Can Do about It.* San Francisco: Berrett-Koehler, 2012.

Congressional Budget Office. "Reducing the Deficit: Spending and Revenue Options." March 2011a. <www.cbo.gov/publication/22043>.

---. "Trends in the Distribution of Household Income Between 1979 and 2007." October 2011b. <www.cbo.gov/publication/42729>.

Conley, Dalton, "Getting into the Black: Race, Wealth, and Public Policy." *Political Science Quarterly* 114.4 (1999): 595-612.

Cowie, Jefferson. *Stayin' Alive: The 1970s and the Last Days of the Working Class*. New York: The New Press, 2010.

Department of Homeland Security, Subcommittee on Investigations. "Offshore Profit Shifting and the U.S. Tax Code – Part 2 (Apple Inc)." 21 May 2013.

Devaux, Marion, and Franco Sassi. "Social Inequalities in Obesity and Overweight in 11 OECD Countries." *The European Journal of Public Health* 6 June 2011.

DiPrete, Thomas, Gregory M. Eirich, and Matthew Pittinsky. "Compensation Benchmarking, Leapfrogs, and the Surge in Executive Pay." *American Journal of Sociology* 115.6 (2010): 1671-712.

Dube, Arindrajit. "Minimum Wages and the Distribution of Family Incomes." Working Paper, 30 December 2013. <https://dl.dropboxusercontent.com/u/15038936/Dube_MinimumWagesFamilyIncomes.pdf>.

Fligstein, Neil, and Taek-Jin Shin. "The Shareholder Value Society: A Review of the Changes in Working Conditions and Inequality in the U.S. 1976-2000." Berkeley Institute for Research on Labor and Employment, Working Paper 88-03, March 2003.

Fox, Cybelle. *Three Worlds of Relief*. Princeton: Princeton University Press, 2012.

Frydman, Carola, and Raven Sakes. "Executive Compensation: A New View from a Long-Term Perspective, 1936-2005." *The Review of Financial Studies* 23 (2010): 2099-138.

Galbraith, James K. *The Predator-State: How Conservatives Abandoned the Free Market and Why Liberals Should Too.* New York: Free Press, 2009.

Gillens, Martin. *Affluence and Influence*. Princeton: Princeton University Press, 2014.

---. "Under the Influence." *Boston Review* 1 July 2012. <http://bostonreview.net/forum/lead-essay-under-influence-martin-gilens>.

---, and Benjamin Page. "Testing Theories of American Politics: Elites, Interest Groups, and Average Citizens." *Perspectives on Politics* 12.3 (2014): 564-81.

Gordon, Colin. "The Computer Did It: Technology and Inequality." *Dissent Magazine* (Spring 2014a). <www.dissentmagazine.org/article/the-computer-did-it-technology-and-inequality>.

---. "The Wage Crunch in Historical Perspective." *Dissent* online, 9 June 2014b. <www.dissentmagazine.org/blog/the-wage-crunch-in-perspective>.

---"The Great Barbecue Revisited." *Dissent* online, 4 July 2013. <www.dissentmagazine.org/blog/the-great-barbecue-revisited>.

---. *Dead on Arrival*. Princeton: Princeton University Press, 2003.

---, and Ross Eisenberry. "As Unions Decline, Inequality Rises." Economic Policy Institute, 6 June 2012. <www.epi.org/publication/unions-decline-inequality-rises/>.

Gordon, Linda. *Pitied But Not Entitled.* New York: The Free Press, 1994.

---, and Nancy Fraser. "Contract vs. Charity: Why There is No Social Citizenship in the United States." *Socialist Review* 22 (1992): 45-68.

Gottschalk, Marie. *The Shadow Welfare State.* Ithaca, NY: Cornell University Press, 2000.

Greenstein, Robert. "Welfare Reform and the Safety Net." Center on Budget and Policy Priorities, June 2016. <www.cbpp.org/research/family-income-support/welfare-reform-and-the-safety-net>.

Hacker, Jacob. *The Divided Welfare State.* Cambridge: Cambridge University Press, 2002.

---, and Paul Pierson. *Winner-Take-All Politics.* New York: Simon & Schuster, 2011.

Hoffman, Beatrix. *Health Care for Some*. Chicago: University of Chicago Press, 2012.

Hudson, Michael. *The Bubble and Beyond.* Dresden: ISLET-Verlag, 2012.

Hungerford, Thomas. "Taxes and the Economy: An Economic Analysis of the Top Tax Rates since 1945." Congressional Research Service, 14 September 2012. <www.dpcc.senate.gov/files/documents/CRSTaxesandtheEconomy%20Top%20Rates.pdf>.

International Labor Office. *Global Wage Report 2012/13: Wages and Equitable Growth.*

Kalleberg, Arne. *Good Jobs, Bad Jobs: The Rise of Polarized and Precarious Employment Systems in the United States, 1970s to 2000s*. New York: Russell Sage Press, 2013.

Katznelson, Ira. *Fear Itself.* New York; W.W. Norton & Company/Liveright, 2013.

---. *When Affirmative Action Was White*. New York: W.W. Norton & Company, 2005.

Kedrosky, Paul, and Dane Stangler. "Financialization and Its Entrepreneurial Consequences." Kauffman Foundation, 15 March 2011.

Keightley, Mark P. "An Analysis of Where American Companies Report Profits: Indications of Profit Shifting." Congressional Research Service, January 2013.

Kessler-Harris, Alice. *In Pursuit of Equity*. New York: Oxford University Press, 2001.

Kim, Daniel, Ichiro Kawachi, Stephen Vander Hoorn, and Majid Ezzati. "Is Inequality at the Heart of It? Cross-country Associations of Income Inequality and Cardiovascular Diseases and Risk Factors." *Social Science and Medicine* 66.8 (2008): 1719-32.

Klein, Jennifer. *For All These Rights*. Princeton: Princeton University Press, 2006.

Kondo, Naoki, Grace Sembajwe, Ichiro Kawachi, Rob M. van Dam, S.V. Subramanian, and Zentaro Yamagata. "Income Inequality, Mortality, and Self-rated Health: Meta-analysis of Multi-level Studies." *British Medical Journal* 339.102 (2009): b4471.

Kristal, Tali. "The Capitalist Machine: Computerization, Workers' Power, and the Decline in Labor's Share within U.S. Industries." *American Sociological Review* 78 (2013): 361-89.

Lardner, James. "A Brief History of the Glass-Steagall Act." Demos, 10 November 2009. <www.demos.org/publication/brief-history-glass-steagall-act>.

Lawrence, Robert. *Blue-Collar Blues: Is Trade to Blame for Rising US Income Inequality?* Policy Analyses in International Economics 85. New York: Columbia University Press, 2008.

Lichtenstein, Nelson. *State of the Union*. Princeton: Princeton University Press, 2002.

Lieberman, Robert. *Shifting the Color Line*. Cambridge: Harvard University Press, 1999.

Lind, Michael. "Private Sector Parasites." Salon, 21 March 2013.

Machin, Stephen, and John Van Reenen. "Changes in Wage Inequality." Centre for Economic Performance, Special Paper 18, April 2007.

Massey, Douglas. "Globalization and Inequality: Explaining American Exceptionalism." *European Sociological Review* 25.1 (2009): 9-23.

McCann, Philip. "Globalization and Economic Geography: The World is Curved, not Flat." *Cambridge Journal of Regions, Economy and Society* 1.3 (2008): 351-70.

McCartin, Joseph. *Collision Course: Ronald Reagan, the Air Traffic Controllers, and the Strike that Changed America*. New York: Oxford University Press, 2011.

Mettler, Suzanne. *Dividing Citizens*. Ithaca: Cornell University Press, 1998.

Mink, Gwendolyn. *The Wages of Motherhood*. Ithaca: Cornell University Press, 1996.

Mishel, Larry, and Alyssa Davis. "CEO Pay Continues to Rise as Typical Workers Are Paid Less." Economic Policy Institute, 12 June 2014. <www.epi.org/publication/ceo-pay-continues-to-rise/>.

---, and Kar-Fai Gee. "Why Aren't Workers Benefiting From Labour Productivity Growth in the United States?" *International Productivity Monitor* 23 (2013): 31-43.

---, and Josh Bivens. "The Pay of Corporate Executives and Financial Professionals as Evidence of Rents in Top 1 Percent Incomes." *Journal of Economic Perspectives* 27.3 (2013): 57-78.

Moody, Kim. *An Injury to All*. New York: Verso, 1997.

OECD. *Less Income Inequality and More Growth – Are they Compatible?* OECD Working Papers, 2014.

Offer, Avner, Rachel Pechey, and Stanley Ulijaszek. "Obesity Under Affluence Varies by Welfare Regimes: The Effect of Fast Food, Insecurity, and Inequality." *Economics and Human Biology* 8.3 (2010): 297-308.

Oliver, Melvin, and Thomas Shapiro. *Black Wealth, White Wealth*. New York: Routledge, 2006.

Ostry, Jonathon, Andrew Berg, and Charalambos Tsanganides. "Redistribution, Inequality, and Growth." IMF Staff Discussion Note (February 2004).

Petit, Becky, and Bruce Western. "Mass Imprisonment and the Life Course: Race and Class Inequality in U.S. Incarceration." *American Sociological Review* 69 (April 2004): 151-69.

Phillips-Fein, Kim. *Invisible Hands: The Businessman's Crusade Against the New* Deal. New York: W.W. Norton & Company, 2010.

Piketty, Thomas. *Capital in the Twenty-First Century*. Cambridge: Harvard University Press, 2014.

---, Facundo Alvaredo, Tony Atkinson, Emmanuel Saez, and Gabriel Zucman. The World Wealth and Income Database. <www.wid.world/#Database>.

Poole, Mary. *The Segregated Origins of Social* Security. Chapel Hill: University of North Carolina Press, 2006.

Rainwater, Lee, Irwin Garfinkel, and Timothy Smeeding. *Wealth and Welfare State*. New York: Oxford University Press, 2010.

Reardon, Sean, Lindsay Fox, and Joseph Townsend. "Neighborhood Income Composition by Household Race and Income, 1990-2009." *The Annals of the American Academy of Political and Social Science* 660.1 (2015): 78-97.

Rogers, Joel. "Divide and Conquer: Further 'Reflections on the Distinctive Character of American Labor Laws.'" *Wisconsin Law Review* (1990): 1-147.

Rosenfeld, Jake, and Bruce Western. "Unions, Norms, and the Rise in US Wage Inequality." *American Sociological Review* 76 (2011): 513-37.

Saez, Emmanuel, and Thomas Piketty. "Top Incomes and the Great Recession: Recent Evolutions and Policy Implications." *International Monetary Fund Economic Review* 61.3 (2013): 456-78.

Schmitt, John. "Low Wage Lessons." Center for Economic and Policy Research, January 2012. <www.cepr.net/documents/publications/low-wage-2012-01.pdf>.

---. "Inequality as Policy: The United States since 1979." Center for Economic and Policy Research, October 2009.

---, and Colin Gordon. "What's So Bold about $9.00 an Hour: Benchmarking the Minimum Wage." *Dissent* online, February 2013. <www.dissentmagazine.org/online_articles/whats-so-bold-about-9-00-an-hour-benchmarking-the-minimum-wage>.

Shapiro, Thomas, Tatjana Meschede, and Sam Osoro. "The Roots of the Widening Racial Wealth Gap: Explaining the Black-White Economic Divide." Institute on Assets and Social Policy, 27 February 2013.

Sherman, Matthew. "A Short History of Financial Deregulation in the United States." Center for Economic and Policy Research, July 2009. <cepr.net/documents/publications/dereg-timeline-2009-07.pdf>.

Smith, Trenton, Christiana Stoddard, and Michael G. Barnes. "Why the Poor Get Fat: Weight Gain and Economic Insecurity." WSU School of Economic Sciences, Working Paper 2007-16.

Stein, Judith. *Pivotal Decade*. New Haven: Yale University Press, 2010.

Stiglitz, Joseph. "The Price of Inequality." Project Syndicate, 5 June 2012. <www.project-syndicate.org/commentary/the-price-of-inequality>.

Stone, Chad, Danilo Trisi, Arloc Sherman, and Emily Horton. "A Guide to Statistics on Historical Trends in Income Inequality." Center on Budget and Policy Priorities, 30 September 2016. <www.cbpp.org/research/poverty-and-inequality/a-guide-to-statistics-on-historical-trends-in-income-inequality>.

Thiess, Rebecca. "Changes in Income Shares Show How Preferential Tax Rates Increasingly Benefit Top Filers." Economy Policy Institute, 19 July 2012. <www.epi.org/publication/income-shares-show-preferential-tax-rates>.

Thompson, Heather Ann. "Why Mass Incarceration Matters: Rethinking Crisis, Decline, and Transformation in Postwar American History." *Journal of American History* 97.3 (2010): 703-34.

Warner, Kris. "Protecting Fundamental Labor Rights: Lessons from the United States and Canada." Center for Economic and Policy Research, August 2012. <www.cepr.net/documents/publications/canada-2012-08.pdf>.

Western, Bruce. *Punishment and Inequality in America*. New York: Russell Sage Foundation, 2008.

---, and Becky Pettit. "Incarceration & Social Inequality." *Daedalus* 139.3 (Summer 2010): 8-19.

Wilkinson, Richard G., and Kate Pickett. *The Spirit Level: Why Equality is Better for Everyone*. New York: Bloomsbury Press, 2009. Results updated at <www.equalitytrust.org.uk>.

---. "Income Inequality and Population Health: A Review and Explanation of the Evidence." *Social Science and Medicine* 62.7 (2006): 1768-84.

Zuberi, Dan. *Differences that Matter*. Ithaca: ILR Press/Cornell University Press, 2006.

Unequal Democracies in Europe: Modes of Participation, Understanding, and Perception of Democracy

Susanne Pickel

Introduction

In comparison to Namibia, Russia, and a number of countries in Latin America, the level of social inequality in the states of the European Union is moderate (World Bank), as political participation, at least in elections, is practiced by about two-thirds of the electorate. However, this does not mean that we can assume that this (albeit, moderate) level of social inequality has no consequences for the democracies of Europe. Socially stratified access to and participation in all forms of political activity have been demonstrated empirically (Merkel and Petri; Schäfer), as has the fact that the higher layers of society in terms of education and income benefit disproportionately from the economic successes of societies and are over-represented in parliaments (Gilens). In addition, their interests are more strongly taken account of by the elected representatives and enforced in the political decision-making process (Flavin; Carnes). It would therefore not be surprising to find that members of these layers, not least as a consequence of their education, should articulate an understanding of democracy that differs from the one held by the less privileged. If such rejections of interests of the less privileged by society are tolerable in the neoliberal market, they do nonetheless seem to be increasingly incompatible with democracy, at least when democracy entails political governance. According to this way of thinking, democracy as social democracy should be neutralized (Streeck 90-97), since it is engaged in regulating market processes. But the needs and demands of many citizens cannot be reconciled with a purely liberal democracy, in which economic markets ignore uneven playing fields. In this essay, I will investigate the impact that social inequality has on the political sphere, on people's understanding of democracy, on the political attitudes of citizens, on their political behavior, and finally on the quality of democracy. But what we can expect to see is not only an effect *within* societies. There are also discrepancies in wealth and education *between* European countries that affect the quality of democracy. To answer these questions, I will analyze and compare macrodata at the country level and microdata at the level of the individual citizen.

Social Inequality, Political Equality, and Political Participation

Social inequality, political equality, and political participation are closely linked: Maslow's "hierarchy of needs" already pointed to the fact that people who are confident in meeting their basic needs are more likely to develop political interests than those who have to struggle to do so on a daily basis. Increased prosperity and more economic resources facilitate investment in education which not only enables people to participate in political activity, but also ensures that they have access to better economic maintenance. At the top of the hierarchy (later interpreted as a "pyramid of needs") are people who live in economically secure conditions and have a high level of education as well as demanding occupations. These help them in their quest for self-realization, political participation, and codetermination (Inglehart and Welzel; Welzel). They are able to take the rules given by the political system as politically equal citizens and to ensure that their interests are taken care of.

Social inequality works the other way. Thomas Piketty has demonstrated that earnings from investments usually grow more quickly than the entire economic output. He considers this to be a major cause of increasing global inequality. Because of 'old' wealth, wealthy people become ever wealthier, without having to generate additional capital. At the other end of society are people who are trapped in material deprivation. Their proportion is particularly high at more than 40% of the population in the EU countries of the east, particularly in Bulgaria, Romania, and Hungary, and particularly low at under 10% in the EU countries of the north.

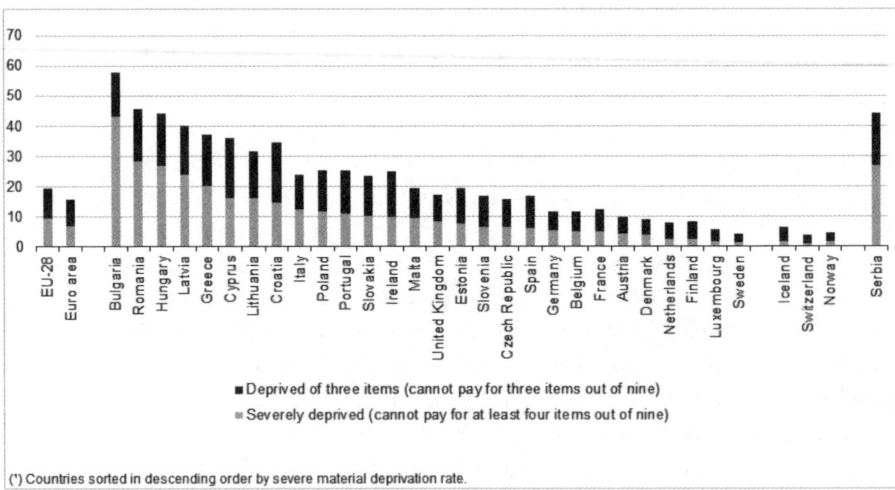

Fig. 1: Material deprivation rate, 2013. Source: EUROSTAT 2015a

When is a person materially deprived? A person is (severely) materially deprived if he or she is not able to afford at least three (four or more) out of nine of the following items, considered to be necessary or desirable: "(1) having arrears on mortgage or rent payments, utility bills, hire purchase installments or other loan payments, (2) not being able to afford one week's annual holiday away from home, (3) not being able to afford a meal with meat, chicken, fish (or vegetarian equivalent) every second day, (4) not being able to face unexpected financial expenses, (5) not being able to buy a telephone (including mobile phone), (6) not being able to buy a color television, (7) not being able to buy a washing machine, (8) not being able to buy a car, (9) not being able to afford heating to keep the house warm" (Eurostat 2015b).

Materially deprived people are not able to participate in social and political activities in the same way as people who are economically better off. They tend to remain at the base of the pyramid, thus not only starting in a worse position in their quest to reach the top at some point but their interests are also represented less well in politics than the concerns of more affluent citizens. This disadvantage has far-reaching consequences: socially disadvantaged people often have poor school-leaving qualifications, are often given only low-paying jobs, often have to rely on state support, and have no time for, or interest in, participating politically. This section of society is left behind and loses touch not only with the more affluent layers of society, but also with the political decision-making process. They participate less often in all forms of political involvement than those who are better placed economically. Despite formal political equality regarding access to the political decision-making process, they suffer the consequences of real political inequality when it comes to asserting their interests effectively.

Social inequality within societies raises considerable problems for equal opportunities among individuals, and differences in the levels of social inequality between European countries further contribute to this gradient of individual opportunities. Past and current debt crises in European countries illustrate this effect. It is not only youth unemployment rates – between 6.9% in Germany and 51.9% in Greece (EU average 19.1%, euro zone 21.2%, Spain 45.5%, Croatia 39% (Statista) – that point to the significant effects of social inequality between European societies. In some EU member states, material deprivation begins in adolescence and reduces the chances that people have of participating equally in economic and political processes at an early age.

The political and economic performance of the respective democracies suffers from the effects of financial crises and leads citizens in European countries with higher social inequality, such as in the southern or eastern parts of Europe, to demand more state involvement. The expectations that people have of democracy, and their ideas of what democracies should do for their citizens, are changing. These observations lead to the following claims: social inequality *within* societies leads to a different expectation of what makes a (good) democracy, to different political attitudes towards, confidence in, and feelings of legitimacy regarding the democratic political system, and finally to a different perception of opportunities for political participation, depending on whether an individual has a better or worse position in society.

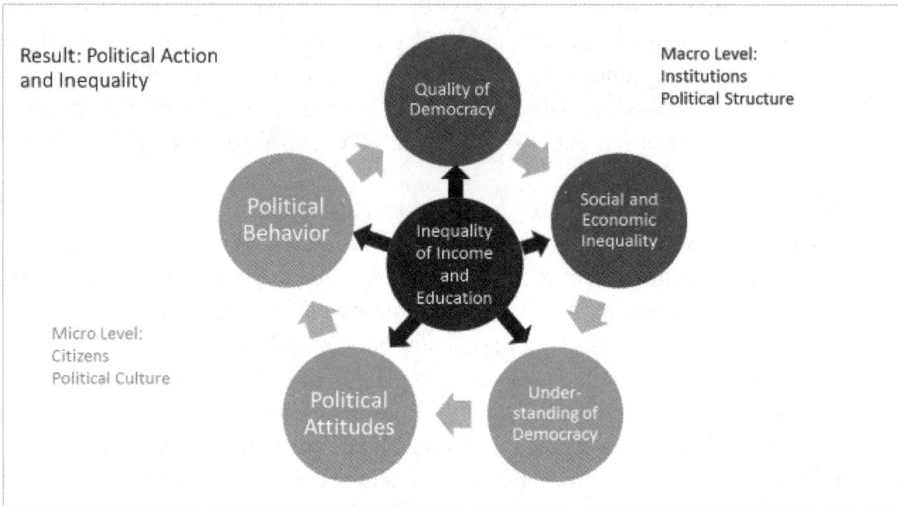

Fig. 2: Social inequality of political participation. Source: author's own diagram

Differences in the level of social inequality *between* the European countries lead to an inequality of opportunity for these countries with regard to whether they can achieve progress in social and economic development, provide their citizens with equal conditions of participation, and achieve a high quality in the realization of democratic principles. Finally, the different playing fields in society as a whole have an effect on individuals who, under the economic pressures that they face, cannot 'afford' any lasting political activity.

Data and Methods

The impact of social inequality on politics and political culture can only be identified through empirical analyses. In order to analyze the impact between societies and within a given society, data is required both on the situation of society as a whole and on the position of individual citizens, their attitudes and behavior, in a society. The macrodata on the characteristics of countries are taken from the Democracy Barometer, the Human Development Report, the database of the World Bank, the GINI index of social inequality (World Bank), and the documentation provided by Transparency International, the Corruption Perception Index (Transparency International). The Democracy Barometer determines the quality of democracies based on the concept of embedded democracy (Merkel), and focuses on the principle of free and fair elections. When there are no such elections, a political system cannot be a democracy. If there are elections, the political system meets the minimum requirement for an electoral democracy. The Democracy Barometer is based on the democratic principles of freedom, equality, and monitoring. These are taken up by the functions of individual liberties, rule of law, public sphere, competition, mutual constraints, governmental capability, transparency, participation, and representation. The Democracy Barometer records the years between 1990 and 2014 for 100 indicators, its values ranging from 0 (worst empirical value) to 100 (best empirical value). Scale values are shown for all principles, too.

The Human Development Index reflects the development undergone by states by combining the gross national income (GNI) per capita, life expectancy at birth, expected years of schooling, and mean years of schooling into an index. The values range from 0 (no development) to 1 (comprehensive development). The GINI index measures the ownership status of citizens: if assets are distributed unequally, it approaches the value of 100; if they are more equally distributed, the value of 1. The index is therefore able to provide a rough picture of social inequality. Transparency International has questioned various sources since 1995, mainly from business, about their experiences of corruption in the public sector in 168 countries around the world, with the results creating the Corruption Perception Index. The higher its value, the less corruption people perceive in a country (value range from 0 to 100). The microdata on the attitudes and social position of citizens are taken from the dataset of the European Social Survey (ESS) of 2012, Questionnaire: "Principle of Equality or Equivalence." It includes 27 European countries (Albania, Belgium, Bulgaria, Cyprus, Czech Republic, Denmark, Estonia, Finland, France, Germany, Hungary, Iceland, Italy, Kosovo, Lithuania, Netherlands, Norway, Poland, Portugal, Russia, Slovakia, Slovenia, Spain, Sweden, Switzerland, Ukraine, United Kingdom), and approximately 1000 respondents per country. The data were subjected to a cross-sectional analysis for 2012. The levels of analysis were merged at the level of aggregate data.

Social Inequality and Democracy: The Citizens' Perspective

We first have to examine the impact of social inequality on the democratic political systems in Europe based on the political behavior of citizens. Which forms of participation are chosen particularly often? Does political participation depend on the socio-structural characteristics (age, gender, education, income) of citizens?

Political Behavior in European Countries

A quick look at the frequencies of political participation in Western and Eastern Europe already shows that citizens opt more frequently for voting than for any other form of participation. On average, three-quarters of Europeans participate in elections to the national parliament. Far behind come petitions, product boycotts, participation in social organizations, and contacting politicians. Overall, the citizens of Western Europe participate more frequently than those of Eastern Europe, although low-input or seemingly non-political forms of conventional and unconventional participation are especially popular in this context.

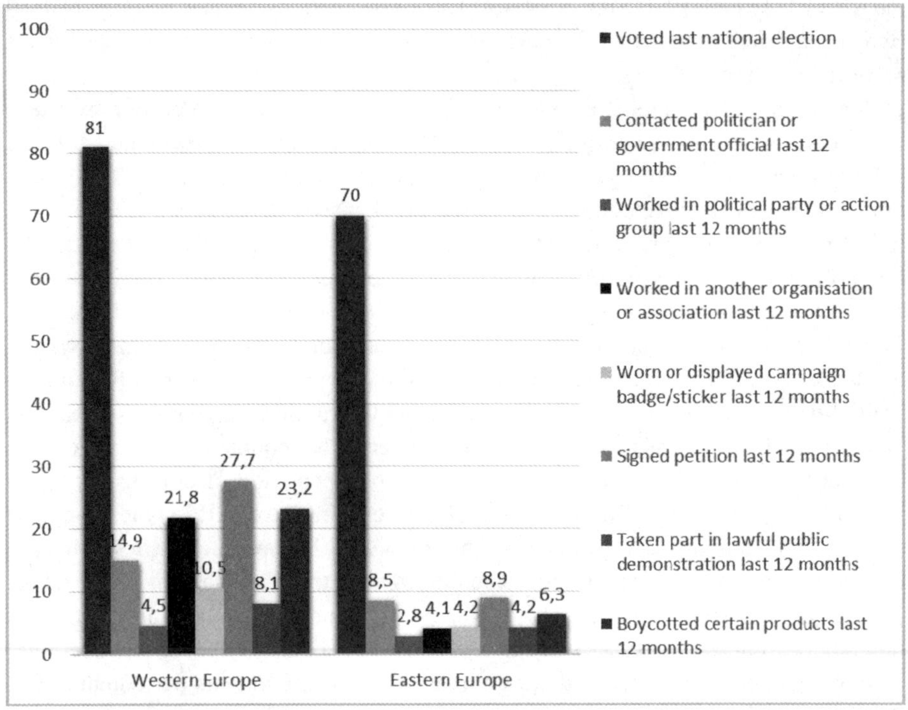

Fig. 3: Political participation in Western and Eastern Europe. Source: ESS 2012; author's own calculations

Voting, Petitions, and Demonstrations

If we look at the core forms of conventional (voting) and legal, unconventional (petitions, demonstrations) political participation, we can see significant differences between countries, as citizens of Western EU member states participate particularly often, citizens of Eastern EU member states are doing so particularly seldom (we should note, though, that the dataset of the ESS includes Norway and Switzerland as representatives of Western European non-EU members, and Russia, Ukraine, and Kosovo as representatives of Eastern European non-EU members).

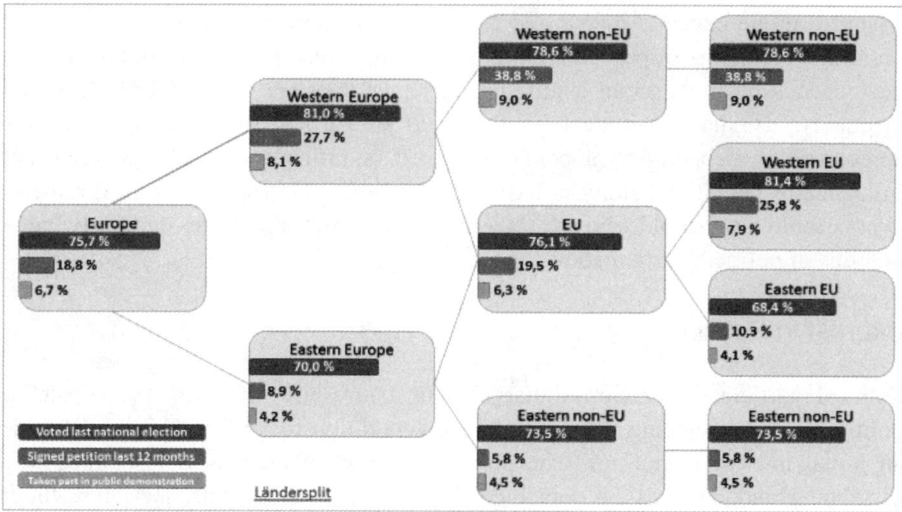

Fig. 4: Voting, petitions, and demonstrations in Europe. Source: ESS 2012; author's own calculations

How can we explain this behavior on the part of citizens? What socio-structural differences can explain whether citizens participate in elections, petitions, and demonstrations? Age is the most important predictor for voting in Western Europe. The older a person, the higher the probability that he or she will take part in elections. Inequality in terms of income has some positive impact throughout Western Europe except in Iceland. Inequality in terms of education is also important everywhere except in Cyprus. That means that social inequality in terms of education and income has an impact on voting behavior. The same holds true for petitions: education and income are the most important predictors of participation in petitions. Whether people sign a petition or not depends on their social status, i.e., whether they are well-off or not. Social inequality has an impact on this kind of participation as well. Taking part in a demonstration depends on a person's age. The younger a person is, the higher the probability that he or she will take part in demonstrations. This kind of political participation is affected by social inequality in some countries only: Switzerland, Spain, Finland, France, United Kingdom, Iceland, Netherlands, Norway, and Portugal. People who are socially underprivileged are also underprivileged in terms of political participation. This rule applies for all Western European countries.

In Eastern Europe, some societies break this rule: a more advanced age is the most important predictor for participating in elections everywhere except in Slovenia, the Czech Republic, and Estonia; here, the most important factor is voters' education. Inequality in terms of education is important in all other countries as well except in Albania, Ukraine, and Kosovo. Inequality in terms of income has some influence throughout Eastern Europe except in Albania, Bulgaria, Lithuania, and Kosovo. Social inequality has an impact on voting behavior in all of

Eastern Europe except Albania and Kosovo. Education and income are the most important predictors of participation in a petition: whether people sign a petition or not depends on their social status, i.e., whether they are well-off or not. Social inequality also has an impact on this kind of participation. Taking part in a demonstration depends on a person's age. It is influenced in all countries but Lithuania by social inequality in terms of education and income. For all Europe, it is noticeable that people who are socially underprivileged are also underprivileged in terms of political participation.

Interest in Politics

Political participation assumes that citizens know how they can participate in political decision-making processes. The precondition for political participation is an initial interest in politics. The political interest of citizens is also unequally distributed and depends on social conditions: there is no participation without political interest and hardly any political interest without education. Political interest is high if people are privileged with a high level of education and income, and if they are older, and often male. They are involved, organized, and assertive. Political interest is low if people are underprivileged with a low level of education and income, and they are younger, and often female. They are marginalized, not organized, and not assertive. The respective data show high, robust correlations (from 0.088 in France to 0.652 in Bulgaria). Levels of education are unequally distributed not only within European societies; the societies themselves also differ considerably from each other. While the proportion of citizens with a minimum qualification from school (*Hauptschulabschluss* or equivalent) in most Eastern European countries as well as in Germany and Iceland is sometimes well below 10%, that figure is between 10 and 25% of citizens in most Western European countries, with France (almost 30%), Spain (about 35%), and Portugal (about 50%) ranging highest (ESS 2012 self-reported education). Differences in school and university education not only influence the political interest of citizens, but also have permanent effects on how people understand democracy, on the democratic political culture, and on the quality of democracies.

Understanding of Democracy

The data provided by European Social Survey 2012 allow us to investigate the ideas that the citizens of 27 European countries have regarding a democratic political order. The variables of the module "Europeans' understandings and evaluations of democracy" (European Social Survey 2013) depict a spectrum of opinion regarding rule of law, accountability, participation, competition, representation, responsiveness, freedom, and equality. If we use a principal component analysis to bundle these variables together, then the attitudes of citizens form specific patterns. These patterns or dimensions can then be assigned to the properties of social and liberal democracies.

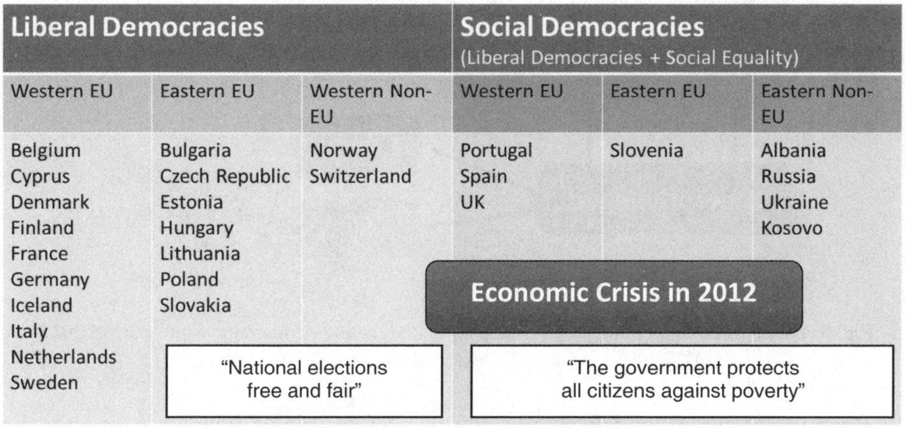

Fig. 5: Liberal and social democracies. Source: ESS 2012; author's own calculations: dimensions of a principal component analysis

It is striking that virtually all EU member countries, as well as the Western states of Norway and Switzerland, favor the idea of a liberal democracy without specific social measures of redistribution. Exceptions are those Western and Eastern countries that at the time of the survey were experiencing an economic crisis; in these countries, state social benefits are seen as a positive feature of democratic political systems. The same applies to those Eastern countries that are not members of the EU and where ideas of the state's duty of care, originating from the socialist period, continue to be important, and are often maintained by the socialist successor parties, at least partly to gain legitimacy. Political socialization and the economic situation do much to explain the different ideas of democracy between the countries.

Whether an individual favors a democracy that is social or liberal in character often depends less on his or her political socialization than on the particular position in society that the individual has. This can better explain the different ideas that exist within societies. In many countries (Belgium, Czech Republic, Denmark, Estonia, France, Germany, Iceland, Lithuania, Poland, Slovakia, United Kingdom), the privileged favor an idea of democracy that corresponds to liberal (market) ideals, while the underprivileged in these countries would like to see more social components anchored in their democracy. These attitudes are in line with the claim that material deprivation more often excludes those citizens affected negatively from the processes of liberal (market) democracies, or discriminates against them politically in addition to their economic disadvantages.

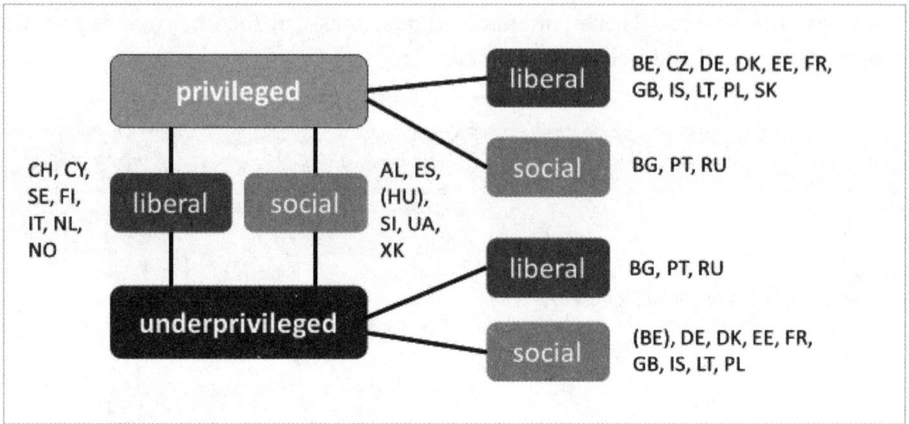

Fig. 6: Effect of being privileged on how people understand democracy. Source: ESS 2012; author's own calculations

In Bulgaria, Portugal, and Romania, the respective groups behave in exactly the opposite way. This may be due to the ongoing economic crises in these countries and their strong social(ist) character. People in Switzerland, Cyprus, Sweden, Finland, Italy, Netherlands, and Norway favor a liberal democracy, no matter whether they are privileged or not, whereas people in Albania, Spain, Hungary, Slovenia, Ukraine, and Bosnia prefer a social type of democracy. People's position in society therefore influences their understanding of democracy, but this does not apply in the same way for all countries. Western and economically successful Eastern countries correspond to general expectations, while countries in economic crises or those relatively distant from the EU have ideas of democracy that deviate from these expectations.

Political culture

Ideas regarding the characteristics of a democracy are the foundation of political culture in European countries. This culture comprises the various attitudes that citizens have towards "political objects," these objects being the political system as such, the institutions, agents, and the role that the political system can play (Almond and Verba). The attitudes, which are also called "political support," towards the political system are referred to as democratic legitimacy; attitudes towards the concrete political system in each country and its institutions, are called "system support of democracy;" and attitudes towards the agents and how they perform, are referred to as "satisfaction with democracy" (Easton). The attitudes reflect the type of democracy in terms of values, system, and performance. The more concrete and therefore more tangible the political objects are for citizens, the more critical their attitudes: democracy as a political system enjoys a high degree of legitimacy throughout Europe. In the Western countries, more than 90% of citizens feel that it is important to live in a democracy, while it is more than 80% in the Eastern countries. The lower percentage in the Eastern countries outside the EU are a result of the lower level of agreement in Russia and the Eastern part of Ukraine (ESS 2012).

Eastern and Western European societies differ even more in how people assess the extent to which their own country is democratic. In Western Europe, about three-quarters of citizens believe in the high quality of their democracies, while in Eastern Europe not even half the citizens do so; outside the EU, it is less than a third of the population. People clearly perceive deficits in the form of democracy in their own country. Almost half of the citizens in Western Europe are satisfied with democracy in their own country as well as with the political and economic benefits that it delivers; in Eastern Europe, about a third; outside the EU, barely a quarter. The benefits of democracy for its citizens' wellbeing are therefore seen particularly critically in the Eastern countries.

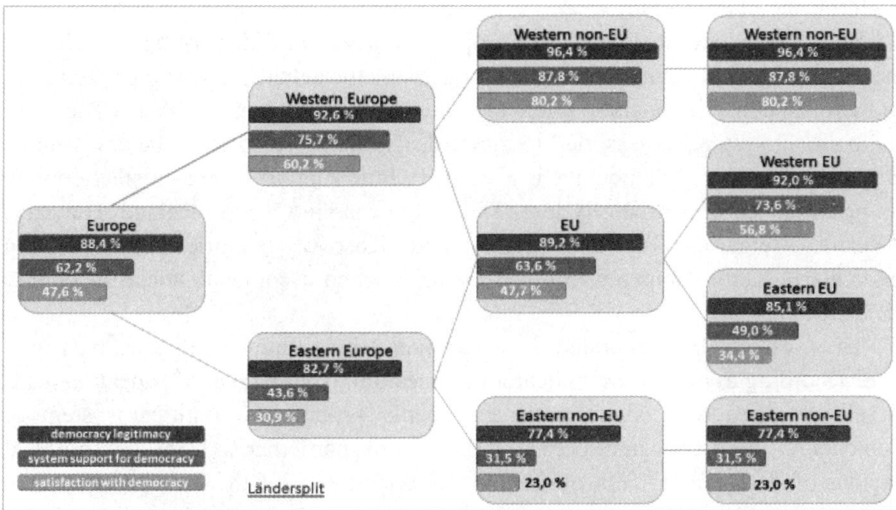

Fig. 7: Political attitudes in Europe. Source: ESS 2012; author's own calculations

Ideas about how a democracy should be constituted, whether liberal or social, shape the attitude towards the legitimacy of democracy itself in all countries. The same applies to people's satisfaction with democracy for virtually all EU member states. Satisfaction with economic performance hardly plays a role at all, however, and, where it does, it has no adverse effect on the fundamental legitimacy of democracy.

In Switzerland, Denmark, Finland, Sweden, Slovakia, and Lithuania, i.e. countries shaped by liberal ideas of democracy, people's expectations of a democracy correspond to the current condition of democracy in their countries. In contrast, people in Ireland, the Czech Republic, Albania, and Bulgaria clearly want to see a stronger orientation in their country towards the liberal model. Russian citizens are also dissatisfied, mainly because their expectations of a model of social democracy are not fulfilled. In all other countries, there is no evidence that ideas of democracy have an effect on how people assess their current democracy. In all countries, feelings of the legitimacy of democracy, satisfaction with both the government and the economy support the positive impression that people have with regard to their own democracy.

Only in Switzerland, Denmark, Finland, France, and Lithuania does people's understanding of democracy as liberal or social play a role when it comes to their satisfaction with how their democracy is performing. Here, citizens are satisfied with the performance of liberal democracy. In contrast, there is greater dissatisfaction with the performance of democracy in Spain, Portugal, and Romania, i.e. countries shaped by social ideas of democracy. In all countries, belief in the legitimacy of democracy, satisfaction with the government and with economic performance have a positive effect on how people assess the performance of democracy.

This means that the citizens of Europe have developed ideas of democracy that are either liberal or social in character, and assess the actual shape and performance of their respective democratic political systems according to these ideals. The more the political systems correspond to these ideals, the more positive the assessment. But the legitimacy of democracy is given very little support where satisfaction with its performance is particularly low. This is the case in Cyprus, Iceland, Hungary, Albania, Bulgaria, Russia, Ukraine, and Kosovo, countries that perform particularly badly compared to other countries when it comes to social inequality (ESS 2012).

These effects are moderated by social inequality within societies, as measured here according to the central indicator of education. A high level of education leads in all countries to a situation where people support the political system of democracy. Well-educated people thus benefit particularly from the political system of democracy. This observation is underlined by the fact that educated citizens in Albania, Spain, Hungary, Slovenia, Slovakia, and Ukraine are dissatisfied with the performance of their democracies, since their demands are simply not met due to political and economic crises. The returns of their education are much lower than in other countries.

Quality of Democracy: The Perspective of Societies

The quality of democracy in terms of freedom, equality, and political control and especially the quality of political equality varies considerably between the European countries. While most Central European democracies share similar quality values, the Scandinavian countries show a particularly high, and the Eastern European countries a significantly lower quality with regard to their democratic political system in general and to political equality in particular. What causes these differences? Social differences were assumed to be one factor, with these differences being depicted by the GINI index. According to this assumption, the lower the social inequality in a society, the higher its quality of democracy. We cannot find a similar effect of social inequality on political equality, however. States with lower social inequality do not necessarily achieve better values regarding the principle of political equality. On the other hand, a higher human development does much to promote not only the quality of democracy, but also the political equality of its citizens. The same applies to the fight against corruption, with even clearer correlation values.

Societies with low social inequality, advanced human development, and a functioning politics of anti-corruption achieve a better quality of democracy and promote the principle of political equality. Differences are particularly apparent here between the Northern European and the (South-) Eastern European countries.

Social inequality (GINI)

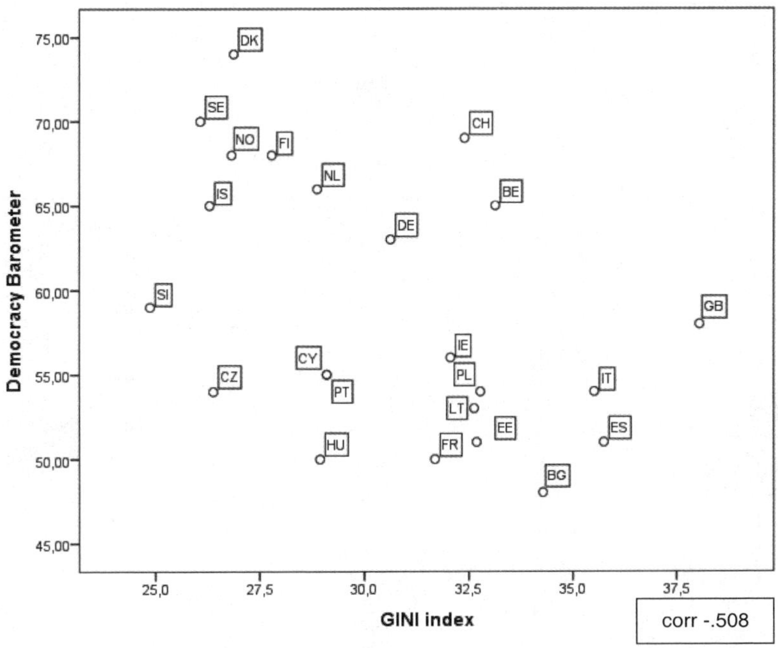

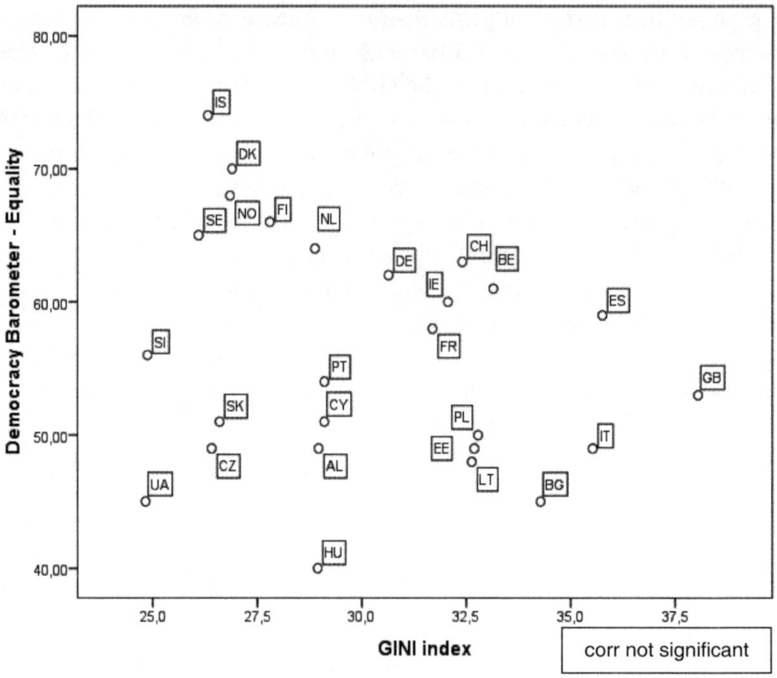

Human development (HDI)

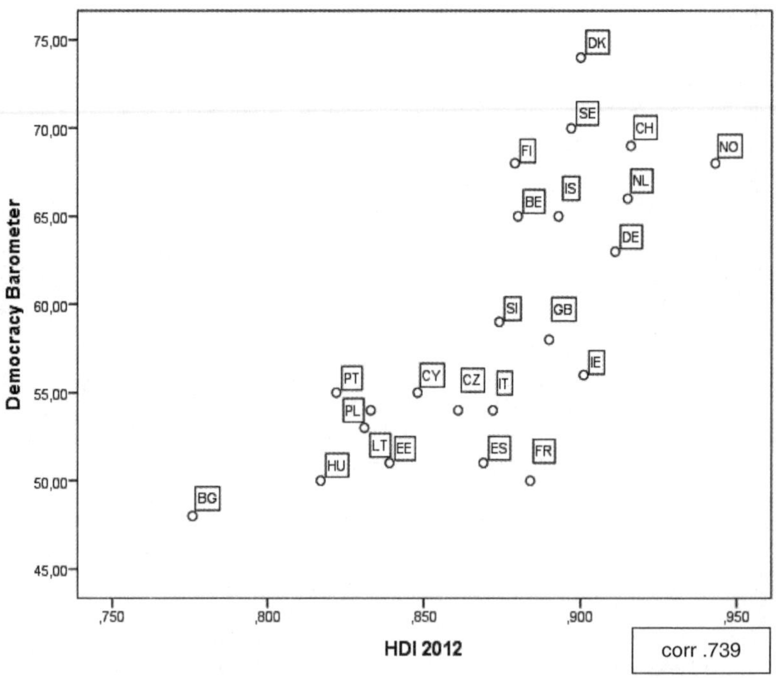

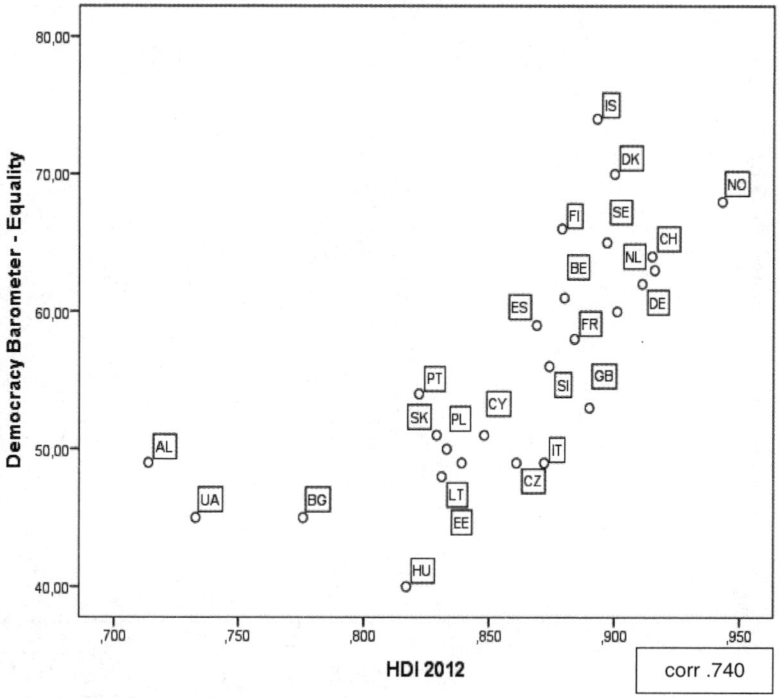

Corruption (CPI)

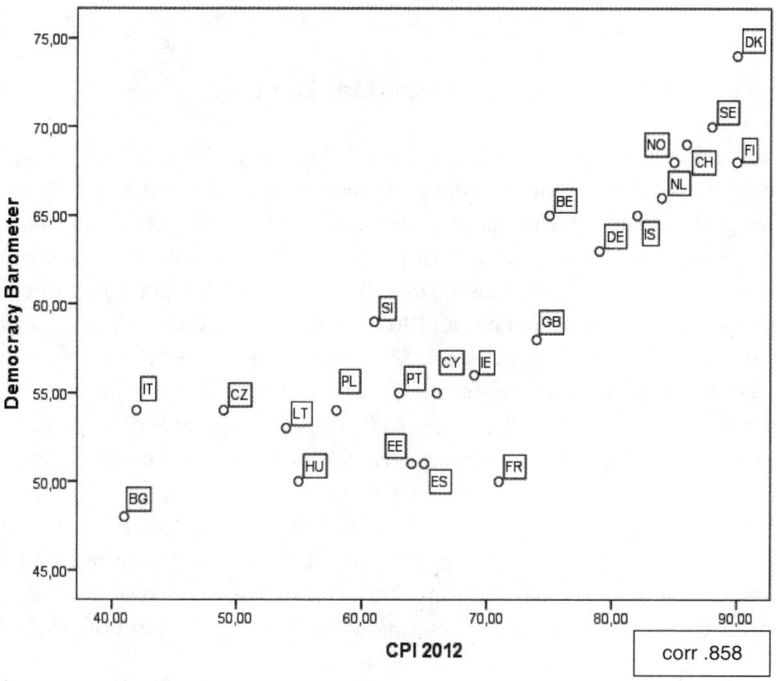

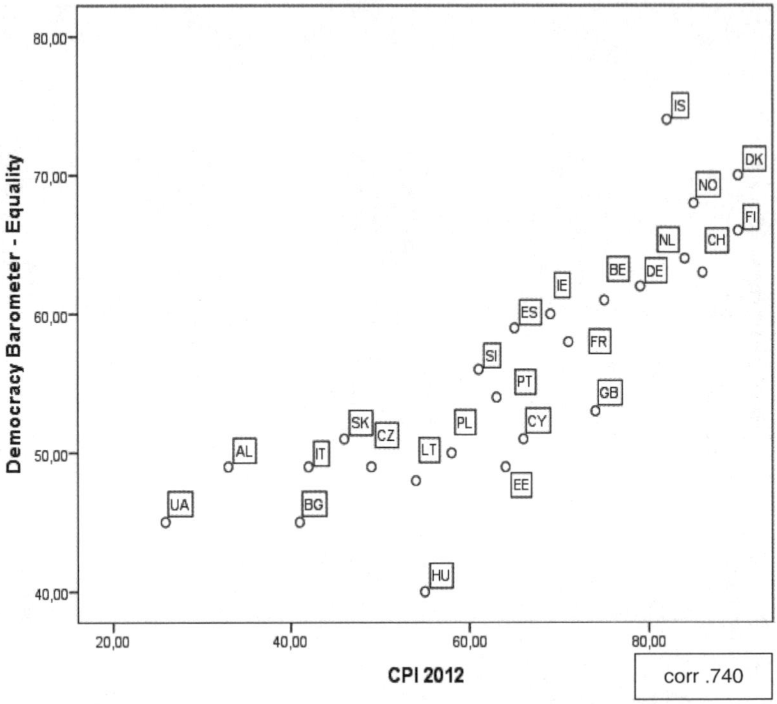

Fig. 8: What shapes the quality of democracy and political equality? Source: author's own calculations

Macrolevel Determinants of Political Behavior

How, then, do all the factors of social inequality, the quality of democracy, human development, people's understanding of democracy, and political culture affect political participation? Differences in social inequality between countries do not result in differences in voter turnout or participation in demonstrations, but they do have a significant impact on how frequently people submit petitions: in countries with a high level of development and low corruption, people submit significantly more petitions than in less modernized countries with corrupt political figures. How people understand democracy affects all forms of participation, albeit in different ways. The belief that free and fair elections are part of democracy encourages voter participation; perspectives influenced by social democracy foster participation in elections and demonstrations; and the support of protection of minority rights has an effect all forms of participation. The higher the legitimacy of democracy in a country, the more people are likely to participate in elections and petitions. Attitudes to the current democratic political system and to the performance of democracy also determine the number of petitions that people submit.

Determinants		Voting	Petitions	Demonstrations
Quality of Democracy		.466	.797	n.s.
Gini Index	Inequality (Macro Level)	n.s.	n.s.	n.s.
CPI	Inequality (Macro Level)	n.s.	.697**	n.s.
HDI (including education)	Inequality (Macro Level)	n.s.	.711**	n.s.
National elections free and fair	Under-standing of Democracy (Makro Level)	.427*	n.s.	n.s.
The media provide citizens with reliable information to judge the government	Under-standing of Democracy (Makro Level)	n.s.	n.s.	n.s.
The rights of minority groups are protected	Under-standing of Democracy (Makro Level)	.416*	.464*	.393*
The government protects all citizens against poverty	Under-standing of Democracy (Makro Level)	.420*	n.s.	.388*
How important to live in democratically governed country	Political Attitudes (Micro Level)	.469*	.570**	n.s.
How democratic [country] is overall	Political Attitudes (Micro Level)	n.s.	.715**	n.s.
How satisfied with the way democracy works in country	Political Attitudes (Micro Level)	n.s.	.647**	n.s.

Fig. 9: Determinants of political behavior. Source: ESS 2012, Democracy Barometer, World Bank, Human Development Index 2013, Transparency International; author's own calculations, multiple regression, sig. < .05, N=27

All aspects of social inequality, the understanding of democracy, as well as the political attitudes that I discussed above therefore affect the participation of citizens in elections, petitions, and demonstrations. Differences in social inequality between countries are reflected in differences in actual political participation.

Discussion: Differences and Inequalities in How People Understand, Participate in, and Perceive Democracy

Differences in the level of social inequality between European states result in differences in the quality of democracy, but not in differences in political equality. Here, a criterion of democracy, "one man, one vote," can be realized. Whether a citizen *can*, in principle, participate formally in the process of political decision-making does not depend on his or her education or income, but whether he or she actually *does* participate depends very much on these factors: as expected, we can establish negative effects of deprivation of political participation. Education and prosperity allow greater participation in political activity. People who are closer to the top of the Maslow pyramid have more interest in, and more time for, politics. In particular, they devote themselves significantly more often to submitting petitions, which, compared to participating in elections or demonstrations, is a time-consuming activity.

People's understanding of what constitutes a democracy also differs between privileged and less privileged citizens, at least in Western Europe. Materially deprived people cannot benefit from economic and political freedom to the same extent as people who are well-off. The latter favor a liberal democracy, while the former favor a social democracy that provides for more redistribution and more care for less economically well-off people. This form of democracy, though, is no longer available in virtually any European democracy. This has not (yet) affected people's assessment of democracy as legitimate, but it has affected their satisfaction with how democratic political systems are implemented and with the current performance of democracy in their own country. The current movements arguing for renationalization are clear indications of a desire for change in the concrete implementation of democracy, especially among people who fear slipping into material deprivation.

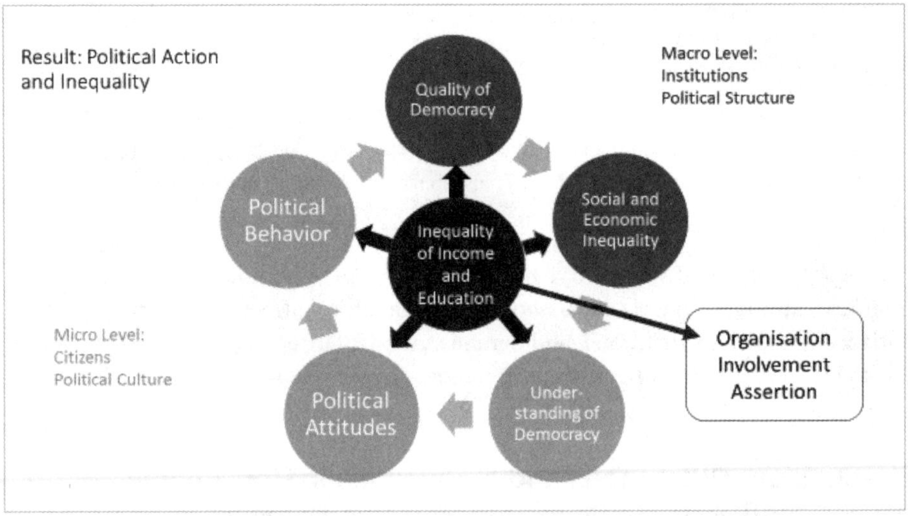

Fig. 10: Political action and inequality. Source: author's own diagram

Overall, we have shown that social inequality, as a feature difference both between and within European countries, has significant effects on people's understanding of, attitudes towards, and participation in democracy. Countries with greater social inequality are usually unable to achieve the same quality of democracy as more egalitarian societies. Privileged people participate more frequently in organizations, they are more involved, and are better able to involve themselves in the political process. This results in a double disadvantage for less privileged people: they cannot participate to the same extent in the political decision-making process, and this process takes their interests into account to a lesser degree. This effect is found in all European countries. The higher the level of social inequality in a country, the more serious are these effects. The more a society is marked by material deprivation and pure market liberalism, the more it undermines the very principles of a democracy that would in fact give all its citizens equal access to the political process of decision-making.

Works Cited

Almond, Gabriel A., and Sidney Verba. *The Civic Culture: Political Attitudes and Democracy in Five Nations*. Princeton: Princeton University Press, 1963.

Carnes, Nicholas. *White-Collar Government: The Hidden Role of Class in Economic Policy Making*. Chicago: Chicago University Press, 2013.

Democracy Barometer. 2016. <www.democracybarometer.org>.

Easton, David. "A Re-Assessment of the Concept of Political Support." *British Journal of Political Science* 5.4 (1975): 435-57.

European Social Survey. 2013. *Round 6 Module on Europeans' Understandings and Evaluations of Democracy – Final Module in Template*. London: Centre for Comparative Social Surveys, City University London, 2013.

---. 2012. Datadownload. <www.europeansocialsurvey.org/data/download.html?r=6>.

Eurostat. 2015a. <ec.europa.eu/eurostat/statistics-explained/index.php/File:Material_deprivation_rate_%E2%80%94_proportion_of_persons_who_cannot_afford_to_pay_for_selected_items,_2013.png>.

---. 2015b. <ec.europa.eu/eurostat/statistics-explained/index.php/Material_deprivation_and_low_work_intensity_statistics>.

Flavin, Patrick. "Income Inequality and Policy Representation in the American States." *American Politics Research* 40 (2012): 29-59.

Gilens, Martin. "Inequality and Democratic Responsiveness." *Public Opinion Quarterly* 69.5 (2005): 778-96.

Human Development Report. *Human Development Index 2012*. <hdr.undp.org/en/content/table-1-human-development-index-and-its-components>.

---. *Human Development Index* 2013. <hdr.undp.org/en/2013-report>.

Inglehart, Ronald, and Christian Welzel. *Modernization, Cultural Change, and Democracy: The Human Development Sequence*. Cambridge: Cambridge University Press, 2005.

Maslow, Abraham. "A Theory of Human Motivation." *Psychological Review* 50.4 (1943): 370-96.

Merkel, Wolfgang. "Embedded and Defective Democracies." *Democratization* 11.5 (December 2004): 33-58.

---, and Alexander Petri. "Partizipation und Inklusion." *Demokratie in Deutschland*. Ed. Friedrich Ebert Stiftung. Berlin: 2011.

Piketty, Thomas. *Capital in the Twenty-First Century*. Cambridge: Belknap Press, 2014.

Schäfer, Armin. "Die Folgen sozialer Ungleichheit für die Demokratie in Westeuropa." *Zeitschrift für Vergleichende Politikwissenschaft* 4.1 (2010): 131-56.

Statista. 2016. *Jugendarbeitslosigkeit in Europa*. <de.statista.com/statistik/daten/studie/74795/umfrage/jugendarbeitslosigkeit-in-europa/>.

Streeck, Wolfgang. *Gekaufte Zeit: Die vertagte Krise des demokratischen Kapitalismus*. Frankfurt a. M.: Suhrkamp, 2013.

Transparency International. *Corruption Perception Index 2012*. <www.transparency.org/cpi2012/results>.

Welzel, Christian. *Freedom Rising*. Cambridge: Cambridge University Press, 2013.

World Bank. *GINI-Index*. 2012. <data.worldbank.org/indicator/SI.POV.GINI>.

Why Don't Americans Care About Inequality?

Lisa A. Keister

There is no question that inequality is extreme in the United States, and some groups are clearly much worse off than others (Collins and Hoxie; Keister 2014; McCall and Percheski; Piketty). There are also some individuals and groups – social activists, some academics – who find this deeply troubling. Yet more general levels of dissatisfaction with the state of inequality in the United States are relatively low; that is, most people are just not overly concerned about inequality. Indeed, dissatisfaction is lower than social scientists predict it to be given the extreme levels of inequality that exist in many countries (Winship), and dissatisfaction is also lower than many activists would like given that apathy typically accompanies it. In this essay, I explore why levels of widespread outrage and calls for change are so low. I start by describing how unequally distributed income and wealth are in the United States, and I highlight some of the important group-level differences in well-being that social scientists now take for granted. I then identify five reasons that these extreme levels of inequality do not lead to more discontent. The reasons I offer are speculative but are based on well-established principles and evidence from the social sciences.

Income and Wealth Inequality

Income and wealth are two of the measures that are most commonly used to assess inequality. The two terms are often used interchangeably, but they have very different meanings and different implications for understanding inequality. *Income* is a flow of funds into the household over time from wages or salaries, businesses, investments (i.e., interest and dividend income), capital gains, government transfer payments, gifts, and other sources. Income can be measured at either the individual or household level, and income from various sources can have different implications for well-being. For example, wage/salary income involves work and time commitments that are very different from those required to manage the investments that produce interest/dividend income or to run a business that produces business income. In contrast, *wealth* refers to the things people own at a single point in time and is usually measured as net worth (total household assets less total liabilities or debts). Assets include real assets (e.g., the home or primary residence, other real estate, business equity, vehicles) and financial assets (e.g., transaction accounts, certificates of deposit, bonds, stocks, mutual funds, retirement accounts). Debts include mortgages, consumer debt, student loans, and other liabilities. *Financial wealth* is total financial assets, a measure of relatively liquid assets such as stocks and bonds that, for most households, refers to non-housing wealth. Financial wealth is particularly significant for understanding resource concentration because ownership of financial assets tends to be even more highly concentrated than ownership of real assets, and financial assets are also often used to exert political influence as they can be used to make large, influential donations. Net worth and financial wealth are both usually measured at the household level because many assets, such as the family home, tend to be jointly owned.

Income and wealth are used as metrics for well-being and inequality because each has important advantages. Income is essential for paying for current needs and desires, and it can provide a degree of social and political power. Income becomes wealth when it is saved, and the advantages of wealth ownership are even more far-reaching. The family home, for instance, has both current use-value and investment value. Similarly, a business can provide current income and long-term investment advantages. Wealth can enhance educational attainment, occupational opportunities, political power, and social influence. It provides a buffer against income interruptions, medical emergencies, and other crises such as accidents and natural disasters (Keister 2014). Wealth can create more wealth when it is reinvested, and it can generate income in the form of interest or dividends. Perhaps most significantly, wealth can be passed to future generations to extend these benefits indefinitely. Total household income and total household net worth have been correlated at about 0.5 to 0.6 since 2001, a pattern that reflects extremes and that underscores the importance of defining income and wealth clearly (Keister and Lee 2014). First, some households have high income from current work but have relatively low savings and, as a result, low wealth; for instance, some top executives, surgeons, and professional athletes have high salaries but relatively low saving rates and thus low wealth. At the other extreme are households with high net worth but low income; for example, a person who inherited high wealth or a retiree who saved consistently over the working years may have high levels of assets but low income from current work. The correlation is further complicated by the fact that those with high wealth are also likely to receive interest/dividend income, highlighting the importance of specifying income and wealth sources.

It has become clear that the distribution of income and wealth are highly unequal in the United States. In recent work, stratification scholars have begun to focus on the one percent – those at the top of the income and wealth distributions – to underscore the degree of inequality and to understand recent patterns in the concentration of financial well-being. The findings are startling. Since 1980, the percentage of total household income going to the top one percent of income earners has risen dramatically: since 2001, this group has received between 17% and 21% of total household income (Atkinson and Piketty; Keister 2014; McCall and Percheski). Consistent with this, median household income was less than $46,000, but the threshold for being in the top one percent by income exceeded

$600,000 in 2010 (Keister 2014). Although the top one percent of income earners lost about 4% of their income share between 2007 and 2010, the next 9% actually gained slightly during that time. This does not suggest that income levels for the top 10 percent increased; rather, it signals a reordering of the distribution as those at the bottom were more likely to lose jobs and thus income (Grusky et al.). Yet, the 2007-2009 recession had a somewhat equalizing effect as the percentage of total income going to top earners in 2010 returned to 2004 levels. The effect of the recession was also clear in changes in the well-being of more average families: median household income fell nearly 8% as a result of the recession, a decline caused by losses in both earned income and capital gains income despite an increase in the prevalence of young adults living with their parents (Keister 2014; Smeeding et al.).

Although it receives less research attention, wealth ownership is even more highly concentrated than income in the United States. Since 1980, the top one percent of net worth owners have held between 33% and 38% of total household wealth or net worth (Keister and Lee 2014; Kennickell; Ohlsson et al.). In 2010, median household net worth was less than $80,000, but the threshold for being in the top one percent of net worth owners was nearly $7 million (Keister 2014; Kopczuk and Saez). Because the 2007-2009 recession eroded both the housing wealth and savings of most households, there were important changes in wealth ownership during these years. Indeed, the share of total net worth held by the top one percent increased between 2007 and 2010 (Keister 2014). Median net worth increased modestly between 2001 and 2004, spiked to more than $126,000 dollars in 2007, and fell by nearly 40% in 2010. During the 2007-2010 period, debt also increased as a share of total net worth across the wealth distribution, and the portion of net worth accounted for by housing wealth rose particularly for those in the lower half of the wealth distribution.

The story gets worse when we dig deeper into wealth ownership. For example, the ownership of financial wealth – liquid wealth that provides a buffer against financial emergencies – is even more concentrated than the ownership of net worth. We now know that the top one percent has consistently owned 35% of financial assets since 2001. The next nine percent of households has consistently owned at least 38% of financial assets, with their share rising to nearly 44% in 2010 (Keister and Lee 2014). Thus, the top 10 percent of wealth owners owned nearly 80% of financial assets in 2010, and the remaining 90% of the population owned 20%. Despite a rise in financial asset values and because of the degree to which financial asset ownership is concentrated, there was only a slight increase in the percentage of financial assets owned by the wealthiest households in the years preceding the recent financial crisis and recession. Between 2004 and 2007, the top one percent increased their share of total household financial assets from 36.6% to 37.6%, while the next 9% increased their portion of financial assets by only 0.1% (Keister and Lee 2014).

Finally, social scientists often use the Gini coefficient to understand the degree to which resource ownership is concentrated. The Gini is a proportion ranging from 0 to 1, with 0 indicating perfect equality and 1 indicating perfect inequality. Conceptually, if a single household were to receive all income or own all wealth, the Gini coefficient would equal 1. The Gini is a common measure of income inequality, and it is becoming standard in research on wealth disparities (Keister and Lee 2014). Fig. 1 shows that the Gini coefficient for income has risen overall since the early 1980s, but it was relatively stable between 2000 and 2013 (author's estimates from the Survey of Consumer Finances; see Keister 2014 for more details). The Gini coefficient for income in the United States is quite high, exceeding 0.5 since the early 2000s. This means that more than half of all income would have to be redistributed to have perfect income equality. Yet the Gini coefficients for net worth and financial asset ownership are considerably higher still: both the net worth and financial assets Gini coefficients have exceeded 0.8 for decades (Keister 2014; Wolff 2010). One surprising pattern is that between 2001 and 2007, wealth inequality did not increase as much as income inequality did; however, it is becoming clear that this reflects the fact that asset values during that period increased, but household debt was also expanding and cancelling out asset gains for many households (Keister and Lee 2014; Wolff 2002, 2010).

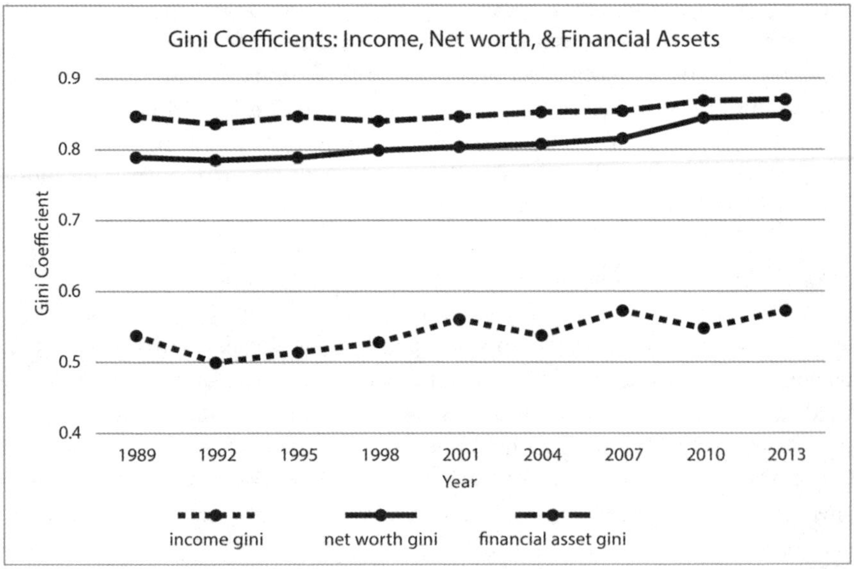

Fig. 1: Inequality trends

The Privileged and the Rest

Details about who has access to income and wealth in the United States are also becoming clear. We now know, for example, that those at the top of the income and wealth distributions are disproportionately male, white, and married. Most have children and are employed full time. They are also much more likely than the typical American to be self-employed (Bricker et al. 2011, 2012; Freeland: Raffalovich et al.). Consistent with this, entrepreneurship is an important way through which people move up within the wealth distribution (Keister 2005), although there is little evidence that having wealth leads to higher rates of business startup (Kim et al. 2003, 2004). In addition, those at the top of the income and wealth distributions tend to be middle-aged, to have at least a college education, and to be employed in professional and managerial occupations (Keister 2014). These patterns have not changed much over the last decade and are similar even at the very top of the income and wealth distributions; that is, these patterns are true even for those in the top 0.5% of these distributions and those in the Forbes 400 (the very wealthiest households). There was some change between 2007 and 2010 (i.e., following the recession) in self-employment. In 2007, 48.6% of the top one percent (defined by net worth) were self-employed (not shown), but in 2010, nearly 56% of the top one percent were self-employed. More detailed analyses suggest that it was the self-employed who were better able to weather the financial storm; this is consistent with evidence that the top one percent of wealth owners experienced the greatest wealth loss during the recession but that their assets allowed them to withstand the crisis better than others (Grusky et al.; Keister 2014).

Why Is There so Little Discontent?

Although inequality is extreme, there is remarkably little discontent about either the overall distribution of resources or the fact that some groups are clearly underrepresented among the privileged. The degree to which Americans care about inequality has been debated elsewhere (see Winship for a summary and discussion of the work), and I will not revisit the details here. A small minority of commentators in this field suggest that Americans are somewhat concerned, but the overwhelming majority of work suggests Americans are simply not bothered by inequality. The reasons for this relative apathy, however, have attracted almost no attention. Of course, speculating about why this is the case is challenging, but I propose that there are at least five reasons that are likely at work. To be clear, I am not arguing that people *should not care* about inequality! On the contrary, I am offering some reasons for the empirical reality that – on average – they *do not care* much.

The first important explanation for the relative lack of dissatisfaction about inequality is *homophily*, the notion that we tend to spend most of our time with people like us. Social scientists have studied homophily – and its opposite, heterophily – across various settings and find that social relations are highly consistent with our tendency to sort ourselves so that we resemble those we encounter regularly. That is, we are typically very similar to our friends, neighbors, work associates, acquaintances, and of course family members on most demographic traits: race, ethnicity, education, family structure, religious beliefs, and political views. We also tend to be similar to those around us on income and wealth measures. By contrast, heterophily is rare. Even within heterogeneous settings (e.g., some schools, workplaces), we tend to sort ourselves into smaller groups or cliques of similar others. As a result, we encounter a small slice of the population on most days and rarely see evidence of inequality. Even those who are extremely rich or extremely poor spend most of their time in the company of other very rich or very poor people, giving them little reason to think about inequality most of the time. Most Americans are certainly aware that Bill Gates – and other very wealthy people – have enormous amounts of wealth and income. However, on any given day, for average families very wealthy people like Gates are no different than people in movies or on television. The result is that inequality is seldom relevant to an average American even if they know it is extreme.

A second reason for the general lack of concern about inequality is the notion that rising tides lift all boats. Even though inequality has grown over time and recently, the general trend in average income and wealth has been upward: median income increased noticeably between the early 2000s and 2007. It was only during the recession that the median household began to notice a sharp decline in financial well-being. Moreover, many families continued to have the same incomes as before the recession, even though unemployment rose and lowered the average household well-being (Keister 2014). Of course, the median household is doing quite a bit worse now than during the financial bubble of the late 2000s, and most estimates suggest that middle-class Americans have not recovered the income and wealth they lost during the recession. By contrast, those at the top of the income and wealth distributions have recovered and thrived, leading to the recent growth in inequality. Despite these patterns, most people compare themselves financially to their parents and grandparents, and most people still see that they appear to be better off then prior generations. They have nicer, larger homes and more consumer products; more families are able to send their kids to private schools and to college; vacations are more common; working conditions in most industries are better; and widespread participation in the stock market through 401k and similar plans gives the impression that wealth is rising.

Third, evidence of upward mobility kindles the idea that poverty and other challenges can (perhaps easily) be overcome. That is, despite overall growth in inequality and the reality that upward mobility of any sort is rather rare, some individuals and groups have been upwardly mobile. This evidence of mobility fuels the idea that anyone can do well with the right effort and under the right conditions. The success of particular individuals is often presented in the popular press – and internalized by many – as evidence that mobility is both common and possible. The Forbes list of the 400 richest Americans is filled with well-publicized examples of people who have gotten rich over their lives: Bill Gates, Mark Zuckerberg, Warren Buffet, Larry Page, Jeff Bezos, the heirs of Sam Walton, Michael Dell, Paul Allen, Oprah Winfrey, etc. Even if many of these people had relatively well-off parents, their stories are frequently portrayed as evidence that with the right combination of motivation and hard work, it is possible to become wildly rich.

In addition to particular individuals who appear to be upwardly mobile, there are entire groups that have experienced upward mobility, furthering the notion that such change is possible. White Roman Catholics in the United States are an important example. In prior generations, non-Hispanic whites raised in Roman Catholic families were among the poorest Americans on most dimensions including income and wealth. In recent years, however, these families have been upwardly mobile as a result of unique fertility, marriage, and education patterns (Keister 2007, 2011). The incomes, educations, and wealth of these individuals are now on par with the mainline Protestants to whom they were often compared unfavorably in the past; indeed, on many measures, the financial status of white Roman Catholics now exceeds that of mainline Protestants. More recent evidence suggests that Mexican Americans may be the next upwardly mobile group. In particular, there is evidence that through business startup, saving, and investing, Mexican-American families with more than a decade of tenure in the United States are also experiencing upward mobility on income and wealth (Keister and Borelli; Keister, Agius Vallejo and Borelli). Although this evidence is preliminary and should be interpreted with the knowledge that Mexican Americans are still experiencing considerable financial hardships on average, the evidence that mobility is possible for this group may well encourage the idea that mobility is common and attainable for anyone.

A fourth reason that many Americans do not care much about inequality is that they are busy, distracted, and stressed. Americans are working long days and experience high levels of stress about the hours, the work itself, and other issues such as health and personal finances much of the time (National Public Radio). The average American household has work and other activities planned from early morning until night, with little time for much else. More households than in previous decades have two adult breadwinners, and this means that other household chores have to be done before and after work hours. Scheduled activities for kids are also higher than in the past, and already-stretched parents have added these activities to their schedules. In recent years, adult children have also added to stress levels as they have moved back home at relatively high rates (Qian). Levels of stress about stagnating incomes and other issues such as health are also high. With all those activities and stress, there is little time to worry about bigger questions like inequality (National Public Radio). As a result, Americans are unhappy compared to other people in the world and emotional conditions are not much better for the very well-off. Indeed, the limited amount of evidence we have regarding the relationship between financial and emotional well-being finds that happiness among Americans rises modestly with income but reaches a plateau at about $75,000 in annual income (Kahneman and Deaton). Moreover, general levels of happiness have declined in recent years particularly among older adults who used to be among the happiness groups in the country (Twenge et al.). Of course, it might be logical to assume that at least some of this unhappiness would be directed at issues of inequities in financial well-being, but the distractions of work, life, and family appear to be overwhelming enough that inequality does not make it onto most people's lists of things to be stressed about.

Finally, it might be that academics and activists are focusing on something different than the average American when it comes to financial well-being. That is, academic research and efforts at social justice often reference inequality and discuss issues to change the distribution of resources without considering the important difference between inequality and poverty. Inequality – distribution of resources across individuals and households – is, indeed, extreme. Poverty – the lack of sufficient resources to live decently or to make ends meet – is also high, but it is not the same as inequality. Even if we raised everyone out of poverty, we could still have very high levels of inequality. That is, all people could have the income and wealth they need to pay their basic expenses, cover emergencies, retire well, and even have a little fun. Yet there could still be very high levels of inequality. The negative consequences of poverty are clear, and there is no question that some groups experience higher levels of poverty than others (Desmond; McLanahan and Kelly; Smeeding et al.). It is also clear that there are negative consequences associated with having insufficient levels of both income and wealth, and that the negative consequences can be passed from parents to children with the resources themselves (Hansen; Wolff and Gittleman). By contrast, the empirical evidence regarding the negative consequences of inequality is more limited. When inequality is high, academics and others often point to issues of power, including political power, that becomes concentrated in the hands of a small group as a consequence, and there is no doubt that this is a problem (Gilens). There is also evidence that those at the top of the income and net worth distributions are similar in their cultural preferences, lifestyles, and voting behavior which implies the existence of a unified upper class that has a preference to maintain its position (Domhoff). However, the upward social mobility in the United States is higher than we would expect by chance, and the propensity to move into top positions increases with education and self-employment (Keister 2005; Keister and Lee 2015). It does appear that people care about poverty, particularly childhood poverty (Pew Research Center), but whether that level of concern exceeds levels of concern regarding inequality is an open question. Future research might usefully study this issue.

Conclusion

Inequality is certainly high in the United States, but levels of discontent regarding inequality are low. In this essay, I summarized some recent and disturbing trends in the rise of inequality. I then explored five potential reasons that Americans seem to have little concern about these patterns. I discussed the role of homophily and proposed that our lack of contact with others who are different from us might be at the heart of the low levels of discontent that we find. I also addressed how rising incomes and wealth, evidence of upward social and economic mobility, and high levels of stress and general unhappiness might factor in. Finally, I speculated that Americans might be more concerned about poverty than they are about inequality, but I pointed out that we have little, if any, empirical evidence to support this claim. Future research might address this issue and might also explore each of these proposed mechanisms in greater detail.

Works Cited

Atkinson, Anthony B., and Thomas Piketty. *Top Incomes: A Global Perspective*. Oxford: Oxford University Press, 2010.

Bricker, Jesse, Brian Bucks, Arthur Kennickell, Traci Mach, and Kevin Moore. "Surveying the Aftermath of the Storm: Changes in Family Finances from 2007 to 2009." Federal Reserve Bank Working Paper 2011. <www.federalreserve.gov/pubs/feds/2011/201117/201117pap.pdf>.

---, Arthur B. Kennickell, Kevin Moore and John Sabelhaus. "Changes in U.S. Family Finances from 2007 to 2010: Evidence from the Survey of Consumer Finances." Federal Reserve Bank Working Paper 2012. <www.federalreserve.gov/pubs/bulletin/2012/pdf/scf12.pdf>.

Collins, Chuck, and Josh Hoxie. "Billionaire Bonanza: The Forbes 400 and the Rest of Us." Institute for Policy Studies 2015. <www.ips-dc.org/Billionaire-Bonanza/>.

Desmond, Matthew. "Eviction and the Reproduction of Urban Poverty." *American Journal of Sociology* 118.1 (2012): 88-133.

Domhoff, G. William. *Who Rules America? The Triumph of the Corporate Rich*. New York: McGraw Hill, 2013.

Freeland, Chrystia. *Plutocrats: The Rise of the New Global Super-Rich and the Fall of Everyone Else*. New York: Penguin, 2012.

Gilens, Martin. *Affluence and Influence: Economic Inequality and Political Power in America*. Princeton, NJ: Princeton University Press, 2012.

Grusky, David B., Bruce Western, and Christopher Wimer (eds.). *The Great Recession*. New York: Russell Sage, 2011.

Hansen, Marianne Nordli. "Self-Made Wealth or Family Wealth? Changes in Intergenerational Wealth Mobility." *Social Forces* 93.2 (2014): 457-81.

Kahneman, Daniel, and Angus Deaton. "High Income Improves Evaluation of Life but Not Emotional Well-Being." *Proceedings of the National Academy of Sciences* 107 (2010): 16489-93.

Keister, Lisa A. "The One Percent." *The Annual Review of Sociology* 40 (2014): 347-67.

---. "Religion and Attainment." *Sociological Focus* 44 (2011): 354-83.

---. "Upward Wealth Mobility: Exploring the Roman Catholic Advantage." *Social Forces* 85.3 (2007): 1195-225.

---. *Getting Rich: America's New Rich and How They Got That Way.* New York: Cambridge University Press, 2005.

---, and Hang Young Lee. "Is the One Percent Permeable?" Duke University Department of Sociology Working Paper 2015.

---, and Hang Young Lee. "The One Percent: Top Incomes and Wealth in Sociological Research." *Social Currents* 1 (2014): 13-24.

---, Jody Agius Vallejo, and E. Paige Borelli. "Mexican American Mobility: An Exploration of Wealth Accumulation Trajectories." *Social Forces* 89 (2014): 763-74.

---, and E. Paige Borelli. "Religion and Wealth Mobility: The Case of American Latinos." *Religion and Inequalities.* Ed. Lisa A. Keister and Darren E. Sherkat. New York: Cambridge University Press, 2013.

Kennickell, Arthur B. "Ponds and Streams: Wealth and Income in the U.S., 1989 to 2007." *Finance and Economics Discussion Series.* Washington, D.C.: Federal Reserve Board, 2009.

Kim, Phillip H., Howard E. Aldrich, and Lisa A. Keister. "Household Income and Net Worth." *Handbook of Entrepreneurial Dynamics: The Process of Business Creation in Contemporary America.* Ed. William B. Gartner et al. Thousand Oaks, CA: Sage, 2004. 49-61.

---. "If I Were Rich? Financial and Human Capital's Impact on Becoming a Nascent Entrepreneur." Paper presented at the annual meeting of the American Sociological Association in Atlanta, 16 August 2003.

Kopczuk, Wojciech, and Emmanuel Saez. "Top Wealth Shares in the United States: 1916-2000: Evidence from Estate Tax Returns." *National Tax Journal* 57.2 (2004): 445-87.

McCall, Leslie, and Christine Percheski. "Income Inequality: New Trends and Research Directions." *Annual Review of Sociology* 36.1 (2010): 329-47.

McLanahan, Sara S., and Erin Kelly. "The Feminization of Poverty." *Handbook of the Sociology of Gender.* Ed. Janet Chafetz. New York: Plenum Press, 1999.

National Public Radio, Robert Wood Johnson Foundation, and Harvard School of Public Health. "The Burden on Stress." 7 July 2014. <www.rwjf.org/en/library/research/2014/07/the-burden-of-stress-in-america.html>.

Ohlsson, Henry, Jesper Roine, and Daniel Waldenström. "Long-Run Changes in the Concentration of Wealth: An Overview of Recent Findings." *Personal*

Wealth from a Global Perspective. Ed. James B. Davies. Oxford: Oxford University Press. 2008. 42-63.

Pew Research Center. "Poverty." 2015. <www.pewresearch.org/topics/poverty/>.

Piketty, Thomas. *Capital in the Twenty-First Century*. Cambridge: Harvard University Press, 2013.

Qian, Zhenchao. "During the Great Recession, More Young Adults Lived with Parents." *US2010 Project* (August 2012): 1-29.

Raffalovich, Lawrence E., Shannon M. Monnat, and Hui-Shien Tsao. "Family Income at the Bottom and at the Top: Income Sources and Family Characteristics." *Research in Social Stratification and Mobility* 27 (2009): 301-09.

Smeeding, Timothy M., Jeffrey P. Thompson, Asaf Levanon, and Esra Burak. "Poverty and Income Inequality in the Early Stages of the Great Recession." *The Great Recession*. Ed. David B. Grusky, Bruce Western, and Christopher Wimer. New York: Russell Sage, 2011. 82-126.

Twenge, Jean M., Ryne A. Sherman, and Sonja Lyubomirsk. "More Happiness for Young People and Less for Mature Adults: Time Period Differences in Subjective Well-Being in the United States, 1972–2014." *Social Psychological and Personality Science* 58 (2015): 1-11.

Winship, Scott. "How Much Do Americans Care About Income Inequality?" *Brookings Briefs* 30 April 2013.

Wolff, Edward N. "Recent Trends in Household Wealth, 1983-2009: The Irresistible Rise of Household Debt." *Review of Economcs and Institutions* 2 (2010): 53-88.

---. *Top Heavy: A Study of the Increasing Inequality of Wealth in America*. New York: New Press, 2002.

---, and Maury Gittleman. "Inheritances and the Distribution of Wea!th or Whatever Happened to the Great Inheritance Boom? Results from the Scf and Psid." *Journal of Economic Inequality* 12 (2014): 439-68.

Inequality, Ethnopolitics, and Social Welfare: US Health Care Reform in the World War I Era

Axel R. Schäfer

Modern welfare states are arguably among the most effective means to reduce social inequality and achieve a measure of distributive justice in twentieth-century liberal, capitalist societies. During the heyday of welfare state-building between the 1930s and the 1970s, in particular, the income gaps in Western countries narrowed markedly. To this day, countries with highly developed welfare states display significantly less income disparity than those with weak systems of public social provision (Schröder 39; Esping-Andersen; Brady).

At the same time, a key prerequisite for higher levels of equality and redistribution, or so much of the social policy literature argues, are ethnic and cultural homogeneity. Scandinavian countries, for example, feature not only extensive welfare states and comparatively low levels of social inequality, they are also ethnically more homogeneous. In contrast, many studies suggest that the United States failed to develop a robust welfare state because of its ethnic and racial heterogeneity. Indeed, in the eyes of many observers the United States is just one manifestation of a larger general dilemma of modern welfare states in the age of global migration, namely, that the more culturally diverse a society is, the more difficult it becomes to establish effective systems of social provision that facilitate a fairer distribution of wealth (Alesina et al.; Alesina and Glaeser).

The most common arguments supporting this conclusion suggest that a mixture of cultural and economic factors militated against the development of more solidaristic, redistributive welfare states under the conditions of ethnic diversity.[1] On the one hand is the cultural problem of creating kinship ties and solidarities with strangers. As the British politician David Willetts put it,

> the basis on which you can extract large sums of money in tax and pay it out in benefits is that most people think the recipients are people like themselves [...]. If values become more diverse, if lifestyles become more differentiated, then it becomes more difficult to sustain the legitimacy of a universal risk-pooling welfare state. (qtd. in Goodhart)

In the words of historian Tony Judt, Western welfare states have usually enjoyed broad-based public support only in "small, homogenous countries." In places "where immigration and visible minorities have altered the demography,"

[1] For the contemporary debate, see Fox 2010: 454-55, 459-60; and Kettunen et al.

however, mistrust has often led to a loss of identification with the social welfare institutions of the liberal state (Judt).[2]

On the other hand, many critics point to the economics of ethnoracial stratification in capitalist societies as the root of weak welfare states. In particular they emphasize the 'dual labor force' in the United States, in which ethnic and racial divisions parallel skills and wage differentials. These racialized work structures, in which managerial and skilled workers with good wages and benefits are overwhelmingly white, and unskilled, low-paid, migratory workers in precarious labor arrangements are primarily nonwhite, generate inter-ethnic workplace conflicts, limit effective transethnic union organizing, and allow employers to draw upon a continuous supply of cheap, docile, and flexible workers. Rather than reducing inequality, social policies are complicit in reproducing these racially and ethnically-based divisions via the creation of fragmented, segmented, and paternalist welfare systems.

Observed through this lense, US welfare state-building often amounted less to an effort to foster social justice than an effort to hierarchize provision along race, ethnic, class, and gender lines. During the New Deal, for example, agricultural, domestic, and service workers were excluded from Social Security, leaving a larger number of women and African Americans without coverage. The G.I. Bill and racially-coded housing policies after World War II mainly provided subsidies for the development of homogenous, racially segregated white middle-class suburbs. And while the most discretionary, stingiest, and politically exposed *assistance programs,* such as Food Stamps, Medicaid, and the now defunct Aid to Families with Dependent Children (AFDC) offer meagre support with many restrictions to a largely minority and female clientele, *social insurance*, such as Social Security and Medicare, are 'respectable' programs that largely serve the white working and middle-classes.[3] Moreover, negative racial and ethnic stereotypes historically formed the conceptual core of a 'poverty knowledge' that located the origins of deprivation in behavioral deviance, moral deficiencies, and cultural pathology, rather than in socioeconomic inequality or the maldistribution of income.[4] Public health policies, for example, were frequently couched in a language which denounced the morality and cultural practices of the "queer conglomerate mass of heterogeneous elements […] [with a] taint of whiskey" (Riis 22).

In the past two decades scholars have probed further the relationship between multicultural societies and welfare states. Crucially, this research has revised the narrative that equates high levels of diversity and immigration with weak support for more universal social provision in two significant ways. First, it has found that "the effect of societal heterogeneity on the welfare state's ability to sustain its legitimacy is limited" (Mau and Burkhardt 226). Other factors, such as institutional

2 See also Gilens; Larsen.

3 See, for example, Mink; Abramowitz; Lieberman; Davies and Derthick; Lasch-Quinn.

4 See, for example, O'Connor; Handler and Hasenfeld 202-05; Mead 2-4, 16-23; and Epstein 8, 204.

structures and the politics of interpretation, need to be taken into consideration as well.[5] In Europe, for example, Belgium has developed an expansive welfare state despite considerable cultural and social heterogeneity. And in North America, Canada happily combines European-style welfare with multicultural politics (Banting 2000, 2010).

Second, scholars have shown that extensive and expensive systems of social provision often base their popular appeal on ethnopolitics. Indeed, ethnoracial segmentation can be utilized to build quite generous systems of social provision for in-groups and thus create attachments to welfare states among this clientele. Historian Cybelle Fox, for example, maintains in a study of American social policy from the Progressive Era to the New Deal that European immigrants benefitted from sustained investment in social welfare programs, whereas Mexicans and blacks were subjected to arbitrary discrimination, niggardly provision, deportation, degrading means, and morals-testing. Even noncitizenship and illegal status did not prevent European ethnics from receiving support. Meanwhile, illegal Mexican migrants who asked for assistance were deported with the help of the very social workers they had turned to for help (Fox).

These segmented, fragmented, and unequal welfare systems did not necessarily feature lower social expenditures than more universal and inclusive arrangements. Indeed, the axiomatic categorization of the United States as a 'laggard' in welfare state development is highly problematic. As Theda Skocpol has demonstrated, for example, the Civil War pension program had by 1890 developed into a quasi-universal system, which gobbled up a large percentage of the federal budget and was more generous and less discriminatory than comparable European systems (1984). Marcus Graeser has shown that the American welfare state is less characterized by its absence than by its multilayered "welfare society." And, as indicated earlier, New Deal and postwar policies subsumed European ethnic divisions while simultaneously reinscribing racial hierarchies.[6]

Social policies based on ethnopolitics have the potential to generate significant electoral support. For instance, despite decades of devolution, privatization, and government retrenchment, neoliberal policies in the United States have not so much undermined voters' attachment to social welfare programs as divided the electorate in line with different levels of benefits. Growing job insecurity, wealth gaps, and the rise of the new precariat have made many in the middle and working classes even more defensive of their privileged position within the system of social provision. The political right thus often has to tread carefully when it comes to dismantling the welfare state. In the United Kingdom for example, its post-Thatcherite despisers fall over each other to guarantee that the National Health Service (NHS), a key achievement of Labour postwar social policies, is protected. And in the United States, the Republicans face the dilemma expressed by one Tea

[5] See also Brady and Finnigan.

[6] On shifting definitions of "whiteness," see Jacobsen 19; Gerstle 162-86.

Party activist when he reportedly demanded of a South Carolina Republican congressman: "Keep your government hands off my Medicare" (qtd. in Rucker; vanden Heuvel). Indeed, the appeal of Republican policies in recent decades was less based on principled antistatism than on what historian Alonzo Hamby has called "reactionary Keynesianism" (340). This combines deep resentment against cultural secularization, social liberalization, racial modernization, and liberalized immigration policies with staunch support for government military spending, economic stimulus packages, punitive intervention, public aid for religious social services, and extensive corporate subsidies.

In summation, on the surface the United States seems to provide a good illustration for the thesis that cultural diversity automatically limits the extent of social provision across a society. A closer look, however, suggests a more complex reading. Generous welfare state provision can thrive in both multicultural and homogeneous settings. Social policies can be employed to advance distributive justice and transcultural solidarity, but also to promote ethnopolitics, social control, and paternalism. Welfare states are thus powerful instrument of ethnoracial inclusion and exclusion, of democratizing the social order, and of hierarchizing it. The alleged conflict between solidarity and diversity, therefore, is not simply a 'given.' Instead, it is the result of historical policy choices and contingent processes that marginalized more ethnically inclusive and racially transgressive approaches. Only in the context of specific social crises, institutional frameworks, and political economies do issues of cultural diversity become virulent.

In the following, this essay explores World War I and the postwar era as one such historical turning point when efforts to bridge social solidarity and cultural diversity yielded to the construction of welfare state structures operating on the basis of ethnopolitics. The essay analyzes this issue by taking a closer look at a crucial pioneer of American social policy – Isaac Max Rubinow – and a specific early twentieth-century reform cause: the campaign for public health insurance. On the one hand it shows that wartime and postwar policies, while leaving a distinctive legacy of government social intervention, channeled health care reform into a model at odds with Progressive-era efforts to establish a transethnic and transracial social welfare system. On the other hand, it recovers a tradition of American politics that sought to turn ethnic solidarity into broader mutualistic cooperation, and to prevent social welfare policy from being instrumentalized by those who wanted to assert ethnoracial hierarchies and inequalities.[7]

Isaac M. Rubinow and the Health Insurance Campaign

Few pivotal figures in the creation of the modern American welfare state were more aware of the problem of how to reconcile social solidarity with cultural

[7] I have explored this in more detail in Schäfer 2014.

diversity, and the concomitant problem of the use of welfare policy to reinforce ethnoracial inequality, than Isaac Max Rubinow (1875-1936). Often referred to as the "greatest American expert of his generation" on social insurance and the father of Social Security, Rubinow embodied the cosmopolitan breadth and intellectual vitality of American reform from the late nineteenth century to the New Deal (Kreader 1988: 36-37). As a German-speaking Lithuanian Jew, his roots were both in the Old World and in the immigrant cultures of New York City; as a socialist, he participated in the raucous urban politics of the Progressive era and repeatedly ran for Congress on a socialist ticket; as a physician, he witnessed first-hand the ravages of urban poverty and frequently refused to charge his poverty-stricken immigrant patients; as a teacher and writer, he taught night classes for foreigners and wrote articles for Russian and Jewish periodicals; and as a professional actuary, he worked for the furtherance of progressive legislation. In the words of his biographer, Rubinow "could have created the appearance of a social movement single-handedly" (Kreader 1980: 289).

Rubinow was the son of an affluent and assimilated Jewish textile merchant in Russian Lithuania. In 1893, aged 17, he moved with his family to New York in the wake of restrictions and pogroms under Czar Alexander III. In the autumn of the same year, he entered Columbia University, and later attended New York University Medical School, where he received his degree in 1898. While working as a physician in the ghettoes of New York City, Rubinow once again enrolled at Columbia to study economics, statistics, sociology, and political philosophy. In 1903, having given up medical practice, he began to pursue a career as researcher, actuary, and statistical expert.

Rubinow moved easily between his identity as Jewish immigrant and as an urban, educated, and morally driven progressive. Working for the US Department of Commerce and Labor in 1908, he helped compile a comprehensive reference work on systems of workmen's insurance. This massive report became a standard reference book for Progressive-era reform. The polyglot and cosmopolitan Rubinow was at an advantage, since US Commissioner of Labor Carroll D. Wright "obliged its researchers to become familiar with European experiments with social insurance" (Kreader 1988: 62).[8] After leaving government service for a career as a statistician in the private insurance business, he established himself as a leading campaigner for public insurance. By 1912, the Progressive Party used his work for a platform that called for the introduction of social insurance. And in 1913, Rubinow published *Social Insurance with Special Reference to American Conditions*, a book which attracted favorable attention in American and European academic and reform circles and became the standard text on the subject at American universities (Kreader 1988: 190).

By 1913, one particular cause dominated Rubinow's social activism: public health insurance. The main lobbyist in this campaign was the American

[8] See also United States Bureau of Labor 978.

Association for Labor Legislation (AALL). Founded in 1906, the organization went from a clearinghouse for information to an advocacy body that sustained the organized social insurance movement in the years before and during World War I. The AALL was dominated by professionals and reformers who had either been trained at German universities, or were avid students of German social reform. Among its most active members were Chicago sociologist Charles R. Henderson, labor advocate John Graham Brooks, and social worker Florence Kelley.[9]

Health insurance was not only close to Rubinow's heart as a physician; the campaign also enabled him to formulate a vision of reform that saw social insurance as a means of furthering industrial democracy, redistributive justice, and ethnic and racial inclusion. A follower of Eduard Bernstein, Rubinow understood social insurance as part and parcel of modern democracy that challenged the established distribution of power and economic resources. Keenly aware of the pitfalls of the dual labor force in the United States he insisted that insurance coverage had to be universal and compulsory. Locating ethnic and racial stereotypes in economic conditions, he saw social insurance as a means of transforming ethnic solidarity into a mutualistic concept of cooperation. He argued that self-governing insurance funds would help build up the working classes' organizational skills, political awareness, moral strength, and intellectual abilities in preparation for the broader socialist emancipation emanating from revolutionary change. His distinctive strand of progressivism merged Bernsteinian revisionism with the social-relational theories of John Dewey and European traditions of mutualism (Rubinow 1913: 480-82, 491; 1904a: 336; 1916; 1903).

In 1916, the AALL published a model health insurance bill that became the centerpiece of its reform campaign. The proposal mainly reflected Rubinow's conception of health insurance. It required compulsory coverage and granted benefits as an entitlement without means tests or questions of fault. Following the German precedent, it called for local, self-governed funds, jointly managed by employers and employees under public supervision with regular membership elections, to deliver medical care and decide upon services. In a departure from the German model, however, the model bill suggested that contributions should also come from the state (Committee on Social Insurance 250-51).

Crucially, the plan combined elements of distributive justice with immigrant claims for cultural recognition: it called on government to put established immigrant traditions of ethnically-based self-help on a sound actuarial and administrative basis. Indeed, Rubinow rarely missed an opportunity to trumpet the immigrant roots of health care reform. In his view, immigrant self-help organizations had pioneered mutualistic forms of health insurance in the United States. In particular, he cited immigrant German *Krankenkassen*, English fraternal orders, Italian societies, and Jewish lodges as having "have laid the foundations of

[9] On the AALL, see Lubove 29, 67; Skocpol and Ikenberry 100.

both the main features of sick-insurance, medical aid and financial sick-benefits" (Rubinow 1913: 283).

On this basis Rubinow saw this model of health insurance as an important step toward overcoming established ethnic, racial, and gender-based divisions in American society. Together with Florence Kelley he was one of the most scathing critics of the discrimination of immigrants in existing American laws. Moreover, Rubinow criticized that both private insurance plans and the federal Civil War pension program excluded African Americans. Indeed, in contrast to most progressives, he was deeply interested in the plight of blacks. He corresponded with W.E.B. Du Bois and wrote the "first extended Marxian analysis of black history in America" which linked the emancipation of African Americans to the emancipation of the working class (Kreader 1988: 79, 81-82, 183).[10] Likewise, Rubinow maintained that social insurance would undermine gender-based discrimination that regarded only men as rights-bearing entities while depicting women as dependent subjects of their care (Rubinow 1904a: 338). Hence, the 1916 AALL plan was not restricted to males, but extended to female workers as well. It also included maternity benefits which did not differentiate between illegitimate and legitimate children, thus avoiding the moralism that haunted the American debate (Rubinow 1905: 50).[11]

Rubinow's vision, however, differed markedly from that of many other progressives in the AALL. Brooks and Henderson, for example, promoted compulsory health insurance primarily as a means of asserting traditional social hierarchies and moral control. Making a clear distinction between industrious and socially useful workers and the *Lumpenproletariat*, Henderson declared that social insurance was neither for the wealthy, nor for the "dependents, defectives, and delinquents," but rather for the "vast majority of those who live on small wages or salaries" (1909a: 43). Social insurance was not designed to expand the service functions of the state or to redistribute wealth, but rather to restore opportunities for social advancement and entrepreneurship in an industrial setting. Henderson, for example, bemoaned that the hope of rising into the "diminishing capitalist-manager class has been definitely abandoned by workingmen and people on salaries." (1909b: 45).

Another school of thought in the AALL, represented by political scientist William Franklin Willoughby and Rubinow's erstwhile economics instructor Henry Rodgers Seager, viewed compulsory health insurance primarily as a utilitarian tool that addressed a social need in a more cost-effective way by taking the matter "out from the domain of litigation and the courts." Neither social ethics nor civic participation, but "efficiency" formed the core of their thinking

[10] See also Robbins.

[11] However, health insurance remained mainly geared toward restoring the health and productivity of male workers. It did not address the problem of women facing discrimination because of pregnancy, left the care of invalids to charity, and excluded casual, farm, and domestic workers. See Gordon 145-81.

(Willoughby 1913: 157, 160-61).[12] Seager and Willoughby modeled their approach on the AALL's other main campaign – the pursuit of workmen's compensation – which reflected more clearly the economic and administrative wishes of the private sector. As Rubinow was acutely aware, however, this latter approach left business in control and denied decision-making power to insured workers (Rubinow 1917: 74-75; Berkowitz and McQuaid 43).

World War I and Health Care Reform

Initially the future seemed bright for the campaign. By 1917 the AALL had succeeded in introducing insurance bills in New York, Massachusetts, New Jersey, and fifteen other states. By 1920, twenty states had considered the model health bill. Commissions or legislative committees had been appointed in nine states, and the majority reported in favor of compulsory insurance. In California and New York, health care legislation was almost passed. And yet, hailed in the early teens of the twentieth century as the next step in social progress, the movement for compulsory health insurance was utterly defeated by 1920. Opponents of the movement, Rubinow bemoaned, were "strong enough to kill even the agitation, the very thought of it, for many years to come" (1934: 209). Reeling from the defeat, those who dominated the AALL in the aftermath of the war decided to cut loose from Rubinow's emphasis on ethnic inclusiveness and to ignore "the foreign-born, socialist, Jewish statistical expert who asked them to learn from Europe" (Kreader 1980: 306-07).

The defeat can largely be attributed to resurgent nativism and the war-related transformation of the popular image of Germany, massive lobbying by organized interest groups in the insurance business, trade union opposition to the scheme, and growing opposition among medical practitioners. Although the reformers had been careful to stress that their reform proposal was not a foreign import but in keeping with American traditions of self-help and democratic participation, their heavy reliance on an idealized image of German social reform proved to be fatal as nativist hysteria merged with the new 100% Americanism of the war years. George Creel's powerful Committee on Public Information commissioned articles exposing the health insurance scheme as a Hun-inspired master plan of the Kaiser to turn Americans into slaves of an autocratic government. Frederick L. Hoffman, a self-educated German immigrant who emerged as a key anti-reform lobbyist, charged that the "German cause of world conquest was largely conditioned by the German conception of so-called social or compulsory insurance" (186).[13] And John O'Reilly of the Kings County (New York) Medical Society denounced the insurance bill as "MADE IN GERMANY as part of the Infamous Kultur and

[12] See also Willoughby 1898; Seager.

[13] For other examples, see Lubove chapter 4; Huthmacher.

imported to this Country by a Russian disciple of Bolshevism and I WON'T WORKISM" (qtd. in Numbers 87). The immigrant roots of social insurance, namely the immigrant German sickness funds and Jewish lodges eloquently defended by Rubinow, now proved a burden in promoting health insurance reform.

In addition, Rubinow and his wayfarers underestimated the effectiveness of organized opposition. Private insurance companies mustered a considerable force against public health insurance, forging alliances with such powerful lobbyists as the National Association of Manufacturers (NMA) and the National Civic Federation (NCF) (Starr 81).[14] In California, for example, where the progressive governor Hiram Johnson had appointed a Social Insurance Commission and the State Medical Society had recruited Rubinow for its campaign, business lobbying nonetheless succeeded in defeating the scheme. They set up the California Research Society of Social Economics, which apparently conducted neither research nor studied economics; instead, it busied itself with distributing pamphlets that showed a picture of the Kaiser over the words "Made in Germany. Do you want it in California?" At the same time, Johnson, who was worried about the heavy financial burden insurance would impose on the state, withheld his support from the AALL plan and proposed a referendum on the issue. When Californians went to the polls in November 1918, they soundly defeated the initiative for compulsory health insurance (Numbers 81).[15]

Furthermore, divisions over the issue within the labor movement weakened the prospects for insurance reform. Rubinow and the AALL had hoped that organized labor would lend its support to the cause.[16] Indeed, influential labor leaders, such as John Mitchell of the United Mine Workers, and William Green of the American Federation of Labor (AFL), embraced the plan. While the tally of supporters sounded impressive, however, overall grassroots enthusiasm for the plan remained low.[17] Moreover, the influential AFL president Samuel Gompers emerged as one of the most vocal critics of compulsory health insurance. Gompers, who had committed the AFL to the war effort, reasoned that fighting the proposal would show labor's patriotism and simultaneously undermine his nemesis, the socialists, who had come out in support of compulsory health insurance (Gompers 173).[18]

14 For a discussion of the National Civic Federation, see Tishler; see also Rubinow 1934: 213.

15 For a discussion of the California campaign, see Viseltear.

16 Eighteen state federations supported compulsory insurance by 1918, in addition to 21 internationals and a range of leading reform organizations, such as the National Consumers' League, the Women's Trade Union League, and various state federations of women ("Prominent Labor Organizations").

17 The Pennsylvania State Federation of Labor was led by a socialist, and the New York unions that favored insurance were in the largely Jewish needle trades. A poll among 13,000 factory workers in Utica, NY revealed that 12,875 opposed compulsory health insurance, and only 112 favored it ("Medical News." *Albany Medical Annals* 40 (1919): 393, qtd. in Numbers 91).

18 Moreover, the AFL had profited under war conditions from higher wages, shorter hours, federal mediation, and union recognition at the expense of more radical labor organizations. In

Another nail in the coffin of the campaign was that a crucial ally abandoned the cause: The American Medical Association (AMA). Initially, the reformers of the AALL and the physicians organized in AMA had formed a united front. Indeed, in May 1916 the AMA hired Isaac Rubinow as secretary of its Social Insurance Commission. This cooperation, however, was sustained for the most part by doctors and administrators affiliated with institutions, governmental bodies, or medical organizations (Numbers 36; "Statements of Prominent Persons"). Meanwhile, to private practitioners compulsory insurance "appeared as a sinister influence upon their entire life" (Rubinow 1934: 213). By 1920, a revolt within the AMA had resulted in the Association's declaring that it was opposed to "the institution of any plan embodying the system of compulsory contributory insurance against illness" ("Minutes of the House of Delegates," qtd. in Numbers 105). In short, the campaigns suffered because enthusiasm for broad-based insurance reform was largely confined to academic and professional supporters. Indeed, Rubinow charged in retrospect that the health crusaders had failed to recognize "the various class and group interests involved" (Rubinow 1934: 210-11).

The high emotional drama of the war years, however, tends to overshadow the fact that the AALL in many ways had actually succeeded in putting health care improvements on top of the public policy agenda. Wartime mobilization turned the security and health of workers into an issue of national interest. The devastating effects of venereal diseases, tuberculosis, typhus, and alcohol on the effectiveness of soldiers caused a public outcry. And the embarrassing fact that 33% of the men examined for the National Army were rejected on grounds of physical unfitness catapulted health care to the forefront of public debates. "[S]uch conditions place a serious handicap upon the social well-being and productive efficiency of the nation," the National Industrial Conference Board, a lobbying agency established by major industrial trade organizations, warned in 1918 (3).

As a result, World War I did indeed pave the way for significant legislation promoting public health and established a precedent for government intervention in the field. The main piece of wartime insurance legislation, the War Risk Insurance Act of 1917, was a case in point. Drawn up by progressives, including Julian Mack and Julia Lathrop, it constituted the most comprehensive government provision for the protection of servicemen to date. It eventually insured four million American soldiers and sailors, offering life insurance, medical care, vocational education, and disability benefits ("War Time Extension of Social Insurance" 188; Bruno 231). Many progressives hailed the Act as a crucial step on the way toward universal coverage. In 1919, AALL president Samuel McCune Lindsay declared that "a new concept of governmental duty and opportunity growing out of [...] the war" will result in generalized health insurance (110).

turn, many AFL unions expressed fear that social insurance would cement low wages, because competitive pressure would force employers to deduct their contribution from wages.

Although War Risk Insurance, consolidated into the Veterans' Bureau in 1921, significantly extended the role of government into the insurance field, and furthered the expansion of the administrative state in the United States, it simultaneously limited and defanged substantive health insurance reform. This was because war-related legislative changes differed in four fundamental ways from the proposals Rubinow and others had put forth:

First, war risk insurance was based on centralized, paternalist government provision, not self-governed, decentralized mutual funds. Pointing out the irony of it all, Rubinow noted that "the 'un-American' institution of state insurance [...] has become more extensive in the United States than it has ever been in Europe" (1917: 74-75). In turn, the precedent set by war risk insurance forestalled reform in the direction of democratic participation. By 1920, for example, 43 states had enacted workmen's compensation legislation and 39 states had passed widows' and orphans' pension laws. While often touted as the success stories of the limited social welfare expansions of interwar years, however, neither contained principles of effective worker representation or control (Kreader 1980: 288; Berkowitz and McQuaid 43).[19]

Second, wartime federal health benefits cemented the selective, exclusionary, and reward-based foundation of American social insurance, following the precedent set by the Civil War pension system. Insurance remained limited to servicemen and never developed into a system of universal coverage. The limited extension to government workers in the 1920s created a new interest group and privileges to be protected, rather than a broad-based system of social security. Wartime and postwar reform thus created a segmented and fragmented system of provision on the basis of exclusionary coverage for "deserving" groups (Chambers 156; Heclo 385). "Are we ready to admit that a life full of toil is of less social value than a life full of play and parade, with a few occasional battles thrown in?" Rubinow asked in 1904 (1904b: 372). The war revealed that the question had been answered in the affirmative: workers and soldiers would continue to be treated according to different standards.

Third, wartime government interventionism was based on 'repressive' concepts of regulation and police power, rather than on 'progressive' notions of industrial democracy and social justice. In addition to the War Risk Insurance Act, the main public health policies encompassed Prohibition, initiatives against public smoking, preventive safety measures, and compulsory physical examinations. Indeed, the only government bodies that broadened their power base during and after the war were the agencies such as justice and interior that were also in charge of political persecution (Rosenthal 295). Meanwhile, many interwar progressives pushed for further regulatory intervention based on the limited police power of the state,

[19] Workmen's compensation laws became a fundamental element of the rudimentary welfare state created during the early twentieth century. They enjoyed widespread support in business circles because they averted the threat of litigation. See, for example, Rimlinger 120; Neubeck and Cazenave. On the maternalist welfare state, see Gordon.

disassociating themselves from Rubinow's mutualistic ideas. As Chicago law professor and AALL member Ernst Freund put it, the "controlling consideration" for social legislation "is the existence of risk or danger, which the police power may seek to minimize" (460).

Fourth, in contrast to Rubinow's efforts to replace private insurance with public provision, the war furthered government-business cooperation. The government machinery put together to organize war production was predominantly staffed by men drawn from industry. Despite Woodrow Wilson's misgiving that "war means autocracy [...] we shall be dependent on the steel, oil and financial magnates," Wall Street's Bernard Baruch, the Burlington & Ohio Railroad's Daniel Willard, and International Harvester's Alexander Legge became wartime icons as enlightened captains of industry (Wilson to Daniels 506; Ferrell). This pro-business stance came to shape the trajectory of progressive reform in the postwar years. John R. Commons' emphasis on employer cooperation in the much-touted "Wisconsin Plan," and Herbert Hoover's concept of the "associative state," for example, promoted public-private partnerships and state subsidies for business planning and research in ways that pioneered the modern *corporate* welfare state (Commons and Andrews; Hawley 116-40). "Progressivism may have laid the egg of the regulatory state, and hatched it," historian Otis Graham concluded, "but the formative war-time years were spent with foster parents from Wall Street" (107).[20]

This also meant that welfare capitalism, rather than democratic participation and economic redistribution, came to be seen as the solution to labor unrest. In 1918, for example, AALL president Irving Fisher sought to make workers into good soldiers by investing in brighter colors, cafeterias, and company-sponsored outings (Fisher 16-17; Howe 171; Schaffer 212). Rubinow deeply disliked the focus on industrial psychology and therapeutic intervention. The therapeutic mindset viewed complaints such as "wages are too low" as reflections of personal discontent, rather than structural inequalities, and sought to adjust individuals to the dominant social order. In contrast, Rubinow continued to emphasize that poverty and deprivation were the result of exploitation and the workings of market capitalism (Rubinow 1926; Kreader 1980: 303).[21]

In summation, the war-related social welfare expansions of government – supported by many progressives – institutionalized the very features that Rubinow had sought to overcome via substantive health care reform: centralized state provision, selective benefits, punitive intervention, and enhanced government-business cooperation. As Rubinow had feared, these features reinforced the established socioeconomic, political, and regional division in the ethnic and racial tapestry of the United States and thus did little to overcome the tension between cultural diversity and social solidarity. State-centered health provision deflected

[20] On cooperation between government and business shaping the nature of federal intervention in the future, see also Cuff; Berkowitz and McQuaid 57.

[21] In contrast, many progressives frequently defined poverty as a problem of insufficient socialization, rather than as a problem of the maldistribution of income; see Sklansky.

from the creation of participatory structures and thus limited the opportunity for turning ethnic solidarity into broader mutualistic cooperation. Selective provision tied benefits to 'deservingness,' a category that was often used as code for ethnic stereotypes and racial prejudices. Police power-based intervention, as in the case of Prohibition, vilified foreign cultures and used moral regulation for the purpose of political repression and assimilation. And business-approved welfare capitalism cemented the divided labor system by limiting benefits to higher skilled workers. In turn, in the interwar years, as Cybelle Fox has noted, European immigrants, Mexicans, and African Americans lived "in three separate worlds of welfare in the first third of the twentieth century, each with its own particular set of race and labor market relations and distinct political systems" (Fox 2010: 455).[22]

Conclusion and Outlook

The history of the campaign of public health care in the early twentieth century illustrates the recent academic literature's two main revisions to the understanding of the solidarity-diversity dilemma of modern welfare states. First, it shows that ethnoracial heterogeneity and extensive welfare states are not inherently at odds, but that specific historical and sociopolitical circumstances stymied the development of more inclusive systems of social provision. Second, it demonstrates how social policy can be turned into a handmaiden of a type of ethnopolitics that creates comparatively generous provision for in-groups while vilifying outsiders.

At the same time, health care reform illuminates both the trajectory of American welfare state development in the twentieth century, and outlines alternative visions to its heavily race, ethnicity, and gender-coded construction. On the one hand, wartime and postwar social policies institutionalized a hierarchical, tiered, moralistic, and paternalist system of social provision that relied for electoral support on privileged groups defending their benefits from those who were excluded. This system was at the root of the inability of the welfare state to bridge the solidarity-diversity gap and to address the socioeconomic problems of ethnoracial inequality. It was overly bureaucratic and centralized, provided limited benefits to 'deserving' beneficiaries, primarily strengthened the police power of government, and promoted welfare capitalism. While this type of interventionism fostered the growth of state administrative capacities and social expenditures within the US's multilayered political system and complex welfare regime, it increasingly sidelined notions of mutualism, cultural recognition, industrial

[22] At the same time, the war and wartime hysteria also reinforced the desire for more ethnically inclusive social policies. These polices, however, while integrating many European ethnics – including the German Americans vilified during the war – simultaneously reinforced discrimination directed against African Americans and Mexican immigrants in the 1920s and 1930s.

democracy, and distributive justice. Established in the early days of welfare state-building, these institutional and ideological framings continued to shape American social politics in the twentieth century. Although this cannot be examined within the confines of this article, they laid the foundations for what Norman Furniss and Timothy Tilton termed the American "corporate-oriented positive state" that focused on macroeconomic intervention, subsidies to the private sector, restrictive police power, and generating economic growth (x).[23]

On the other hand, the health insurance campaign outlined a different model of welfare state development that offered a route toward reconciling high levels of cultural diversity with comprehensive systems of social provision. Rubinow and his wayfarers formulated a distinctive 'cultural social politics' that combined distributive justice, the participation of immigrants without forcing them to give up their cultural heritage, and a 'transnational' sense of social solidarity.[24] Rejecting both assimilationist concepts of the melting pot and the notion of fixed ethnic identities, they wanted, in the words of philosopher John Dewey, to create "new civic and political agencies" to generate the bonds of mutuality and reciprocity that sustained social cohesion beyond racial and ethnic exclusiveness (Dewey and Tufts 439, 481).[25] For this purpose they called less for centralized state provision than for the creation of mutualistic insurance funds, government support for immigrant self-help institutions, non-discriminatory coverage, and a fair distribution of the financial burden.

Unearthing the institutional and intellectual roots of modern social policy thus helps recover conceptions of social politics that sought to reconcile democratic participation, cultural recognition, ethnic pluralism, and distributive justice. However, the contemporary debate about this issue mostly features either "economistic" efforts to show that cultural diversity is economically beneficial, or multicultural identity politics that celebrate "sheer difference" (Hollinger). The former reduces all public policy debates to issues of profit and loss, the latter essentializes cultural separateness. Only in recent years have scholars begun to recover the progressive tradition in social politics that Rubinow and others had outlined. Tony Judt, for example, argues that the lack of the "web of reciprocal services and obligations that bind citizens to one another via the public space" explains to a large extent the failure to reconcile high levels of immigration with public support for comprehensive systems of social provision. Sociologist Richard Sennett suggests that an excessive focus on the politics of (ethnic) solidarity, rather

[23] Furniss and Tilton juxtapose this with a social security state that emphasized minimum standards, and a social welfare state that operated on radically democratic and egalitarian principles. See also Skocpol and Ikenberry 91. I have discussed this further in Schäfer 2000, 2004.

[24] For details on cultural social politics, see Schäfer 2013.

[25] According to Dewey, an expanded public sphere of control could provide opportunities for equal participation and communication that would facilitate both collective social progress and individual ethical development.

than on the more mutualistic concept of cooperation, was at the basis of this political disaffection with welfare states. Philosopher Nancy Fraser argues for "participatory parity," a norm requiring social arrangements that enable all members of society to interact with one another as equals in ways that encompass both distributive justice and address claims for cultural recognition (5). And journalist Barbara Ehrenreich calls for progressive social policy to be intellectually rooted in the "social infrastructure for a revitalized democracy," namely, meaningful civic participation via a reconstructed public sphere of control (193). As Rubinow knew only too well, recovering this dimension of progressivism is crucial for challenging the dominant narrative that assumes that high levels of immigration and diversity cannot be reconciled with solidaristic, redistributive welfare states.

Works Cited

Abramowitz, Mimi. *Regulating the Lives of Women: Social Welfare Policy from Colonial Times to the Present*. Boston: South End Press, 1988.

Alesina, Alberto, and Edward Glaeser. *Fighting Poverty in the US and Europe: A World of Difference*. Oxford: Oxford University Press, 2005.

---, Edward Glaeser, and Bruce Sacerdote. "Why Doesn't the US Have a European-style Welfare State?" National Bureau of Economic Research Working Paper Series, Working Paper 8524, October 2001.

Banting, Keith G. "Is There a Progressive's Dilemma in Canada? Immigration, Multiculturalism and the Welfare State." *Canadian Journal of Political Science /Revue Canadienne de Science Politique* 43.4 (2010): 797-820.

---. "Looking in Three Directions: Migration and the European Welfare State in Comparative Perspective." *Immigration and Welfare: Challenging the Borders of the Welfare State*. Ed. Michael Bommes and Andrew Geddes. London/New York: Routledge: 2000. 113-33.

Berkowitz, Edward, and Kim McQuaid. *Creating the Welfare State: The Political Economy of Twentieth-Century Reform*. Lawrence: University Press of Kansas, 1992.

Brady, David. *Rich Democracies, Poor People: How Politics Explain Poverty*. Oxford: Oxford University Press, 2009.

---, and Ryan Finnigan. "Does Immigration Undermine Public Support for Social Policy?" *American Sociological Review* 79.1 (2013): 17-42.

Brooks, John Graham. *Compulsory Insurance in Germany*. Revised edition. Washington, D.C.: Government Printing Office, 1895.

Bruno, Frank J. *Trends in Social Work, 1874-1956: A History Based on the Proceedings of the National Conference of Social Work*. New York: Columbia University Press, 1957. Repr. Westport, CT.: Greenwood Press, 1980.

Chambers, Clarke A. *Seedtime of Reform: American Social Service and Social Action, 1918-1933.* Minneapolis: University of Minnesota Press, 1963.

Committee on Social Insurance. "Health Insurance: Tentative Draft for an Act." *American Labor Legislation Review* 6 (1916): 239-68.

Commons, John R., and John B. Andrews. *Principles of Labor Legislation.* New York: Harper & Brothers, 1920.

Cuff, Robert D. *The War Industries Board: Business-Government Relations During World War I.* Baltimore: Johns Hopkins University Press, 1973.

Davies, Gareth, and Martha Derthick. "Race and Social Welfare Policy: The Social Security Act of 1935." *Political Science Quarterly* 112 (1997): 217-35.

Dewey, John, and James Tufts. *Ethics.* New York: Henry Holt, 1908.

Ehrenreich, Barbara. "The New Right Attack on Social Welfare." *The Mean Season: The Attack on the Welfare State.* Ed. Fred Block et al. New York: Pantheon Books, 1987. 161-95.

Epstein, William M. *The Dilemma of American Social Welfare.* New Brunswick, NJ: Transaction Publishers, 1993.

Esping-Andersen, Gøsta. *The Three Worlds of Welfare Capitalism.* Cambridge: Polity Press, 1990.

Ferrell, Robert H. *Woodrow Wilson and World War I, 1917-1921.* New York: Harper & Row, 1985.

Fisher, Irving. "Health and War." *American Labor Legislation Review* 8 (1918): 9-17.

Fox, Cybelle. *Three Worlds of Relief: Race, Immigration, and the American Welfare State from the Progressive Era to the New Deal.* Princeton, NJ: Princeton University Press, 2012.

---. "Three Worlds of Relief: Race, Immigration, and Public and Private Social Welfare Spending in American Cities." *American Journal of Sociology* 116 (2010): 453-502.

Fraser, Nancy. "Social Justice in the Age of Identity Politics: Redistribution, Recognition, Participation." WZB Discussion Paper, FS I 98-108 (1998).

Freund, Ernst. *The Police Power: Public Policy and Constitutional Rights.* Chicago: Callaghan & Co., 1904.

Furniss, Norman, and Timothy Tilton. *The Case for the Welfare State: From Social Security to Social Equality.* Bloomington: Indiana University Press, 1977.

Gerstle, Gary. *American Crucible: Race and Nation in the Twentieth Century.* Princeton: Princeton University Press, 2002.

Gilens, Martin. *Why Americans Hate Welfare.* Chicago/London: University of Chicago Press, 1999.

Gompers, Samuel. "Labor versus Its Barnacles." *American Federationist* 23 (April 1916): 268-74.

Goodhart, David. "Discomfort of Strangers." *The Guardian* 24 February 2004.

Gordon, Linda. *Pitied But Not Entitled.* Cambridge: Harvard University Press, 1994.

Graeser, Marcus. *Wohlfahrtsgesellschaft und Wohlfahrtsstaat: Bürgerliche Sozialreform und Welfare State Building in den USA und in Deutschland 1880-1940*. Göttingen: Vandenhoeck & Ruprecht, 2009.

Graham, Otis L. *The Great Campaigns: Reform and War in America, 1900-1928*. Huntington, NY: Robert E. Krieger Publishing, 1980.

Hamby, Alonzo. *Liberalism and Its Challengers: From F.D.R. to Bush*. New York: Oxford University Press, 1992.

Handler, Joel, and Yeheskel Hasenfeld. *The Moral Construction of Poverty: Welfare Reform in America*. Newbury Park: Sage Publications, 1991.

Hawley, Ellis W. "Herbert Hoover, the Commerce Secretariat, and the Vision of an 'Associative State,' 1921-1928." *Journal of American History* 61 (1974): 116-40.

Heclo, Hugh. "Toward A New Welfare State?" *The Development of Welfare States in Europe and America, 1850-1950*. Ed. Peter Flora and Arnold J. Heidenheimer. New Brunswick: Transaction Books, 1981. 383-406.

Henderson, Charles R. *Industrial Insurance in the United States*. Chicago: University of Chicago Press, 1909a.

---. "The Logic of Social Insurance." *Annals of the American Academy of Political and Social Sciences* 33.2 (1909b): 41-53.

Hoffman, Frederick L. *Facts and Fallacies of Compulsory Health Insurance*. 2nd ed. Newark, NJ: Prudential Press, 1920.

Hollinger, David. "How Wide the Circle of the 'We': American Intellectuals and the Problem of the Ethnos since World War II." *American Historical Review* (1993): 317-37.

Howe, Frederic C. *Socialized Germany*. New York: Charles Scribner's Sons, 1914.

Huthmacher, J. Joseph. "Urban Liberalism in the Age of Reform." *Mississippi Valley Historical Review* 49 (1962): 231-41.

Jacobsen, Matthew Frye. *Whiteness of a Different Color: European Immigrants and the Alchemy of Race*. Cambridge: Harvard University Press, 1999.

Judt, Tony. "What Is Living and What Is Dead in Social Democracy?" *The New York Review of Books* (online) 17 December 2009.

Kettunen, Pauli, Sonya Michel, and Klaus Petersen (eds.). *Race, Ethnicity and the Welfare State: An American Dilemma*. Cheltenham, UK: Edward Elgar, 2015.

Kreader, J. Lee. "America's Prophet for Social Security: A Biography of Isaac M. Rubinow." Ph.D. diss: University of Chicago, 1988.

---. "Isaac Max Rubinow: Pioneering Specialist in Social Insurance." *Compassion and Responsibility: Readings in the History of Social Welfare Policy in the United States*. Ed. Frank R. Breul and Steven J. Diner. Chicago: University of Chicago Press, 1980. 288-311.

Larsen, Christian Albrekt. *The Rise and Fall of Social Cohesion: The Construction and De-Construction of Social Trust in US, UK, Sweden and Denmark*. Oxford: Oxford University Press, 2013.

Lasch-Quinn, Elizabeth. *Black Neighbors: Race and the Limits of Reform in the American Settlement House Movement, 1890-1945*. Chapel Hill, University of North Carolina Press, 1993.

Lieberman, Robert. *Shifting the Color Line: Race and the American Welfare State*. Cambridge: Harvard University Press, 1998.

Lindsay, Samuel McCune. "Next Steps in Social Insurance in the United States." *American Labor Legislation Review* 9 (1919): 107-14.

Lubove, Roy. *The Struggle for Social Security, 1900-1935*. Cambridge: Harvard University Press, 1968.

Mau, Steffen, and Christoph Burkhardt. "Migration and Welfare State Solidarity in Western Europe." *Journal of European Social Policy* 19.3 (2009): 213-29.

Mead, Lawrence M. *The New Politics of Poverty: The Nonworking Poor in America*. New York: Basic Books, 1992.

Mink, Gwendolyn. "The Lady and the Tramp: Gender, Race, and the Origins of the American Welfare State." *Women, the State, and Welfare*. Ed. Linda Gordon. Madison: University of Wisconsin Press, 1990. 92-122.

National Industrial Conference Board. *Sickness Insurance or Sickness Prevention*. Research Report 6. Boston: NICB, 1918.

Neubeck, Kenneth J., and Noel Cazenave. *Welfare Racism: Playing the Race Card against America's Poor*. New York: Routledge, 2001.

Numbers, Ronald L. *Almost Persuaded: American Physicians and Compulsory Health Insurance, 1912-1920*. Baltimore: Johns Hopkins University Press, 1978.

O'Connor, Alice. *Poverty Knowledge: Social Science, Social Policy, and the Poor in Twentieth-Century U.S. History*. Princeton: Princeton University Press, 2001.

"Prominent Labor Organizations Already on Record for Health Insurance." *American Labor Legislation Review* 8 (1918): 319.

Riis, Jacob. *How the Other Half Lives: Studies Among the Tenements of New York*. New York: Charles Scribner's Sons, 1890.

Rimlinger, Gaston. *Welfare Policy and Industrialization in Europe, America, and Russia*. New York: Wiley, 1971.

Robbins, I. M. [Isaac M. Rubinow]. "The Economic Aspects of the Negro Problem." in 16 installments. *International Socialist Review* 8-10 (February 1908-June 1910).

Rosenthal, Uriel. "Welfare State or State of Welfare? Repression and Welfare in the Modern State." *Comparative Social Research Vol. 6: The Welfare State, 1883-1983*. Ed. Richard F. Tomasson. Greenwich, CT: JAI Press, 1983. 279-97.

Rubinow, Isaac M. *The Quest for Security*. New York: Henry Holt and Co., 1934.

---. "Needed: A Social Insurance Revival." *Survey Midmonthly* 15 May 1926: 233-34, 283.

---. "Health Insurance through Local Mutual Funds." *American Labor Legislation Review* 7 (1917): 69-78.

---. "Brief for Health Insurance." *American Labor Legislation Review* 6 (1916): 229.

---. *Social Insurance: With Special Reference to American Conditions*. New York: Henry Holt and Co., 1913.

---. "Civic Lessons from Europe: Compulsory Insurance." *Chautauquan* 41 (1905): 48-59.

---. "Compulsory State Insurance of Workingmen." *Annals* 24 (1904a): 331-42.

---. "Labor Insurance." *Journal of Political Economy* 12 (1904b): 362-81.

---. "Edward Bernstein and Industrial Concentration." *International Socialist Review* 3 (1903): 486-89.

Rucker, Phlip. "Sen. DeMint of S.C. Is Voice of Opposition to Health-Care Reform." *Washington Post* 28 July 2009.

Schäfer, Axel R. "Beyond 'Uplift' and 'Efficiency': Isaac M. Rubinow and Transatlantic Progressivism, 1900-1930." *Transatlantic Social Politics, 1800-Present*. Ed. Daniel Scroop and Andrew Heath. London/New York: Palgrave, 2014. 129-63.

---. "Transnationalism and the Welfare State: Cultural Social Politics in Europe and the United States in the Interwar Years." *Beyond the Nation: Pushing the Boundaries of U.S. History from a Transatlantic Perspective*. Ed. Ferdinando Fasce et al. Turin: Otto Editore, 2013. 273-93.

---. "German Historicism, Progressive Social Thought, and the Interventionist State in the US since the 1880s." *Markets in Historical Contexts*. Ed. Mark Bevir and Frank Trentmann. Cambridge: Cambridge University Press, 2004. 145-69.

---. *American Progressives and German Social Reform, 1875-1920: Social Ethics, Moral Control, and the Regulatory State in a Transatlantic Context*. Stuttgart: Franz Steiner Verlag, 2000.

Schaffer, Ronald. *America in the Great War: The Rise of the War Welfare State*. New York: Oxford University Press, 1991.

Schröder, Martin. "Welfare States and their Inequality as a Result of Cultural Differences Instead of Varieties of Capitalism." *Understanding Inequality: Social Costs and Benefits*. Ed. Amanda Machin and Nico Stehr. Wiesbaden: Springer VS, 2016. 39-67.

Seager, Henry Rodger. *Social Insurance: A Program of Social Reform*. New York: Macmillan, 1910.

Sennett, Richard. *Together: The Rituals, Pleasures and Politics of Co-operation*. London: Allen Lane, 2012.

Sklansky, Jeffrey. *The Soul's Economy: Market Society and Selfhood in American Thought, 1820-1920*. Chapel Hill: University of North Carolina Press, 2002.

Skocpol, Theda. *Protecting Soldiers and Mothers: The Political Origins of Social Policy in United States*. Cambridge: Harvard University Press, 1995.

---, and John Ikenberry. "The Political Formation of the American Welfare State in Historical and Comparative Perspective." *The Welfare State, 1883-1983*. Ed.

Richard F. Tomasson. Comparative Social Research 6. Greenwich, CT: JAI Press, 1984: 88-148.

Starr, Paul. "Transformation in Defeat: The Changing Objective of National Health Insurance, 1915-1980." *American Journal of Public Health* 72.1 (1982): 78-88.

"Statements of Prominent Persons in Favor of Health Insurance: Physicians and Nurses." *American Labor Legislation Review* 8 (1918): 324-27.

Tishler, Hace Sorel. *Self-Reliance and Social Security, 1870-1917.* Fort Washington: Kennikat Press, 1971.

United States Bureau of Labor. *Workmen's Insurance and Compensation Systems in Europe.* Twenty-Fourth Annual Report of the Commissioner of Labor, vol. 1. Washington, DC: Government Printing Office, 1911.

vanden Heuvel, Katrina. "Keep Your Hands Off My Medicare!" *The Nation* 3 May 2011.

Viseltear, Arthur J. "Compulsory Health Insurance in California, 1915-1918." *Journal of the History of Medicine* 24 (1969): 151-82.

"War Time Extension of Social Insurance." *American Labor Legislation Review* 8 (1918): 188-89.

Willoughby, William Franklin. "The Problem of Social Insurance: An Analysis." *American Labor Legislation Review* 2 (1913). 153-61.

---. *Workingmen's Insurance.* New York: Thomas Y. Crowell, 1898.

Wilson, Woodrow to Josephus Daniels. *Woodrow Wilson: Life and Letters.* Vol. 6. *Facing War, 1918.* Ed. Ray S. Baker. Garden City, NY: Doubleday & Page. 1927-39.

Creeping Commodification and Resistance to its Inequalities: Chicago's South Side Blues-Scape

David Wilson

Introduction

With a vengeance real-estate and finance capital exert their power in the US city. A new kind of elite re-making – land and blocks re-made into globally declarative, posh play areas – now characterizes large US cities (Jefferson). Up until now, this restructuring has been most evident in and near downtowns. But now, the new affluent takeover of the city, under the guise of requiring that cities be globally competitive, moves far beyond downtown cores. Redevelopment governances (alliances of local government, prominent developers, realtors, city growth organizations) serve up a discourse (their cities must compete for resources in supposed new global times) that drives a new upscaling and expansion of elite patterns of consumption. Affluent homes and spaces replace poor and working-class apartments, stores, and houses with upper-income aesthetics and sensibilities extended to new terrains. Well-coordinated landscapes of pleasure and affluent residency are cultivated, producing what Gordon MacLeod terms "cathedrals of consumption" across the city (609).

This takeover and re-making now grips America's quintessential city, Chicago, most recently its historically neglected South Side 'blues-scape' (blues clubs and their blocks). Once consigned to policy oblivion, this two square mile area, encompassing nine aging blues clubs, today attracts considerable attention and looms ambiguously in a rapidly changing city (see map). A creeping commercialism across the South Side, from an aggressive rediscovery of the South Side by the redevelopment governance, now re-makes many of these South Side clubs. This spread of commercialism was barely imaginable twelve years ago, with most of the South Side institutionally treated as Chicago's core "ghetto" (Venkatesh; Wacquant). But now, a governance-led redevelopment pushes a restructuring by proclaiming something compelling: a rich South Side history. Beneath troubled and struggling neighborhoods, they declare, are once industrious and sturdy communities whose histories and social bases need resurrection. A rediscovery of the black experience now increasingly centers what the governance terms black culture, raw blues musical performance, and exotic black ways as objects of bourgeois fascination.

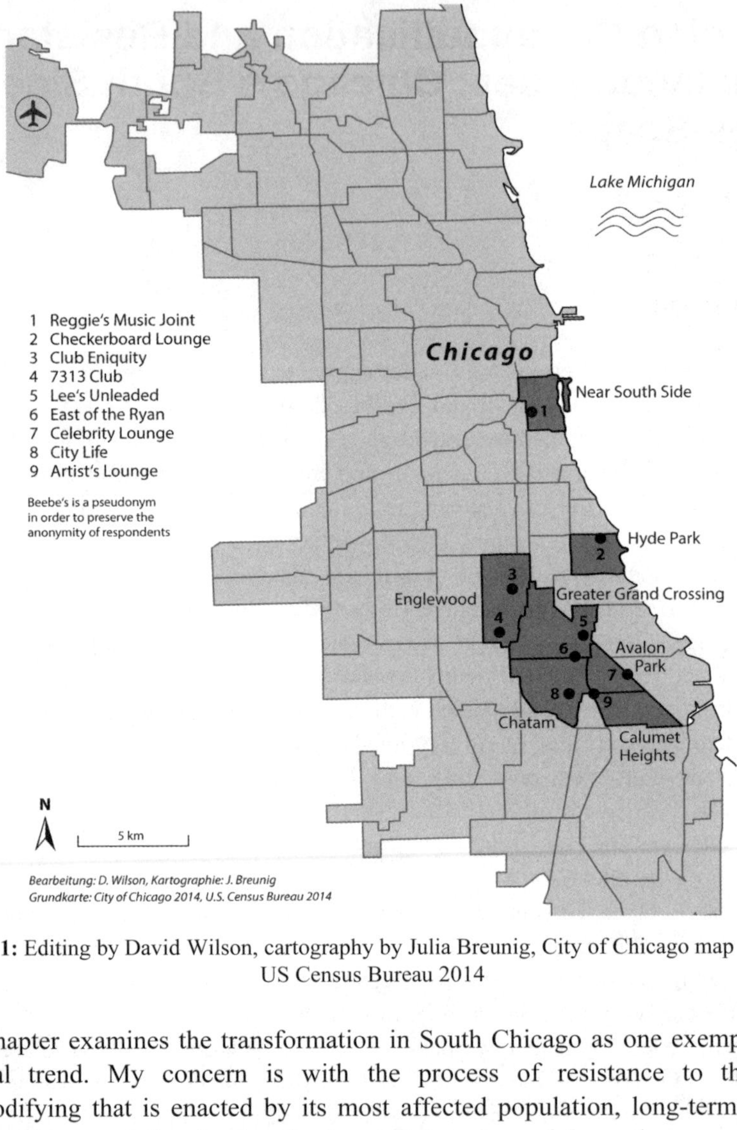

Fig. 1: Editing by David Wilson, cartography by Julia Breunig, City of Chicago map 2014, US Census Bureau 2014

This chapter examines the transformation in South Chicago as one exemplar of a national trend. My concern is with the process of resistance to this club commodifying that is enacted by its most affected population, long-term regular patrons. This population for decades has relied on these clubs as they are presently constituted to provide them enrichment and pleasure. These clubs continue to be dominated by a cadre of long-term regulars who cherish the club's music, social ways, and symbolic content. This population's intense loyalty to the clubs is best described as extraordinary. Yet now these clubs are in danger of changing and for these clubbers there is much to lose. So, what do these clubbers make of this? How do they respond and act in response to this looming change? Is there meaningful resistance to this club commodification?

My goal to excavate activism to the commodification of blues clubs has received too little attention by urban analysts. It reflects a trend: studies of this kind of current governance restructuring typically present a powerful, brutish governance that all but bulldozes its way to produce predictable, decisive effects on passive beings. In our case, regular patrons have been posited as essentially passive and socially placid beings who fail to meaningfully engage their changing club realities. I desire to move beyond the now standard story of current neoliberal governances as always mastering and bluntly producing their desired redevelopment. This prominent story line, for all of its insight, too often neglects turbulence, contradictions, and human interpretation on the ground. My analysis, then, examines the agency and dexterity of this patron population as they operate in a richly specific time and place.

A detailed, ethnographic analysis of one paradigmatic South Side club, Beebe's, suggests an amazingly complex patron negotiating this commodifying blues venue. This finding further explodes the myth of simple interpreting black subjects in communities of social isolation and "American apartheid" with a twist (Massey and Denton; Pattillo). Active and reflexive African Americans construct club beliefs and activities through three interconnecting and seemingly contradictory templates: material concerns, neoliberal beliefs, and class-race identity nourishing. Poor African Americans, through these, ultimately use a complex positionality and improvisational strategies to produce knowledge about the club. These blended templates sometimes conflict but are always made consistent with one another in an adaptation that involves melding them, smoothing them over, and making them compatible.

From this, I further chronicle, these clubbers become galvanized, via use of a sly politics of resistance, to keep the club intact in its current form. A set of techniques advances this politics: coding and exhibiting bodies, performing social engagements, and infusing strategic meanings in language. Yet it is a distinctive kind of resistance few analysts have noticed, what I term "leisure as resistance," which meshes frequently non-recognized political practices with overt strivings for pleasure. Leisure here cannot be reduced to a resistance politics, but becomes its fertile carrier and purveyor. Club commodifying is interpreted with some ambivalence, but emotive attachment to the present club compels attempts to control this space via placing political content in leisure. This population ultimately practices a politics of cunning, artfulness, and dim coercion which nourishes positive identities, hope for the future, and comfort from a life of racism and material struggle.

Beebe's

Beebe's, my empirical focus, is like many South Side blues clubs beginning to feel the pervasive South Side commodifying. On the one hand, the club has experienced little conspicuous physical change. It continues to barely subsist in its severely disinvested low-income economic setting; funds to upgrade are scant (owner Jackie Smith frequently bemoans the club's economic plight). In this context, its exterior is still a gritty, industrial-looking front set within a block of seemingly abandoned buildings. A faded white sign "Beebe's" is the only evidence that a vibrant music scene lies behind a seemingly falling-apart building. The interior has been the same for more than two decades (dominated by black painted walls and faded red carpeting covering all floor space). No bay windows, ample walking space for customers, or track lighting exists at Beebe's. A no-frills decorum wraps around a tiny stage which can barely accommodate five musicians at one time. Behind the stage are faded, unframed posters and photographs of South Side musicians who have played at the club. A crowded, dimly lit room with smoke wafting across the floor and tables still dominate the ambiance. Ashtrays (only occasionally cleaned) adorn the tables.

Yet, this social space now exhibits a few subtle alterations amid the South Side commodifying. Notably, Beebe's recently instituted a $7 cover charge for its live shows after decades of having free admission (it is open and offers live music on Fridays, Saturdays, and Sundays). Owner Jackie Smith has instituted this reluctantly, with an eye to attracting more affluent customers to her club. While deeply desiring to operate a local neighborhood club, one that attracts desired locals and talented local musicians, another desire is to create what Foucault would call a "total blues upgrade space" (1970). This cover charge is potentially one small step to this eventual creation. This imagined space is what Jackie Smith terms "a smart, appreciated musical venue [...] with top-notch players [...] and a profitable, electrifying electricity [sic]." It would be underwritten by "attentive, great audiences paying a fee to be at the club [...]." Smith here imagines a place "with thankful customers buying drinks and eating the place up [...] where alive, diverse people and crowds who know the music know that they are seeing some of the best blues in the world." Her club, in this idealizing, would be an in-demand forum for the blues, and a wondrous producer (performer) and consumer (customer) experience.

The Contemporary Redevelopment Governance and Its Plans

The center of this South Side story is Chicago's redevelopment governance post 2000, that has moved into an aggressive 'transform Chicago' mode. This entity, led by Mayor Richard Daley, pushed harder to upscale and re-aestheticize Chicago's social and cultural fabric. Daley and the governance's highly effective new oratory – global-speak – now booms across Chicago. This oratory had arisen in the 1980s and spoke of the need to redevelop Chicago as an emergent global city. But now, this rhetoric invokes an ominousness and foreboding city reality, as it glaringly provokes the public (Koval et al.; Wilson 2007). "For the first time," the *Chicago Tribune* opined, "Chicago can be a global city – if it wants to be. But does it want to be?" (2000). To the *Tribune*, "Chicago virtually symbolized the Industrial Era and was one of its big winners [...]. But the Global Era presents new challenges.

Chicago is not meeting them [...]. A city that loses the world's attention will wither into a backwater, much as once-mighty cities such as Venice remain today, picturesque and ignored." It is now or never, to the *Tribune*, "city eclipse is at the doorstep [...]" (2004).

In the post-2000 period, Chicago's redevelopment governance has changed its vision of and relation to the South Side. This now taut, bold governance has extended its tentacles geographically and has deepened its rediscovery of so-called South Side authenticity. Incorporating this terrain into their go-global redevelopment scheme, they increasingly speak of a culturally and socially recoverable part of Chicago and have inaugurated bold restructuring efforts. The governance has activated a powerful, area-specific discourse, the need to re-culturalize the South Side to help the area and advance the go-global Chicago redevelopment project, which has been at the center of its restructuring efforts. It now speaks of this terrain as the city's next 'cultural catch' that is deftly framed in the complexities of a contingent cultural moment – the need for Chicago to become fully global. This framing, elaborately seizing the day's concerns and anxieties, drives an ambitious restructuring.

Initially, governance efforts concentrated in a small south-central terrain and were tangibly brick and mortar, i.e., they physically moved Chicago's gentrification frontier beyond the South Loop into adjoining North Bronzeville. Bronzeville gentrification began in the late 1990s fueled by a rhetoric of "an area [...] seeking to re-claim its soul" (Reardon 11). The area, once housing primarily low- and moderate-income households in a widely disinvested terrain (Boyd), came to house patches of upscale condominiums, restaurants and shops in the early 2000s. This persisted, spurred especially by Quad Cities Development Corporation, a city-based development group that focused on the Bronzeville area. Post 2000, they have worked to attract boutique businesses to Cottage Grove Avenue (between 43rd and 47th Streets), bigger gentry stores to State Street, and new upscale housing along State, Cottage Grove, and Martin Luther King Drive (Wilson 2012). Mayor Daley, underscoring the area's symbolic transformation, moved into a Near Bronzeville condo and bucked a decades-old tradition of Daley's living in blue-collar Bridgeport.

But the move to restructure continued. The tactic shifted, given the reality of a more difficult-to-change middle and deep South Side. Emphasis shifted to the realm of discourse with attempts to re-engineer middle-class imaginings of South Side recreational and residential possibilities (that today is most responsible for creating the 'commodification creep' across the South Side and its blues bars). To be sure, physical change picked up in some areas south of Bronzeville (south of 49th Street) post 2005. New condos, single-family homes, townhouses, and retail development came to dot blocks in the Washington Park, Chatham, and Woodlawn communities (see Bergen). But the reality has not matched the rhetoric. The *Tribune*, for example, portrays a deluge of exciting, new South Side investment:

> [D]evelopers are expanding out of downtown and steadily breaking ground on $300,000-plus condos and town homes [...]. On the South Side, public housing high-rises are nearly all demolished. And the transformation of once run-down graystones and six-flats into elegant homes is exciting. So is seeing art galleries on King Drive and cafes on 47th Street. (2007)

The cherry on the topping: "A new Starbucks on the South Side has been a cause for cartwheels" (ibid.).

Blues bars and blues blocks have become one leading edge of this rhetorical rediscovery. Offered as places of raw, authentic black culture and performance, they have been strategically sanitized as milieus for 'outsider' public consumption and recreational pleasure. These clubs, in the process, have been served up as metaphors for the new South Side outsider (incoming black gentrifiers and leisure seeking North Siders and tourists) to live or recreate here. Working through the go-global rhetoric, this push has been steady and aggressive.

Yet, we should not interpret the local governance's attempt to re-make Chicago's South Side blues-scape as an attempt to break down the city's long entrenched race-class divisions. Chicago has a long, virulent history of segregating working-class and poor African Americans that has been personified in the systematic constructing and isolating of its South Side. By the early 1930s, this core of the area, bounded by 31st Street on the north, 63rd Street on the south, and between State Street and Cottage Grove Avenue, housed more than 300,000 African Americans (Koval et.al.). By 1960, this number had increased to more than 750,000 (U.S. Census Bureau). In this space, paraphrasing a conversation with the historian James Barrett, black life in all its vibrancy, hopes, dreams, and despairs, became confined and cordoned off. Formal government policies and informal social stigma that created and maintained this segregating persist to this day (Wilson 2007).

Five Weeks at Beebe's

It's 10 pm on a Sunday evening, and the lights dim in Beebe's Lounge on South 78th Street. Like other South Side blues clubs I have visited this month, people quickly hush, hear the introduction of the evening's first band, and let out a thunderous clapping. The crowd has steadily grown, anticipating a club favorite, Tommy Ariva and His Band of Blues, who play here nearly every Sunday night. Few seem to care that Beebe's sits on a decrepit corner of disinvested buildings and stores. People seem to easily erase the reality of a drab interior and the trappings of a middle-class forgotten, decayed block and side of town. Enthusiasm for the music and for being in this social milieu overwhelms the décor of drab orange curtains draping a few dirty windows. The bulk of the audience is regulars; many have been coming to Beebe's for years. Small groups of inquisitive non-regulars dot the room. Some are nearby men and women out for good music, others offer themselves bodily as intrigued, voyeuristic outsiders intent on immersing themselves in their sense of a mysterious world of black blues. In all cases, bodies, mannerisms, and social conduct unmistakably signal a distinct sense of self, values, ideals, and expectations for the evening.

Long Term Regulars

Complex Beings and Sense of Beebe's

Club regulars, the dominant group this evening and most Sundays, surge into the slowly commodifying club just before Tommy and band begin. Upon arrival, they produce knowledge in the club's flow of activities that is important to this study: it is keenly read and assimilated by owner Jackie Smith. This is the group Jackie feels the greatest affinity for and desires to please, and who she derives enormous satisfaction from. Jackie closely reads this group, and ritually tracks their sensibilities and actions throughout evenings. They are, as she said that evening, the "kind of folk from her cut of life." Their sensibilities, values, and demeanor, she asserts, are also hers. She repeatedly spars with them and reprimands them for social excesses, but identifies them as "her own." As we now see, club regulars exhibit a strong oppositional streak to the club commodifying. Yet, among some regulars, there is an acceptance of this as they believe that their coveted Beebe's could benefit from this change. To understand this, we must know how they socially construct the club and themselves that is now discussed.

Club regulars make and view Beebe's in a prominent way: as a refuge from persistent feelings of material and emotive tumultuousness. Club dynamics and the broader world, in this way, interconnect. Here a tough, gritty life outside the club punctuates them with a haunt which is carried into the club. Many are low-wage workers; material standing is often unstable and afflicting. Many work in the new burgeoning post-industrial economy and workfare economy of Chicago as burger makers, fast-food floor cleaners, maintenance workers, retail hawkers, and the like. Some are retired or semi-retired, but all struggle to produce a livable income. One middle-aged man, in discussion with me this evening, touches upon the haunt and the problem of minimal opportunity: "it's a real tussle to stay afloat now […] many people don't realize what it's like out there […] it's scrapin' by and holdin' things together with hope and dreams […] lots of crappy jobs out there […] it's amazin' so many are survivin'." More succinctly, one younger man says to me: "it ain't simple throwin' off this bizarre life […] there's so little money to be gained […] but life is always gonna be tough, I just got to keep pushin'."

The haunt is often exacerbated by a new normal strand of thought in Chicago and beyond: the individual as culpable agent. Here, Larner's neoliberal-infused everyday works its way into everyday human thinking. Daily engagements with neoliberal-inflected people and institutions in life paths (who talk, reference, insinuate, and sanction these sensibilities) affect these patrons. In this context, their current plight becomes tied up with, in their own words, "being responsible, choosing persons […] to be what we are." Not surprisingly, a sense of blame for their circumstances is seldom discussed with us and others, and outside of highly general references to "a man out there that hurts working black people," there are no recurrently identified targets or causes for their plight. Often, the issue of cause is simply erased (many find this a painful topic to discuss). "Cause for my money struggles? It's not relevant," one man told me this evening, "why get into that? It's bullshit, you just got to cope, keep moving forward […] one step at a time."

Seeing Beebe's as an escape, these patrons fervently strive to create a positive race-class identity and construct a positive scene here that is at the heart of their opposition to the club commodifying. They seek to make this club operate the way they desire through creating and imposing a desired social order. Beebe's becomes a space to momentarily dull the fear and disillusionment and to extract social entitlement and social relish. William Wimsatt's postindustrial torment, transported into the club, becomes a semiotic trace to be contained, managed, and dulled by the building of positive possibilities. As a retired man this evening told me, "is my life hard? Yeah, man, I can go into it for hours, no point in borin' you […] but at Beebe's, this stuff is pushed to the side, I'm kind of startin' all over […] here I feel good – about my friends, myself, my community, you know what I'm saying? I don't know if it's being re-born, but it fuels me […] the music, the people." One woman, a club regular for more than five years, termed Beebe's "my extension of home […] where I don't really bring my worries."

In this vein, hope is etched across the club's vastness: in faces, bodies, musical instruments, social relations, and aging pictures and posters on the wall. Musicians, club owners, waitresses, club outsiders, strangers, and casual acquaintances become characters in a human staging of hope. Positive meanings (nostalgic remembrances, current social recollections) are continuously infused in a place's fabric (its bar, stage, bands, pictures draped on the stage). A space of identity nourishment and social contentment is produced; unmasking possibility and potentiality in their lives is vital. Beebe's becomes a space of elaborate constructing and choreographing tuned and refined to a group's social desires and needs. "I love Beebe's," one elderly man at the bar told me, "it's my refuge, ya know, where I like to go and get away from the other stuff […] all is good here, man, you can't beat it […] the world's tough out there, putting food on the table can be difficult sometimes, I ain't kiddin' […] just give me Beebe's […]."

Beebe's is ultimately constructed through a relentless dialectic of making and obliterating. Obliterating, on the one hand, negates any signifier – a social relation, an object – that invokes the trace of the haunt (e.g., meanings elicited from a face, a customer look, a social act like brusque treatment of a club regular). Club regulars treat these as kinds of ruptures that must be fixed immediately. Such signifiers become either banished to the realm of repugnant (and cast as worthy of being expelled from the club) or re-coded to be re-fitted into a space's desired fabric. This erasure, following Berger and Luckmann, is a human affirming maneuver to eradicate fears and ambivalences. Making, on the other hand, involves building iconographies that can constitute and regularize positive identities. Discursively seized objects, as hollow and open-ended symbolic elements, become adroitly re-coded to a group's specifications. As one club regular said to me, "look, I and we […] make Beebe's something meaningful to us […] we do that every evening […] this is our place, our time for sunning in the blues […] we keep it real, the place we can fall back on […]."

These patrons often put a best face on their drive to erase the haunt at Beebe's. A widely invoked narrative, replete with melodrama and pathos, renders them indomitable beings in a heroic drama. The narrative features epic battles of personal will and strength, continuously being waged to tackle their worlds. Amidst bouts with household troubles, hunger, withered savings, piling up debt, they persist as humor-intact, courageous beings. The most commonly invoked trouble – job loss or job instability – is cast as a nuisance that has them trudging on and keeping their spirits up. In theme, they are being battered and hammered, but will not be torn and broken. The narrative ultimately converts a bitter pill (the trace of the haunt) into a personally empowering story. Tough, plundering social and material realities are identified, but so too are acts of compensatory personal courage and fortitude. The drama suggests active, adroit beings that continuously cope to retain positive identities. Even as these patrons construct Beebe's as an escapist solution to fears, personal strength and personal confrontation are illuminated.

These patrons expediently assume a number of roles in the narrative: omniscient narrator, courageous survivor of a harsh world, and self-reflective, grieving person. Collectively, these offer a dignified South Side person whose deft maneuvers enable a family- and community-minded individual to remain loyal to these allegiances. "We," one patron notes, "know the score and stay true to our families and our neighborhoods […] even as we have to f___n fight to stave off all kinds of unspeakable s__t […] there's no one or thing to really help us, it's our guile, you know, our know-how, that allows us to stay what we are." This construction fervently refutes its mainstream competitive construction, the acutely disturbing subculture-of-poverty notion, which these patrons fully know about. These patrons never acknowledge it, but they reach deeply into the realm of cultural understandings and choose what they desire to display and embellish and what needs to be renounced. Their response narrative rescues them from the taint of dysfunctionality and hedonism.

Bodying and Social Relations of Club Regulars

Club regulars also mobilize their bodies to communicate their opposition to the club commodifying. These apparatuses, as in-motion, symbolically etched elements, move across the club cutting into a social space as things to be continuously interpreted. Bodies so used mediate and help generate club norms and protocols as they bound from bar to stage to dance floor to tables. Never operating in isolation, this bodying produces knowledge as they are interpreted through language, meanings, and social relations. One more time, power and influence is wielded in the whirl of taken-for-granted club practices. Movement carries messages that are unmistakable if you look for them. Many seem to extract the messages at the tables, bar, and on the floor, and they are often overtly sanctioned by the exuding of joyous responses.

These patrons tonight dress, move, and order their bodies as club regulars that spotlight and support the club's current character. Bodying as a to-be-seen process conveys meanings especially as nattily attired blues beings: bodies notably fit into a mix of tight-fitting and loosely attired clothes that range from casual to careful glittery. One woman, in the front, wears tightly fitted jeans and shirt as she dances to Tommy's music in a kind of frenetic ballet. One nearby man wears a flowing orange-fitted shirt and nappy polyester pants as he taps politely to the music. Another man, in the middle of the room, stylizes elements from both of these; he wears a taut, cut-away shirt jacket set against tight, form-fitting jeans. In each case, knowledge-making is immediate. For all to see are people professing an allegiance to the symbols and styles that patrons commonly associate with down-home blues music. Let me elaborate.

For all to see, then, club regulars stylize something important to them: a sense of the blues self. Presented in theatrical motif are blues-infused, proud African-American beings. In symbolism, blues lovers and proud, resilient black people have come to the club. "Blackness […] and our love of the blues," to one of these stylizing people, "is in the look […] and dress […] the way we present ourselves […]." This evening, she notes, its symbols – strong gaits, proud stances, blues-trained facial etchings, hyper-colored shirts and berets – glisten across the club. Confident strolls, to her, are at the core of this. To another women at the bar, there is a way to see Beebe's, "you get trained to see the blues all around you […] in the dress, moves […] that keeps it [the club] bluesy and good […]." Club patrons, normed to see this sense of authenticity and distinctiveness in bodies, routinely inspect and appraise them. This producing becomes one central element in a micro-social space (the club) ablaze with ritualized signifiers.

This bodying communicates something else: the sense of the good club and the bad club. As people bodily revel in the bounty of a space, they signal it as vibrant and pleasurable. Luminous people are projected to find their place and groove at Beebe's and implore all to recognize the need for this kind of presently constituted club. No other kind of Beebe's will suffice, it is communicated. This bodying, in the process, becomes semiotically aligned with other symbolic assemblages in the club: the pictures behind the stage, the bold bar, and the tiny stage that are seized and endowed with self and club-affirming meanings by these patrons. Pictures of prominent musicians having played at Beebe's (B.B. King, Buddy Guy) hang behind the stage; they are symbolized as "carriers of the good stuff that has come to Beebe's." The bar and stage, similarly, are "the antiques of the place […] the timeless part of the club that makes Beebe's what it is […]."

So, as Tommy breaks into Mustang Sally in the middle of the evening, two tables of regulars up front move to the beat and mouth the lyrics. The two men wear relaxed jeans and button-down shirts, the two women 'catchy blues' pants and sweaters. A woman at the bar, noting this attire to me, said: "that's it, that's what I'm talking about […] that's the blues look […]." They, like the club's musicians, are performative. Their bodying also makes them powerful symbolic items which reference a sense of the proper blues club. This bodying ultimately speaks to what the club should rightfully include, sanction, incorporate, and privilege. Similarly, three tables of women in the back move their heads to the music and flash smiles to the players. All are clad in Beebe's standard uniform for blues regulars: relaxed jeans, tight-fitting tops, and high-heels that seamlessly mesh with the club's dominant aesthetic. For all to see are pulsating, time synchronized bodies of blues insiders that sanction the club's proper atmosphere.

It follows in the communication that other versions of Beebe's are inappropriate and undesirable. A strong sense of a desired kind of club pushes any sense of alternative to the realm of problematic. Offers of the ideal club (one that offers blues music, a nostalgic blues terrain, informal and breezy patterns of social relations) serve up its oppositional binary (offerings of other kinds of music, an emotively bereft music venue, staid patterns of social relations). One, upon invoking, always references and plays off against the other in a simultaneous centering-decentering project. A terrain of ideals, aggressively forwarded through sets of representations, purges all other visions of club normalcy.

In this context, the bodying communicates opposition for one practice widely seen as a commercialized endeavor at Beebe's: the subtle alteration of music. Long-term patrons view any new kind of music at Beebe's as an owner effort to attract more affluent people. This is read as a signal of not just the possible loss of blues music, but of the club's present composition. In their eyes, blues music is the lynchpin of Beebe's as a form of music and a symbolic and social ensemble and should not be changed. These patrons, sensitive to any belief of tear in the club's social fabric, often fear the worst. Realizing they can not legislate or punish an owner attitude, they strike out to lampoon alternative forms of music into oblivion. As a kind of politics, it can be remarkably subtle.

So, this evening, anger breaks out as alternative music is briefly introduced. With Tommy on break, quasi disco music shoots across the club. Bodies immediately show contemptuousness. Bodies turn away from the stage, heads nod in disapproval, and disdain bordering on nastiness is etched on faces. One clubber this evening goes so far as to briefly caricature in body movement a disco dance, gyrating John Travolta style across the club to the derisive laughter of friends. Asked about this later, the man said to me: "its' f____ disco man, it has no place in here, I don't know why Jackie [club owner] brings that stuff out […] it's f___n s___ […] this is a blues club […]." Fifteen minutes later, when hard rock music replaces the disco, the response is the same (minus the parodying). Conversation between patrons shows anger. At one table, a man proclaims to a small group: "blues is Beebe's, and that's the end of it […] no more bullshit – this stuff has no right being here."

But all is not so simple: this bodying by some regulars also communicates something different – an acceptance of selective kinds of club commercializing. I reference a parallel track of thinking in a complex human consciousness. A number of regulars tonight slide into a sense of select club commercializing as desirable. The process – seemingly contradicting the opposition to club commercializing – illustrates Michael Dear's notion that all people (including these patrons) are anything but internal unities (2000, 2010). They are, instead, contradictory creatures who are rife with ambivalences and uncertainties.

In this context, some regulars support the new commercial practice of a cover charge to enter the club (instituted last year). Many see this as a way to impose a degree of social discernment that controls the entrance of "riff-raff." The cover charge: "yeah, it's okay," a 58-year old women said to me, "it kind of classes the place up a bit […] not everyone can now come in […] Beebe's has a bit of a better clientele […]." Many identify this act as helping to make the club more reflective of proud, industrious black people. Agreeing to this cover charge, borne of a desire to control the club's iconography, is not seen as a major threat to the club's current social makeup, and would supposedly remove any sense of what one 64-year old regular termed "the ghetto influence" from Beebe's. "Bringing in some new blood," this regular said to me, "would not be bad […] it could spice the club up a bit and spruce this place up a bit too […] I'm for it […] and it removes the sense of slum […] you know what I'm saying […] from this place […] this is a good club […] it should stay that way."

What these regulars reject here is a long-term, haunting icon that they want out of the club: the poverty-stricken, decayed, pathological presence (person, club, neighborhood). Many of these patrons despise this icon (a symbol historically and currently used to crudely caricature their neighborhoods, families, and selves) (see Hooks; and Mercer on this point). The stereotypes in this icon are put to me as "hurtful," "racist based," and "simple attempts at putting the black man down." In this context, any visual references to this in the club are assaulted, and visual references contrary to this tend to be favored. The result is significant: this population adopts a way of thinking about the club that opens up this venue for more white bourgeois usage (that also aligns them this way with the city's redevelopment desires). The anger associated with this icon ultimately enables some signs of upgrade and newness to be welcome.

Thus, as Tommy performs his first set, the commonly understood bodily signifiers of black poverty and black decay are absent across the club: tattered clothing, ripped clothes, poorly fitting shirts and pants (see McCarthy). Such dress, to one bar patron I talked to, "is the s__ we don't want around here […] they [anyone] can take it to the park." At the same time, none of these patrons bodily project themselves as either physically fragile ("weakened-by-poverty black bodies") or hyper-masculine ("over-compensating black bodies"), two widely understood signifiers in mainstream thought for black poverty and black pathology (see Mercer). Displays of muscles, hulking bodies, and at the other extreme, tenuous limbed beings, are out. A group's repugnance for being tattood as decayed and lazy or socially disorganized has been normalized in the club's bodying habitus.

There is more paradox. Among regulars, fear also exists about a possible middle-class takeover of the club – South Side transformation (a black middle-class gentrification) is now apparent to all. A symbol of this kind of change entering the club, the stray white patron, thus becomes an Othered subject. These entrants, identified as outsiders or non-South Siders, are widely projected as being at Beebe's for a dubious reason: to try and regale in a music and aesthetic that they barely understand. "The blues is not their world," one long-term patron noted, "these guys [...] I see at the club [...] we all know they're outsiders and they're here to try to get a taste of the blues [...] but this is not their scene, and they shouldn't pretend it is." "These cats," the man says, "I don't think they really have a commitment to Beebe's, and they probably don't know what they're seeing, the pure blues thing is not easy to understand [...]. I think it's beyond their experiences." Outsider bodies are eyed as carriers of a potential contagion and become objects to be peripheralized.

One more time, a group responds harshly to two aforementioned abstract conceptions: the ghetto and ghetto populations. Regulars at Beebe's, we now know, resent these monikers and spurn their associations as hurtful stereotypes and misconceptions. The dynamic again is to practice a symbolic eradication that removes Beebe's and themselves from this taint. In this context, the paradox emerges: some club regulars show support for the club's possibility to bring in more affluent customers. An imaginative gatekeeping has the door cautiously swinging open to allow entry to outsider populations that help crush any hints of a 'ghetto club.' These entrants, not seen as ideal patrons, nevertheless are seen to, in the words of one 25-year-old regular, "help to keep the club going [...] often help keep the club upright and are not a ghetto influence or anything [...] as long as it's not kids with their pants falling down coming into the club."

Discussion and Conclusion

A new city transformation – land and blocks converted to globally declarative, affluent play spaces – now marks many major American cities (Wilson 2004, 2007; Wyly et al.). This re-making now moves far beyond downtown cores to engage a new terrain: once flagrantly peripheralized black communities and their blues-scapes. In Chicago, its South Side blues-scape (a scatter of nine aging blues clubs) experiences this, attracting intense media attention after being consigned to policy oblivion for decades. Chicago's redevelopment governance, one more time, harnesses the power of the state and planning apparatus to achieve its objectives. A mobile, quick-acting capitalism strikes out to expand this class' consumption field that works through productions of elaborate imaginaries and city need. At a rhetoric's core, a supposed new hyper-competitive reality makes Chicago easily discardable as a place for investment, production, and business. Against this supposed reality, Chicago is now a threatened but still historically resilient locale that once again must act innovatively to survive.

Multiple scenarios exist for how this commodifying will proceed and what this blues-scape will become. A dominant vision, one that needs interrogating, suggests that power is overtly and bluntly applied in a hegemonic process and these clubs will simply be overwhelmed by capital's creeping, infiltrating prowess. Blues clubs, in this vision, will soon be one more re-made city element that will be normalized under a creative destruction ethos (spatially extending the go-global restructuring project). A powerful streak of determinism, but also a sense of intense realism and reference to on-the-ground history, cuts through this vision. Yet, this vision may be too simple, i.e., it ignores that these core South Side clubs have defied the odds before and have been remarkably resilient in the face of different kinds of economic pressures (from both intense commodification and economic decline). Moreover, there is evidence that these clubs contain a potent mixture of vibrant human agency, unpredictable human vision and social constructing, and intense personal striving for pleasure and meaning that make the operation of this commodification influence unduly complex.

My results corroborate this idea of a complex commodification process and unpredictable club futures. At the core of this commodifying, this study suggests that regular patrons, the historic bread-and-butter of the clubs, are reflexive people and will not easily cede this social space to others. They engage, internalize, and work through three central forces to constitute their club reality and their responses: new neoliberal subject realities, governmentality, and class-race identity constitution. These multi-scaler, worked-through 'templates' guide a multi-textured, complex patron production of knowledge about the club and its relation to personal goals, values, and desires. These interconnections are crucial: they intermix the patron's drive to embolden their identities, upgrade their enriching as cultural beings, and service fellow 'subaltern' people. The process of club commodification, I conclude, is anything but a dominant, hegemonic imposition on agency-bereft people.

Finally, why do I take on the issue of how commodification operates on this floor space? These blues clubs and communities, again, face turbulent times. As they currently exist, the core group of clubs, thinned by economic attrition over time and also now a focus for affluent upscaling, may soon disappear or be substantially altered. This would prove scarring to these South Side neighborhoods; these clubs are a substantive social and cultural resource. Whether 'authentic' or not, they continue to be an important social glue in their communities. Yet, I am not convinced that stepped-up attempts to commodify them will be successful, the forces of resistance may prove stronger. The remarkable survivability of these nine resilient clubs, with their staunch club owners and dominant club populations, may be sufficient to thwart capital's overtures. Many club owners here, it seems, have a reverence for this regular patron population. As the long term group in these clubs, owners revere them as fellow 'subalterns.' This is thus a keenly gauged population by owners who desire to satisfy and nurture them. Predicting these club's evolution, then, is difficult, and we must await this deepened interface of capital and community in the upcoming months and years.

Works Cited

Barrett, James. Discussion with Historian. University of Illinois at Urbana-Champaign, 13 January 2012.

Bergen, Kathy. "Community's Promise Attracting Money, Faith." *Chicago Tribune* 16 March 2008: 5.1.

Berger, Peter, and Thomas Luckmann. *The Social Construction of Reality*. New York: Basic, 1966.

Boyd, Michelle R. *Jim Crow Nostalgia*. Minneapolis: University of Minnesota Press, 2008.

Chicago Tribune. "Language and Perception: Selling the South Side." 11 February 2007: 1.

---. "21st Century Chicago: Transformed Windy City Has A Truly Global Reach." 17 October 2004: 2.1.

---. "Here's Our Chance to Be Global." 23 April 2000: 2.1.

Dear, Michael. "Topogenesis: Spaces and Flows in the Production of Urban Space." Plenary Lecture at the First International Conference on Spaces and Flows, Los Angeles, 3 December 2010.

---. *From Chicago to Los Angeles: Making Sense of Urban Theory*. Thousand Oaks: Sage, 2000.

Foucault, Michel. *The Archeology of Knowledge*. New York: Pantheon, 1970.

Hooks, Belle. *Outlaw Culture*. London: Routledge, 1993.

Jefferson, Brian. "Zero Tolerance for Zero Tolerance?: Analyzing How Zero Tolerance Discourse Mediates Police Accountability Activism." *City, Culture and Society* 6.1 (2015): 9-17.

Koval, James P., Bennett, Michael I.J., et al. *The New Chicago*. Philadelphia: Temple University Press, 2006.

Larner, Wendy. "Neoliberalism?" *Environment and Planning D: Society and Space* 21 (2003): 509-12.

MacLeod, Gordon. "From Urban Entrepreneurialism to a 'Revanchist City'? On the Spatial Injustices of Glasgow's Renaissance." *Antipode* 34.3 (2002): 602-24.

Massey, Douglas S., and Nancy A. Denton. *American Apartheid: Segregation and the Making of the Underclass*. Boston: Harvard University, 1993.

McCarthy, Cameron. "Danger in the Safety Zone; Notes on Race, Resentment, and the Discourse of Crime, Violence, and Suburban Security." Unpublished manuscript. University of Illinois Department of Speech Communication. 1995. Available from author.

Mercer, Kobena. *Welcome to the Jungle.* London: Routledge, 1997.

Pattillo, Mary. *Black Picket Fences: Privilege and Peril among the Black Middle Class*. Chicago: University of Chicago, 2013.

Reardon, Patrick. "Can Bronzeville Reclaim Its Soul?" *Chicago Tribune* 21 May 2000: 10-16.

United States Census Bureau. Data on Housing, Population, and Demographics. U.S. Department of Commerce. 1960.

Venkatesh, Sudhir and Isil Celimli. "Tearing Down the Community." *Shelterforce Online* 138 (November/December 2004).

Wacquant, Loic. *Urban Outcasts.* Cambridge: Polity Press, 2008.

Wilson, David. "Chicago's South Side Blues Clubs: The Latest Struggle." Unpublished manuscript. 2012. Available from author.

---. *Cities and Race: America's New Black Ghetto.* London: Routledge, 2007.

---. "Toward A Contingent Urban Neoliberalism." *Urban Geography* 25 (2004): 771-83.

Wimsatt, William. *No More Prisons.* New York: Soft Skull, 1997.

Wyly, Elvin, Markus Moose, et al. "Cartographies of Race and Class: Mapping the Class Monopoly Rents of American Subprime Mortgage Capital." *International Journal of Urban and Regional Research* 33.2 (2009): 332-54.

On a Paradox of Urban Inequality: The Brazilian *Favela* between Spatial Visibility and Social Invisibility

Eberhard Rothfuß

Introduction

> I can tell you that there are thousands of people here that have no idea that this is a favela. They believe that a favela is made out of cardboard and two sticks, where there is only garbage and crooks. And that is not the truth. That is an untruth. There are workers… they are people without possibilities. They don't exist for them. But they are real… it is as if this part of the city was not a part of the city at all, they are invisible. (2007/8/58.)[1]

Cities represent both an exterior form of urbanity and social life as well as a tangible representation of the ideas and ideals of city planners and architects. They are a triumph of the visible. In spite of the lack of coordinated planning and formal architectural knowledge implemented in their construction (Berenstein), however, it is evident that the Brazilian *favelas* are an integral part of the visual cityscape. Because of their central geographical position in the inner cities of Brazil and, as a result of the media narratives which construct them as spaces of the abnormal, violent, and precarious, they have become some of the "most visible living environments in the world" (2007/5/38). This does not mean, however, that visibility must necessarily correspond to the social and individually experienced understandings which the residents possess with regard to these spaces:

> They [the *favelas*] are the most visible living environments in the world! Yes, the most visible, but our elites pay no attention to them because of the inhumane conditions which are prevalent there. Sometimes there is no sewage disposal or no water, for example there is electricity, but it is stolen from the utility pole, light isn't paid for, it's terrible […]. (2007/5/38)

The point which is being made is that the Brazilian *favela*s are, on the one hand, in terms of their media coverage and stigmatization, the most visible urban spaces in

[1] The quotations are selected from of the large data pool of interview transcriptions which were conducted between 2005 and 2008 (see in detail Rothfuß). The quotations are specified with year/number of interview/page.

Brazil. On the other hand, however, with regard to societal recognition and human relevance of the *favela* residents, these disadvantaged urban spaces remain socially invisible. This involves a double humiliation of the Brazilian declassed class. They live in a permanent humanitarian state of emergency that the philosopher Žižek describes as a "condition, in which sections of society become invisible in the slums and where there is an underlying civil war."[2]

(In)Visibility and Space – Conceptual Remarks

> Look here, for me the Favela is invisible, because I can say, that I don't even want to get close to it, but if you look at it from far away, you don't even have the courage to go into it because the houses are made of cardboard, that means… the living environment is visible because you know that people live there in bitter poverty. (2007/5/38)
>
> The Favela is a disguised space. It is not, as if it wouldn't exist, it is disguised. They are behind walls, because they are also close to rich neighborhoods, you understand? Close to neighborhoods of the upper-middle class, middle class and upper class. So they (the walls) are necessary. These people that live there without education, without training, they are necessary, so that these people who live in the better-off neighborhoods can use their services. (2007/2/15)

Both the perception and the real consciousness of a space are determined in a decisive manner by the local subjects and whether or not they connect their memories with spatial experience. These memories are, on the other hand, experiences made by the people themselves and perceived by their bodies through the sensory organs. In line with body phenomenology ("Leibphänomenologie"), perception is an active relationship between one or more subjects, objects, places, and spaces (Merleau-Ponty). Remembrance is both a prerequisite and a result of this process. To remember is equally a part of the work. But how can the privileged remember something, in the manner illustrated above, if they haven't perceived these spaces through their own personal sensory experience? "The majority of the middle-class don't know the favelas. No, they don't know any, they weren't ever in a favela" (2007/8/58).

With this perspective, the decisive factor can be seen which determines the separated, misunderstood and rejected nature of certain living environments in the Brazilian cityscape, as well as the tensions between recognized and unrecognized spaces and their respective residents.

2 Own translation; the original reads: "Zustand, in dem Teile der Gesellschaft in den Slums unsichtbar werden und es einen unterschwelligen Bürgerkrieg gibt" (Žižek 2013: 111).

> The upper class doesn't go into the favelas. They [the favelas] are invisible to them. They do know that they exist, because they read about them. Only through the media and the newspapers do they get their information about them, that's it. They don't go any further than that. (2007/7/51)

Is there a connection between this lack of direct spatial experience and the reduced empathy towards the people who live in these environments? Is it the result of the conceptions and value judgments of these spaces that are derived exclusively from the narratives presented in the media? Perhaps. After all, building an opinion in this way, i.e. without personal experience, results in people outside the *favela*s allowing their own actions to be determined by the media-supported concepts of otherness: "You know, but no one wants to get out of their car and park in front of this modest door, where there is not even a sidewalk, sometimes the streets don't have a sidewalk. They don't want to leave their cars on such streets because it is dangerous" (2007/7/52).

Through the rejection and avoidance of interaction with these areas, indifference and reification grow, while empathy declines. By reification, Honneth (2005, 2012) describes a kind of reduced attentiveness, causing the fact of recognition to fall into the background and thus to slip out of sight. Reification in the sense of a denial of recognition therefore means that in the course of acts of cognition an advanced capitalist society and its members lose more and more attentiveness to the fact that this cognition owes its existence to an antecedent act of recognition. By speaking here of mere objects or 'things,' Honneth means that, in this kind of an amnesia, subjects lose the ability to understand immediately the behavioral expressions of other persons as making claims on us. We may indeed be capable in a cognitive sense of perceiving the full spectrum of human expressions, but we lack, so to speak, the feeling of connection that would be necessary for us to be affected by the expressions we perceive. Recognition then clearly means the opposite of reification as the moral necessity of the 'good life.'

In the Brazilian urban context, reification leads to a situation in which *favela*s exist only in an abstract form in the minds of the inhabitants of the 'formal city.' *Favelas* are not part of their perception of the world; they are denied, or have become irrelevant, if not invisible:

> They are really invisible and they [the rich] are never going to wonder why they are poor, why I am rich, why I am rich and they are poor. They [the rich] are never going to understand, that if one would reach his hand out to someone in the favela, that it could make something possible for them, one mustn't adopt [him] and take [him] home. (2007/8/62)

By examining the field of perception, and the categorical duality of *visible* vs. *invisible,* an opportunity would appear to arise in which recognition theory can be applied to reflect on specific spaces and the individuals who inhabit them. With regard to modern capitalism, Castells brought attention to the condition of personal irrelevance (as social invisibility) in its reference to the development of the dual city in Latin America, the USA, and Europe: "We move from a situation of social exploitation to one of functional irrelevance. We will live to see the day when it will be a privilege to be exploited, because worse than exploitation is ignorance" (213).

Also for Offe (274) as well as Bude and Willisch, the 'unnecessary' must be differentiated from the 'losers': The losers are at least still taking part in the societal struggle over resources and recognition in the social space; the unnecessary, however, are completely excluded from participation in this game, they are of no (current) relevance and don't even have the privilege of belonging to the losers. Both winners and losers are part of the sphere of inclusion, while the unnecessary are to be located in the realm of exclusion (Schroer 36; Nassehi).

The question of whether spaces have value in the sense of recognition and societal visibility and relevance has implications for the cartographic existence of spaces as well. That *favela*s are cartographically ignored in Brazil can be seen in the following pictures, both of which illustrate different visual realities. Fig. 1 represents an excerpt taken from a commercial standard map of Rio de Janeiro, showing the district of *Botafogo* in the center. In the area of the slope northwest of it (where *Morro Santa Marta* is written), there is no indication of a settlement.

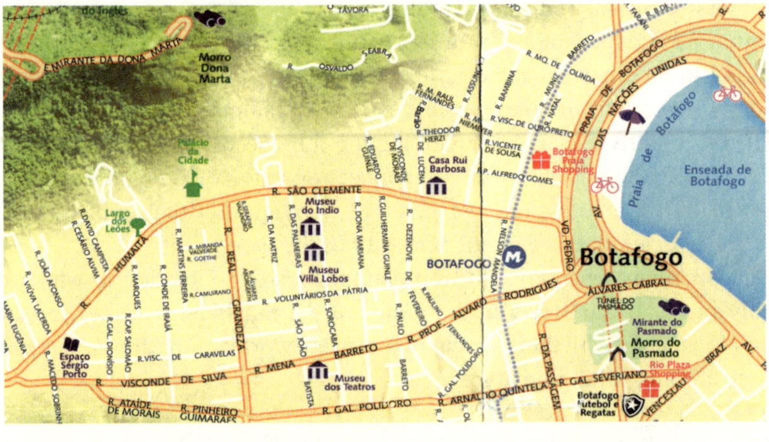

Fig. 1: *Favelas* as invisible cityscapes: Excerpt from map of Rio (Melhoramentos); © Riotur, Empresa de Turismo do Municipio do Rio de Janeiro

In contrast to this, the photo taken from *Corcovado* (Fig. 2) clearly shows the *favela Dona Marta* in the foreground. Jaguaribe and Hetherington have also brought attention to this phenomena of non-representative representations in their contribution "*Favela* Tours: Indistinct and Mapless Representations of the Real in Rio de Janeiro." Is it possible to establish here that the *favela*s often lack representation because through them the paradox of the urban becomes visible?

Could it perhaps be because they represent all of the things which the dominant citizenry attempts, with their collective powers, to dismiss and distance itself from: the suppressed, excluded, disorderly and the autonomously structured?

Fig. 2: Rio de Janeiro: View from Corcovado in the direction of Botafogo; © Eberhard Rothfuß (09/2010)

Spatial Visibility and Social Invisibility

This section will deal with the relationship between the visible and the invisible. Here, I do not mean a spatial/optical (in)visibility but, rather, visibility in a social sense:

> The blacks are an invisible people for the middle and upper class! If one isn't somehow able to get himself noticed, by studying or presenting himself, he will continue to belong in the statistics of the invisible, to the people… that think: "ah, in the favela there is nothing, which is useful." (2007/8/58f.)

This quote from a dark-skinned woman reflects a collective perception with regard to her societal status. The invisibility of a person means an undeniable feeling of non-existence and, as a result, an absolute lack of worth and self-esteem. To count as non-existent is to endure an insufferable subject status. The tragedy of daily personal irrelevance can be seen in the following picture.

Fig. 3: The routine of misery: Social invisibility? © Eberhard Rothfuß (10/2007)

This picture shows, on the one hand, the emotional and perceptual numbness and nonchalance of the city dwellers described by Simmel, and, on the other hand, the irrelevance as well as the socially and recognition-theoretical invisibility of the subject lying on the sidewalk. The positioning in public manner raises the question whether this individual attempts to escape the poverty and loneliness of the capitalistic state by demonstrating a physical and material existence and is in this way obtaining at least some form of visibility. Is this maybe a last option for them to attract attention and reaffirm their existence? Is there, perhaps, also a moral 'invocation' implied, in the sense of Althusser, with regard to the mercilessness of the daily Brazilian reality?

> The feeling of sensitivity and responsibility is missing, I believe that concerns everything. Responsibility, sensitivity, altruism are missing, these belong together and create a common basis of empathy. Not emotions, only rationality, that's how they are often dealing with the situation, that one lives in the same city and thinks, that there are poor here, that there are needy, and walks right past. (2007/8/63)

From a cultural-historical perspective, there are many accounts of situations in which the ruling classes demonstrated their superiority over the subordinated by pretending not to recognize them. In his work *Nacktheit und Scham* ("Nakedness and Shame"), Dürr, for example, has shown that the nobility felt legitimized to undress themselves in front of their servants, since they were in a certain way seen as non-present, or even non-existent. This kind of social inexistence correlates with the societal deficit of recognition which was conceptualized by Honneth (1995) in his book *The Struggle for Recognition*. On the social-philosophical basis provided by Hegel and Mead, Honneth reconstructs three distinct forms of recognition (love, rights, and solidarity) which, in the societal spheres of western modernity, are prerequisites to develop and ensure a healthy individual relationship with the self. The ambition of the subject to obtain societal conditions in which they can develop an undamaged sense of identity and personal integrity or, in other words, the dependence on social recognition, appears for Honneth to be an anthropological constant. This normative layout of social cohesion is delivered through *The Struggle for Recognition:* "The conditio humana as a whole is characterized by the fact, that individuals are enabled for social citizenship through reciprocal recognition, which leads to a positive self" (Honneth 1995: 119). The basic human need for inter-subjective recognition in a society, or rather the lack of recognition and its implications, is an explicit topic in the novel *Invisible Man* by Ralph Ellison. In this first-person narrative, the dark-skinned protagonist describes his experiences of being confronted with a very subtle form of racial humiliation through the white population in America in the 1960s: A form of invisibility in irrelevance which has to do, not with a physical absence, but with a social non-existence manifested in a kind of "looking through," an intentional form of "not-seeing" (Honneth), a subtle form of moral contempt:

> I am an invisible. No, not that phantom, which haunted Edgar Allen Poe, also not any of those movie theater ectoplasm, like they are produced in Hollywood. I am a real person, of flesh and bones, of nerves and fluid – and one could even say, that I have reason. But still I am invisible – but one doesn't want to see me. […] My invisibility is also not determined by a special biochemical constitution of my skin. The invisibility that I mean, is the result of a peculiar mechanism in the eyes of those with which I come in contact, the construction of their inner eyes, the very eyes with which, through their physical eye, they see reality. I don't complain and I don't protest. Sometimes it can even be good to be invisible, but mostly it is depressing. One comes often into contact with them, who see so poorly. Sometime one even doubts one's own existence. (Ellison 7)

The narrator explains his experience of invisibility, in which he places responsibility on a certain construction of the inner eyes of the whites who are constantly looking through him. Here it is not their physical eyes, which are not able to see him, the equivalent of an actual blindness, rather a kind of disposition that doesn't allow him to be perceived (Honneth 2003a: 10).The book's prologue later on describes his reaction to the experienced invisibility when he, in an attempt to make certain of his own existence, feels the need to violently lash out. By provoking "others" in this way, he hopes to achieve some form of "recognition" from them (Ellison 7). For a person suffering from invisibility, this is a method to gain attention. It is with visible reactions that the protagonist forces the others to acknowledge him, to provide him with that which he had been denied. Is this kind of violent action not also comparable to the passive physical presence of the people on the sidewalks of Brazil? The conscious confrontation with a precarious body compels the pedestrians at least to step over it in order to continue on their way. They position themselves as an obstacle, thus a physical resistance, to the commuters. Is this a last attempt to raise awareness and protest against the current unjust conditions? In a milder but no less obtrusive and thus comparable style to Ellison's "invisible man," a woman from Calabar articulates her perception with regard to her daily experienced subject status in society. It is exactly this kind of "looking-through" her social environment which she perceives as a powerful feeling of humiliation:

> Yes, sometimes a look is enough to feel misplaced, you know, misplaced in the sense of inferior [...]. There are those stores, where you go in and no one pays attention to you. If you approach a saleswoman, you have a request, then they look through you, as if you were air. (2005/7/69)

The 'intentional not-seeing' of the under-class by the middle and upper class (and certainly at times by the under-class as well), that is to say, their experienced social irrelevance within capitalistic Brazilian society, could represent the disciplinary counter-concept to the slave pillory of the middle of the nineteenth century. At that time, rather than being ignored, the slaves were presented in public displays of power, and their punishment was made consciously visible in order to effect deterrence and act as a warning.

Fig. 4: The *Pelourinho* (slave pillory) in Vila do Conde, Northern Portugal: instrument of power, achieved through the public displays of discipline and humiliation. © Eberhard Rothfuß (09/2010)

Fig. 5: Largo do Pelourinho, former slave market of Salvador da Bahia. © Eberhard Rothfuß (04/2004)

The name *Pelourinho* is a testament to the earlier location of legal procedures and criminal sentencing. Thus in Vila do Conde (Northern Portugal), on the square in front of the parish church, a stone pillar was erected, and, at least in colonial times, considered to be a pillar of shame. In Salvador da Bahia, the *Pelourinho* was found at a place by the same name, *Largo do Pelourinho,* where, until 1835, the slave market was held. Slavery was abolished in Brazil in 1888 with the promulgation of the *Golden Law.* As a result, the feudalist societal system dissolved, but the hierarchical system of status and class would remain intact. Accordingly, a new instrument of domination had to be contrived to replace the visible disciplining and shaming of the slaves, and to further maintain and justify the authority of power exerted by the privileged sections of society and serving their interests. Would not the implementation of an alternative model of social invisibility of the descendants of the slaves be necessary? One which could, with more and less subtle mechanisms, undermine the standing of the marginalized minority within society and invoke defensive measures of apathy, shame, and resignation?

> Mostly I feel excluded, as if I just wasn't there, if one isn't attributed the smallest of value by the people. If one looks for work, it's already enough to say: "I live in Calabar," and the people don't want to give you work, because they think, the district is bad, so you coming from this world are also bad. (2005/13/100)

The subject experiences social invisibility through the lack of responsive recognition from the social environment that would normally be expected because expressions of positive acknowledgment of the subject are *per se* inalienable. Behind the empirical statements of the social invisibility that poor people have suffered from, there is the recognition-theoretical phenomenon of the "Peripheral Modernity" of Brazil as based on colonial-historical conditions (Souza). Honneth (2003b: 10) sees social invisibility as a moral episteme of recognition. Seen this way, the term 'invisibility' follows, not in the cognitive or optical sense, but rather as a socially defined fact. It becomes clear that through this process of moral contempt in the form of worthlessness of the under-class – Souza speaks of the *ralé* (riff-raff, rabble), a class of "human trash" – a fundamental deformation is created which is necessarily composed of a system of reciprocal recognition. The execution of this practice of selective contempt and humiliation of the majority by the minority of the privileged has been at work in Brazil since the sixteenth century.

> Generally, the difference between *seeing* and *recognizing* becomes clear through the dualism of the anthropological categories of *visibility* and *invisibility*: "While by cognizing a person we mean an identification of him as an individual that can gradually be improved upon, by 'recognizing' we refer to the expressive act through which this cognition is conferred with the positive meaning of an affirmation. In contrast to cognizing, which is a non-public, cognitive act, recognizing is dependent on media that express the fact that the other person is supposed to possess social 'validity.'" (Honneth 2003b: 115)

The consequence of this suffered invisibility, that is to say, the denied acknowledgment of value and importance of the subject, results in a refusal of the positive recognition of the *favela* residents by the privileged and the accompanying internalization of a negative self-identification be the under-privileged.

Shame and Negative Self-Relationship

> It is the weakness of will [...]. If you are poor and you have nothing, your will is also weak [...] and the people here are all poor. [...] it is my own fault, you know, that I haven't exerted myself enough, to educate myself well in order to get a better job. (2005/12/98)

The people that are ruled over compose the majority of Brazilian society. From generation to generation they have internalized and accepted the prejudices and the shame forced upon them by the ruling class. Scott calls this the "ideological support" of the subaltern, which contains an affirmation and recognition of the hegemonic conditions. A result of the denial of recognition is articulated in the fact that the shamed also shame themselves. This shaming takes place within the disregarded communities. The blacks don't pay attention to or value each other anymore. This is seen as a form of racism, just like that between whites and blacks: The blacks themselves don't like each other. The black (person) makes no impact on his location, on others like him. In this way social and racial discrimination are created (2007/21/168).

> Slavery was abolished in 1888, however, the blacks experience much discrimination against themselves up until the present day, because they have few possibilities to study at school, to get a good job. And until the present the employers have found no way, how they could fight against the racial and social discrimination in Brazil. (2007/21/166)

The internalization of a negative self-relation over generations through the structural inequality of slaves is apparent until today in the internalized ways and means, from above and below, in the daily practices of the subaltern. "I believe, that nothing has changed, basically nothing. Slavery still exists. Only on paper it no longer exists, only liberation" (2007/16/138). The ruled have overwhelmingly incorporated the belief in their own inability which results in a collective process of "social shame" (Neckel) that has taken hold in these sections of society. Neckel explains in *Status und Scham* that the meaning of such feelings of shame and inferiority are crucial for the production, especially the symbolic re-production of social inequality in modern society as it is founded in the ideology of performance and competition (for further considerations see Deffner). Neckel's examination shows, through concrete examples, the meaning of social recognition in the sense of Honneth (1994) which stands in direct relation to the experience of shame and shaming within the social stratigraphy. Thus, for a "critical theory of shame," only a "critique of domination" is possible (ibid. 191). In this way, social shame is established through the experience of one's own 'status of deficit':

> In this case we can pronounce a justification on the black class. On the other hand, one could pronounce one's own justification. And another thing, that I have learned to understand, not only from these justification-T-shirts '100% black,' rather the majority of blacks, that are actually black, they rarely marry other black women, they don't get married with another black woman, they have no relation to other black women. What do they do then? They find themselves a European. That means, they flee from themselves, they deny their origins, are ashamed of them. (2007/14/110)

The individual self-esteem is created within a socially hierarchical system in which social prestige follows the generally accepted, societally sanctioned norms. The more modern capitalist societies are characterized by tendencies of individualization, the greater the risk that the subjects will blame themselves for their social status and failure to reach certain achievements. The paradox of social shame in modern society lies in the invisibility of the condition that Neckel has so aptly described: "The unequal distribution of social recognition that manifests itself in the shame of inferiority corresponds to a power-based unequal distribution of the chance to live/chance of survival that finds its cultural opposition in the generalized social claims to autonomous individuality" (own translation).[3]

The profound deficit of recognition substantially hinders the growth of self-esteem, which can manifest itself in a collectively shared negative relationship to the self. This is an expression of the recognition of one's own inferiority and suggests an act of shaming as well as the simultaneous establishment of the superiority of one group over the other. Neckel describes the personality-related shaming also as an effective tool that can be implemented in the struggle for recognition and the perpetuation of the social order. In this way, the 'social shaming' functions through the privileged classes as an effective instrument for securing and maintaining unequal power relations.

Spatial Invisibility as a Prerequisite for "Geographies of the Possible"

In this chapter I will look at the great paradox of the empirical analysis: that the irrelevance and invisibility of the subject can create "Geographies of the Possible" which wouldn't have come into being through control, discipline, and panoptical visualization. This condition also bears a moment of freedom, autonomy, and spontaneity. The unconventional city space of the *favela* can offer a lifestyle which is, at times, less burdensome than that of the 'formal city.'

> If we want to have parties, we have them. [...] everything happens on the streets, everyone can come and no one is bothered by the music. You can't live anywhere as free as here. In a certain way, we are actually the privileged here in Calabar! Living in the city center near to the shopping center and the beach. We have everything that we need to live. And no one bothers us here. The rich [people] would never set a foot in the favela! The police are also not very present here. They are scared to come here to us. We feel good here in the crooked streets. (2006/18/269)

The complex and impenetrable labyrinths that are the *favela*s provide the people living there with protection from the shame and contempt of the outside world.

[3] Original German quotation: "[Die] ungleiche Verteilung sozialer Anerkennung, die sich in der Scham der Unterlegenheit zum Ausdruck bringt, [entspricht] eine[r] machtgestützte[n] Ungleichverteilung von Lebenschancen, die ihren kulturellen Widerspruch in den verallgemeinerten sozialen Ansprüchen einer autonomen Individualität findet" (Neckel 193).

This protective function is confirmed as well by Deffner when she proposes: "For the *favela* residents, the *favela* represents, apart from the shameful side, a space which is actually protected from shame and shaming" (183; own translation). One could thus say that as a consequence of suffered social invisibility, feelings of irrelevance arise among the privileged. This has to do with a depreciation of the living environment of the others and an appreciation of the own living environment. "To know that I would have your personal life, would please me; to have money to lead a better life, to relax, but I wouldn't like to have their lives: Without community, less friends, loneliness – well I believe that a portion of them are just unhappy" (2007/17/145). It is greed, discontentment, and a joyless life that the people from Calabar see in their middle-class neighbors, that they are unhappy because they lack a space in which they can be free. A form of self-confidence shows here, questioning the societal focus placed on material wealth, which ultimately presents a challenge for those in power by the satisfaction and happiness of those lacking in possession and status. This articulated perception of the 'weak' is also connected to the question of recognition. Even while being dismissed in the greater societal context and considered irrelevant, it remains possible to give and receive respect and recognition within one's own (spatial) environment.

The *Favela* as a Space of Recognition

> In Calabar everyone respects me and I respect everyone. (2007/17/150)

In the following, I would like to discuss the more positive connotations associated with the *favela*. The *favela* is perceived as a respect-giving and protective space in which its residents can feel secure. The collectively inhabited and lived space requires the residents to take care of one another in a kind of community of fate against the outer world of rejection and contempt. In this way, the emphasis on respect as a central category appears as a constructed internal practice, for the *favela* is its own universe, containing all the positive and negative earthly attributes of urban existence. Nevertheless, the statement is socially real and true, in that it is connected to a daily experience, which guarantees those who live there an affirmative recognition, much in contrast to the public and private spaces of the 'formal city.'

> I'm really fighting for it, I fight against the inequalities. I am a part of a youth group here in Calabar and I try to do something against social inequality and everything else. But it is very difficult here, because the people here don't have any possibilities. But nothing is impossible. The heads of the youth today are very corrupted. They have a problem and they think that they will never be able to solve it, then they get mixed up with drugs, with the crooks. That is what

> they want, what the government wants, that the blacks will all become and stay drug dealers and crooks, that way they can be finished with them, because they just want to stay amongst themselves. We have to fight, fight very hard, so that we don't do them this favor. And that is what I am doing, I am doing my part, I am part of a youth group, from Pagode Bands, I try to animate the youth, that are now arriving, I take them to my place, so that we can make music (Pagode), so that they can learn to play instruments, so that their thoughts are occupied, and they don't join the crooks. I always do what I can. (2007/17/151)

Honneth (1995) argues that recognition is the kernel of social conflicts as they originate in a collective experience of "social disrespect" that people have to fight against. At the level of collective recognition, the spheres of recognition *rights* and *social solidarities* are relevant, and Honneth excludes the first sphere of recognition *love*, as it "does not entail moral experiences that could lead, of their own accord, to the formation of social conflicts" (1995: 162). On the contrary, "the forms of recognition associated with rights and social esteem, by contrast, do represent a moral context for societal conflict, if only because they rely on socially generalized criteria in order to function" (ibid.). The shift from one level to another is motivated by the fact that "individual experiences of disrespect are read as typical for an entire group, and in such a way that they can motivate collective demands for expanded relations of recognition" (ibid.). Bringing attention to social inequality, and including the struggle into the realm of possible actions from within the *favela*, symbolizes the desire and determination in standing up for justice. It is not resignation, but rather affirmative action that can be observed here. A further positive aspect that the *favela* provides its residents can be seen in the cultural and creative practices which are facilitated within its spatial boundaries:

> The culture is very vibrant. We are very rich in culture here. We make music, we sing, we play instruments, there is everything here. Theater, whatever you can imagine is there. There are all kinds of artists there, but they don't leave. There is a Capoeira group there. All Capoeira groups from Salvador, from the neighborhood, present themselves wherever there is space for them, they travel and just do these kinds of things. (2007/16/31)

This creativity and socio-cultural practices also serve to strengthen one's pride in the sense of having accomplished something without external support. There is a clear awareness about it, to live in a decent area with proper neighbors, which is still completely neglected and as a result has even greater problems than others: "Here is no place in the jungle! It is a place like any other, that has social problems, there are thieves, there is everything, but it is only a little more, because there is no support, there is no one who does anything for these people, who stray from the right path" (2007/17/146).

Intuitive Notions of Justice from the "Under-Class"

The above exploration has shown how and where forgotten recognition could be observed in Salvador. Those who must endure the denial of recognition are fully aware of it.

> You know, to be rebellious without a cause is horrible. Because the recalcitrance and anger effect the position you take on society. To endure situations, to be forced to leave… there must be a cause. You can't criticize just to put something down. (Hölldampf and Rothfuß 33)

Being aware of one's own inferiority, disadvantage, and subaltern status is an essential prerequisite for daily practices of resistance against prevailing conditions of misery and inequality. As described by Paulo Freire in *Pedagogy of the Oppressed,* it is precisely with this consciousness that the possibility for struggle arises that can recognize the opaque societal structures of inequality and hence generate new potential for more just conditions. The statements of the *favela* residents reflect a pronounced perception of injustice, which is confirmed by Honneth when he writes of a "consciousness of injustice" of the underclass which is constructed by experiences of contempt and humiliation (1995: 212). Thus the point of reference for a renewed Critical Theory of the Frankfurt School is, from his perspective, not an orientation on positivistic moral principles such as those propagated by Habermas, rather an experience of infringement upon "intuitively-given notions of justice" (ibid.). Honneth considers this a human intuition, founded upon the motivation of social protest and the perception of injustice of the lower classes. As a result Honneth places, in contrast to Habermas, the crucial normative prerequisite of all communicative action in the acquirement of social recognition. So Honneth conceives recognition as the fundamental, over-arching moral category, potentially encompassing redistribution, while Nancy Fraser argues that the two categories are both fundamental and mutually irreducible (see in detail Fraser and Honneth).

The interviewees respond to this effect, outlining many differing instances and facets of unjust treatment in their daily lives. In particular the formal legal dimension is articulated: "The Brazilian justice is not a real justice, it is a justice, which only exists on paper" (2007/21/170). The conflict between a societal status of recognition or contempt can be seen most clearly along the lines of demarcation between those of black and white complexion. The daily experiences of discrimination and the denial of societal recognition based on skin color seems ubiquitous for those affected. The stereotype that "blacks" are thieves would appear impossible to overcome:

> Because in every era the black [person] was a thief, those who stole the most, were black. And up until today this person, the authority has found no

> possibility to fight discrimination, because everyone says, the black is a thief, the black is just that. (2007/21/166)

One receptionist articulates a personal experience of disrespect:

> What can I say, about the [black] skin color, they believe I am trash. Because I am only an assistant receptionist in the management. Because of my skin color they believe that I am trash. So that is an inequality. (2007/19/156)

A life of disillusion seems to be collectively shared, the perceived racial injustice and discrimination is ubiquitous. It is appalling that discrimination cases often do not lead to penalization. The belief in a just state in Brazil has been severely weakened:

> This happens often, for I believe that there is no justice as such in Brazil. Because when this happens, there are some cases that make it to court, only that this isn't official, it would have to be punished, since racial, social and any other kinds of discrimination are a crime. It is a crime, legally it is a crime, only that it isn't always punished. What happens? I believe that a lot of discrimination happens, since it is not strictly punished as it should be. Because of that there is still so much discrimination. (2007/20/162)

Often, discrimination is perceived as hidden and the unequal status between black and white is based on the kind of work which they respectively perform. This is especially clear in the consumption sphere of malls and shopping centers when one looks at who is there to work and who is there to spend free time. The blacks are security guards, salespeople, and workers whereas white people are the consumers:

> It has to do with a kind of hidden and indirect discrimination. In McDonalds for example, and in many shopping centers here, especially in Bahia. In Bahia, Salvador is the city that has the most blacks, but it is also the city, in which there are the most signs of discrimination, here in Salvador. In Shopping Barra for example, the blacks are policemen, security guards, or working in clothing stores to maintain security. But in Shopping, in McDonalds, one doesn't see many whites working, one only sees… or if one doesn't see many blacks working, then one sees more whites. The policemen are mostly black. But one doesn't see many whites working in the stores. (2007/21/168)

From a political perspective, the people on the lower rungs of the social ladder are aware that the political elite of Brazil wouldn't show any interest in aligning their standard of living with that of the underprivileged. And why should they? Why should they voluntarily, or out of conviction, decide to forego their own privileges? A former employee of the citizen's collective of Calabar articulates a clear plea regarding the status of unjust living conditions through the political class of Brazil, which she describes as "palliative" politicians:

> It is indeed so, that the blacks were freed, but what kind of qualifications did they have? They didn't have any qualifications and thus remained slaves. Now they were indeed free, but now they were slaves for capital, because they wouldn't have otherwise survived. Even though political measures were construed, these were only palliative measures, no effective measures to bring an end to inequality. They are political measures that only meant to solve small problems, to ease the situation, to trick the citizens, but in truth – I tell you – the elites have an interest in maintaining this inequality, so that they can keep their status quo. That is how I see it. (2007/15/111)

The people are completely aware that Brazilian politicians make no attempt to fundamentally reform unjust structures, they rather seek to enact palliative measures upon the unjust system while maintaining the status quo, a notion which is statistically confirmed by an inequality index which has remained invariably high for decades. With regard to inequality, however, arguments are paradoxical. In this way, social status is not determined by the color of the skin; rather, in capitalistic Brazilian society, human value and recognition can be equalized through the attainment of material possessions in the sense of 'money makes equal': "Since value here in Brazil means that only he who owns something is of value. That means that with money you can be either black or white" (2007/21/169). This unveils a strong anti-cultural point of view, exposing a "Culture of Poverty," like the one critically formulated by Lewis.

Final Remarks

As invisible as the *favela*s were in the daily perceptions of the middle classes, they would become present as discursively constructed spaces of fear and violence which, through the threat that they pose to middle classes, turned into a phantasmagoria of horror. This stigmatization of the *favela* contrasts with the perspective of those granted a high degree of daily freedom by living in the *favela*. The denial of recognition from the privileged class and the reactionary perceptions of inferiority as well as the domination through shaming are shown in Brazilian society to be an undeniably powerful instrument for the perpetuation of social inequality. But what remains relevant in the end for the people in the marginalized districts? To go through the urban world in embarrassed resignation, or to become aware of one's own subaltern status and to make the best of it?

The intuitive perception of injustice from the under-class can be observed in the Nietzschean desire "to be a complete person" and thus fight for one's own integrity and dignity. The attribution of a position of shame to the *favela* residents from the side of the powerful was only partially successful: The shamed have proven resistant and have not allowed themselves to be dominated so easily. Statements from *favela* residents have shown more of a pragmatic inflection of "making-with" in order to "do something with it." It is a "faire avec", like in the formulation from De Certeau: "If one does not have, what one loves, one has to love what one has" which is of great significance here (31). Could not even the "real existing slums" become spaces of the counter-class to the nascent "symbolic class" (managers, journalists, PR people, academics, artists, etc.) who engage in the new class struggle of global inequality through acts of self-dignity and political mobilization (Žižek 2013: 107)? Žižek clearly perceives the emancipatory and revolutionary potential of these city spaces when he writes: "We should look for new forms of social consciousness that will emerge from the slum collectives: They will be the nucleus of the future" (2014: 107).[4]

Works Cited

Althusser, Louis. "Ideology and Ideological State Apparatus." *Lenin and Philosophy and other Essays*. Ed. Louis Althusser. New York: Monthly Review Press, 1971. 121-76.

Berenstein Jacques, Paola. "Eine Ästhetik mit Hüftschwung: Von den *Favela*s lernen." *City of COOP. Ersatzökonomien und städtische Bewegungen in Rio de Janeiro und Buenos Aires*. Ed. Stephan Lanz. Berlin: b_books, 2004. 61-74.

Bude, Heinz, and Andreas Willisch. *Exklusion: Die Debatte über die "Überflüssigen."* Frankfurt a. M.: Suhrkamp Verlag, 2008.

Castells, Manuel. "Die zweigeteilte Stadt: Arm und Reich in den Städten Lateinamerikas, der USA und Europas." *Die Welt der Stadt*. Ed. Tilo Schabert. München: Piper, 1990. 199-216.

Certeau, Michel de. *The Practice of Everyday Life*. Berkeley/Los Angeles: University of California Press, 1984.

Deffner, Veronika. *Habitus der Scham – Die soziale Grammatik ungleicher Raumproduktion. Eine sozialgeographische Untersuchung der Alltagswelt Favela in Salvador da Bahia (Brasilien)*. Passau: Selbstverlag Fach Geographie der Universität Passau, 2010. *Passauer Schriften zur Geographie* 26.

Dürr, Hans P. *Nacktheit und Scham*. Frankfurt a. M.: Suhrkamp, 1988.

Ellison, Ralph. *Invisible Man*. New York: Vintage, 1952.

Fraser, Nancy, and Axel Honneth. *Redistribution or Recognition? A Political-philosophical Exchange*. London: Verso, 2003.

Freire, Paulo. *Pedagogy of the Opressed*. New York: Continuum, 2007.

4 My translation of: "Wir sollten nach neuen Formen des sozialen Bewusstseins Ausschau halten, die aus den Slum-Kollektiven hervorgehen werden: Sie werden die Keimzelle der Zukunft sein."

Habermas, Jürgen. *The Theory of Communicative Action*. Vol. 1 & 2. Boston: Beacon Press, 1985/1987.

Honneth, Axel. *Reification: A New Look at an Old Idea*. (Berkeley Tanner Lectures). Oxford: Oxford University Press, 2012.

---. *Verdinglichung: Eine anerkennungstheoretische Studie*. Frankfurt a. M.: Suhrkamp, 2005.

---. "Unsichtbarkeit: Über die Moralische Epistemologie von Anerkennung." *Unsichtbarkeit: Stationen einer Theorie der Intersubjektivität*. Ed. Axel Honneth. Frankfurt a. M.: Suhrkamp, 2003a. 10-27.

---. "Recognition: Invisibility: On the Epistemology of 'Recognition.'" *Aristotelian Society Supplementary* 75.1 (2003b): 111-26.

---. *The Struggle for Recognition: The Moral Grammar of Social Conflicts*. Cambridge: Polity Press/MIT Press, 1995.

---. *Kampf um Anerkennung: Zur moralischen Grammatik sozialer Konflikte*. Frankfurt a. M.: Suhrkamp, 1994.

Hölldampf, Katja, and Eberhard Rothfuß. "Auto-organização Urbana em Vecinidades Desprivilegiadas: As Possibilidades e Limítes de Articulação Autónoma em Salvador da Bahia." *GeoTextos* 9.1 (2013): 11-40.

Jaguaribe, Beatriz, and Kevin Hetherington. "*Favela* Tours: Indistinct and Mapless Representations of the Real in Rio de Janeiro." *Tourism Mobilities Places to Play, Places in Play*. Ed. Mimi Sheller and John Urry. London: Routledge, 2004. 155-66.

Lewis, Oscar. "The Culture of Poverty." *On Understanding Poverty: Perspectives from the Social Sciences*. Ed. Daniel P. Moynihan. New York: Random House, 1969. 187-99.

Merleau-Ponty, Maurice. *The Phenomenology of Perception*. Translated by C. Smith. London: Routledge, 1965.

Nassehi, Armin. "Exklusion als soziologischer oder sozialpolitischer Begriff?" *Mittelweg* 36.5 (2000): 18-25.

Neckel, Sieghard. *Status und Scham: Zur symbolischen Reproduktion sozialer Ungleichheit*. Frankfurt a. M.: Campus, 1991.

Offe, Claus. "Moderne 'Barbarei': Der Naturzustand im Kleinformat?" *Modernität und Barbarei: Soziologische Zeitdiagnosen am Ende des 20. Jahrhunderts*. Ed. Max Miller and Hans-Georg Soeffner. Frankfurt a. M.: Suhrkamp, 1996. 258-89.

Rothfuß, Eberhard. *Exklusion im Zentrum: Die brasilianische* Favela *zwischen Stigmatisierung und Widerständigkeit*. Bielefeld: transcript, 2012.

Scott, James C. *Weapons of the Weak*. New Haven/London: Yale University Press, 1985.

Simmel, Georg. *The Metropolis and Mental Life*. New York: Free Press. 1976.

Schroer, Markus. "Die im Dunkeln sieht man doch: Inklusion, Exklusion und die Entdeckung der Überflüssigen." Mittelweg 36.5 (2001): 33-46.

Souza, Jessé. "The Singularity of the Peripheral Social Inequality." *Imagining Brazil*. Ed. Jessé Souza and Valter Sinder. Lanham, MD: Lexington Books, 2009. 9-36.

Žižek, Slavoj. *Fordern wir das Unmögliche*. Hamburg: Laika-Verlag, 2014.

---. *Demanding the Impossible*. Cambridge: Polity Press, 2013.

Moving In and Out, Up and Down: Real Estate in Twenty-First Century Drama

Julia Faisst

While the term inequality implies a state of disparity, it conversely points to the want of equality between persons and the objects they have access to or own, such as real estate. In the context of African-American history, however, there has long been a double bind when it comes to "property consisting of land and the buildings on it" in general, as well as to the "interest vested in this," that is property relations in particular ("Real Estate"). Once the capitalist infrastructure that was America's plantations had begun to be built, owning first and foremost referred to being owned: slaves were owned by their masters. A fictional but mundane insistence on not being handed down property in the form of a household item such as a chafing dish by a well-meaning but condescending white employer on a moving day in the 1950s, might thus be experienced as more freeing than accepting it. As African American Albert, husband to domestic servant Francine, replies fervently to such an offer in Bruce Norris's dramedy *Clybourne Park*: "Ma'am, we don't want your things. Please. We got our own things" (52). That said, either the acquisition or the holding on to residential property, especially in the purview of private homes that become increasingly contentious, is one of the major topics of the contemporary real estate dramas this essay addresses: the aforementioned *Clybourne Park* and Lisa D'Amour's *Detroit*, both of which premiered in 2010.

Clybourne Park, a play about racialized housing inequalities, is a response to Lorraine Hansberry's 1959 *A Raisin in the Sun*, a landmark play based on the author's family's battle for housing equality, which culminated in the case Hansberry v. Lee. *A Raisin in the Sun* revolves around a black family which attempts to purchase a home in a white Chicago neighborhood in the segregated 1950s.[1] Its updated version, *Clybourne Park*, as well as *Detroit*, are dramas that explore housing inequality and urban neighborhoods in transition after the 2007-2008 real estate crisis.[2] Between inclusion and exclusion, and amidst growing

1 On the struggle for homeownership and African-American suburbanization after World War II from a sociological perspective, see Wiese.

2 While not its main theme, the precariousness of the idea of home and owning property is also treated in D'Amour latest play, *Airline Highway*, set in the underbelly of a post-Katrina and rapidly gentrifying New Orleans. In this play, an underclass community of outsiders working in the service and entertainment industry in and around the French Quarter (including strippers, prostitutes, and entertainers in seedy bars) is threatened by the prospect of eviction from the once flamboyant but ill-maintained Hummingbird Hotel (a wobbly banister, a gutter pipe badly fixed crashing down on party guests, "Oh, I bet the foundation is shot anyway, I mean this hotel is built on soup") they call home. At times, they feel a great sense of belonging ("I'm right here. I'm home"), as well as pride in the shared "kingdom" they have created and

diversification, its resident-protagonists move both in and out, up and down. This essay zooms in on how twenty-first-century drama negotiates housing aspirations in dilapidating and then gentrifying urban neighborhoods in Chicago and Detroit. Thereby, it engages critically with the ways in which African-American and white communities, lower- and middle-class alike, find their neighborhoods threatened, and their hopes for upward mobility and senses of belonging challenged. My inquiries into processes of disinvestment, disintegration, and subsequent re-evaluation and gentrification of housing aim to shed light on contemporary dramatic depictions of both spatial inequality and housing discrimination from the double perspective of class and race.

To be sure, the middle-class homes in the real estate dramas discussed here no longer serve as idealized loci of social equilibrium, as they still might have in nineteenth and early twentieth-century domestic dramas. Therefore, they can no longer be equated with apparent economic or social stability, untainted by the historical forces of class distinctions and divisions. On the contrary, residential location (besides work, consumption, and family dynamics) is considered here as one "substantive are[a] of personal and social experience" where a middle-class way of life is sought and negotiated in the first place (Blumin 1989: 11). The idea of home, to borrow from Amy Schrager Lang, thus "reaches far beyond the domestic setting to capture what is lacking and what is to be desired, what has been lost and what is to be gained in the navigation of class" (12). While negotiating economic and racial inequality, *Detroit* and *Clybourne Park*, as two cases in point, conceptualize the home as an imaginary locus where encounters across classes and races – as well as the possibility of changing one's social position – are as intimately tied up with the desire to gain property as much as with the fear of losing it.

Hereby, class belongings (including, at the lowest end of the spectrum, poverty) are marked by successive layers of change, similar to a notion of domestic space which has been considered dynamic at the latest since the spatial turn. Rather than as an economic state endured by low- or no-income citizens, poverty is therefore considered a relative, mobile, and cross-class term, a "state that people fall into and out of from many positions" (Jones xiii). This would include the suburban inhabitants who populate the two plays and who seemingly embody middle-class values. As both a process of social differentiation and a "dynamic category that develops structurally and thematically across textual space," poverty is part of the

feel they own ("All this is ours!"). When they face how financially and socially downtrodden they are in their more pessimistic moments, however, they feel like "carrying [their] whole life around in a backpack" (18, 144, 121, 106). "Bait Boy" Greg, who claims he understands himself as having been "airlifted out" the community by moving in with a rich 'Hotlanta' cougar, presents yet an alternative, if equally precarious vision of 'owning' property: "I live in a real nice house that I did not buy, I do not own, but I do my fair share, I do the dishes, I fix the ceiling fan, I built Zoe a bookshelf [...] I participate in the household, and that is what you call sweat equity" (142).

class formation that pervades literary (and other) culture (Jones xiii). The same dynamic quality pertains, I would claim, to inequality as well; especially since, to paraphrase Cora Kaplan, it is the inequalities – historical and current ones – that underwrite class (10). As E.P. Thompson already insisted in his preface to *The Making of the English Working Class* in the early 1960s, class – and, by extension inequality – is a fluid "*historical* phenomenon," and, as such, a relational "relationship [...] embodied in real people and in a real context" fostered by both cultural and social forces (rather than a 'category' or 'structure'): "something which in fact happens (and can be shown to have happened) in human relationships," that is in everyday experiences of ordinary people in close physical contact – such as the neighbors residing next to each other in *Clybourne Park* and *Detroit* (9, emphasis by the author).

How the history of inequality is played out between neighbors can be seen in *Clybourne Park*'s debate over the arrival of whites in the black neighborhood:

> STEVE. – The history of America *is* the history of private property. / LENA. That may be – / STEVE. Read de Tocqueville. / LENA. Though I rather doubt *your* grandparents were *sold* as private property. / STEVE. Ohhhhh my *God*. Look. Look. Humans are *territorial*, okay? [...] *you guys* have this territory, right? And you don't like having it *stolen away* from you, the way white people stole everything else from black America. *We get it*, okay? And we *apologise*. But what *good* does it do, if we perpetually fall into the same, predictable little euphemistic tap dance around the topic? / KEVIN. You know how to *tap dance*? (Norris 100)

By way of allusions to historical figures such as Alexis de Tocqueville and historical institutions such as slavery, the contemporary anxiety over holding on to one's residential property is pitched against the backdrop of two versions of historical narratives which are at odds with each other: namely, on the one hand, the narrative of private property accessible to all, and, on the other, that of unequal property relations in the United States. De Tocqueville, for one, deemed property to be within the reach of every member of a community.[3] An economic system like slavery, however, can only be based on property rights by negating these very rights to black Americans: human beings to whom property law is applied.

The vagaries of multiple versions of history notwithstanding, the idea of private property in general, and homeownership in particular, runs deep through what Tocqueville deemed the most democratic of nations, as well as the real estate plays discussed in this essay. The characters in D'Amour's *Detroit*, like in *Clybourne*

[3] As De Tocqueville writes in *Democracy in America*: "In America, the most democratic of nations, those complaints against property in general, which are so frequent in Europe, are never heard, because in America there are no paupers. As everyone has property of his own to defend, everyone recognizes the principle upon which he holds it" (<http://xroads.virginia.edu/~hyper/detoc/1_ch14.htm>).

Park, desire to hold on to the idea of private homeownership – even if it's the bank that owns the house: "KENNY You own your house, right? / BEN Of course. Well, I mean the bank owns it – / KENNY Shit then, private property. You gotta hang on to that house, Ben" (68). The political comedy is set in the neo-liberal age of financialization that Judith Butler and Athena Athanasiou label "debtocracy," that is "a fundamental technology of biopolitical governmentality" (11). Housing debt as "a political and moral economy of life itself," according to the two authors, points to the original meaning of 'economy': "the allotment and management of the *oikos* (the house, the household) as the site par excellence of human capital" (Butler and Athanasiou 12). The title of my essay, "Moving In and Out, Up and Down" may appear like a quip, yet it points out today's rather ironic correlation of the act of moving houses with the reason and/or result of this very move: a moving up or down along class lines, that is a significant change in class belonging, with a particular focus on changes of the middle class. While residents move in and out, changes in neighborhood configurations ensue: "[c]ommunities change," as Lindsay, a young white gentrifier, puts it in response to an objection that the neighborhood Clybourne Park is "intended to house a community of working-class families" (Norris 94). Class and racial alliances are re-evaluated and redrawn.

At the intersection of housing and social justice, the two acts of *Clybourne Park* take place in the living room of a bungalow in a fictional Chicago neighborhood. The first act, set in 1959, revolves around a white middle-class family and neighborhood association representative Karl Lindner who, out of fear of changes in racial configurations and rising property values in the neighborhood, tries to persuade the family to not sell the house to the African-American Younger family. In the second act, set today, the neighborhood, which had turned primarily black and undergone a period of decline in the fifty years past, is now slowly gentrifying. A young, white couple intends to purchase and fix up the dilapidated house. The black descendants who had inherited the historical home and speak out against raising the property value that would come with renovating it challenge this plan. *Detroit* features two married (white) couples, one middle class (if economically uncertain), and one working class: next-door neighbors who mutually enforce their housing-tract angst in what slowly turns into an urban wasteland over patio barbeques in an America that is being downsized. The title and location of the play refers, on the one hand, to the city, but mainly to the state of collapse not only the city of Detroit faces in an exemplary way. Its stage directions set the action in a place "Not necessarily Detroit" (D'Amour 2011: 5), and thus point to the ubiquity of what Nancy Lee Peluso and Michael Watts call "violent environments," that is, as Ann Laura Stoler phrases it, environments made violent "not by a scarcity of resources but by grossly uneven reallocation of access to them" (5).[4] Nonetheless, the play reveals its site-specificity in the questions that

4 As Norris explains in an interview, the neighborhood of Clybourne Park is ubiquitous as well: Pretty much every big city has some version of this. [...] There is no actual Clybourne Park in

some stage directions consist of and that exude the ominous atmosphere pervading a place that is being destroyed: "What are the sounds? Is it the neighborhood sounds, only processed? Or is it construction because they are knocking down the house a few blocks over?" (D'Amour 2011: 65). Frank, the owner of the house the working class couple squats in and Kenny's great-uncle, likewise refers to the place as one that is as much falling into disrepair as Detroit currently is, when he reminisces about the heyday of suburban homeownership:

> To be honest, it hurts my heart to come back here. Half the houses falling apart, the others so fancified they seem untouchable. I mean, how are you going to ask for a cup of sugar from someone who lives in *that* place? [...] This is not what the developers intended. They wanted you to have neighbors. (D'Amour 94-95)

In Frank's view, dilapidation and subsequent gentrification destroy the idea of the neighbor-friendly development that proudly used to call itself the "Bright Houses" division. Fittingly, both the advertisement slogan of the neighborhood, "Come to the Light," and its streets names accord to the utopian optimism of prefabricated housing for each and everyone of the middle class in the 1960s, as well as a belief in the power of science which was deemed capable of engineering an amenable environment: Sunshine Way, Fluorescent Avenue, Helium Lane, Solar Power Lane, or Rainbow Road (D'Amour 47). In Frank's days, it did not matter that all new houses looked similar; on the contrary, their architectural conformity served as the ultimate marker of safety: "It was a new house!" he exclaims. "You were living in Bright Houses. It was like stealing second base. You were safe" (92). In Sharon's and Kenny's days, however, the Detroit of 2011, the big "Bright Houses" sign has fallen "backward a long time ago" and is "all overgrown with weed and ivy" (46). Crucially, in a city like Detroit, this kind of "ruination is made," as Stoler phrases it, and its debris is, like the ruins, "constructed" (x). In *Clybourne Park*, rather than renovating these human-made ruins (constructed by a financialized, neoliberal economy, so to speak), the white couple moving into the black neighborhood opts for re-building their house from scratch: "We *talked* about renovation. [...] Because the houses are *so* charming [...] – but when you figure in the crack in the subfloor and the cost of lead abatement – and in a market

Chicago. Or, to be strictly accurate, there is a playground called Clybourne Park [sic] on Clybourn Avenue, but there is no neighborhood called Clybourne Park. That is something Lorraine Hansberry made up. [I]t would be Wicker Park or Ukrainian Village [...] Wicker Park is a neighborhood that was mostly Latino for about 25 years, and it's very close to where Cabrini-Green used to be. Cabrini-Green was a big, dangerous housing project, which is about three or four blocks from where Steppenwolf Theatre [where the play made its world professional premiere] is now" (Norris in Basso). Incidentally, Archibald Clybourne, after whom the play lot and the street were named, was one of earliest settlers in the area: "From the perspective of the Potawatomi Indians living then, I suppose you could call him one of the first gentrifiers" (Bill Savage cited in Piepenburg).

like this one? It just made more sense to start from scratch" (Norris 71). To outwit a bad real estate market, their pragmatic approach to acquiring a home is paradigmatic.

To be sure, *Clybourne Park* presents the idea of neighborhood as threatened much less by poor construction or maintenance, but by the members of differing classes and races moving in that might lower the real estate value of its homes. Karl expresses this fear as follows: " – and *some* of us, […] those who *don't* have the opportunity to simply pick up and move at the drop of a hat, then *those* folks are left holding the bag, and it's a fairly *worthless* bag" (Norris 43). In other words, neighborhood is conceived of as exclusive. As the neighborhood association representative puts it crudely to a neighbor who is willing to integrate: "But I'll tell you what I *can't* support, and that's disregarding the needs of the people who *live* in a community […] you can't live in a *principle*, can you? Gotta live in a *house*" (35). Karl's idea of maintaining property value is to defend neighborhood boundaries against the threatening influx of members outside the community – which would render existing inequalities visible in the first place. His firmly closed-off mind does not even stop short of including, in a veritable band of imagined outsiders, the communists: "Well, do the boundaries of the neighborhood extend indefinitely? Who shall we invite next, the *Red Chinese*?" (36).

In both plays, the idea of neighborhood preservation and its potential integration in times of gentrification revolve around discussions of food. Upon inviting their new neighbors Kenny and Sharon, who met in rehab and have no furniture but bad credit, to their home, Mary shows off her supposed expertise in all things gourmet:

> All right, everybody, so we've got some dates wrapped in bacon drizzled with some chili oil, and this is Danish Havarti that I mashed with some basil and it is really great with this special olive oil – you just need a little. These are slices of 'heirloom tomatoes' – do you know what that is? I drove all the way to Whole Foods to get them. (D'Amour 34)

Sharon, who is eager to return the favor and invites Ben and Mary over, has neither the skills nor the money to pull of an equally exquisite meal. To hide her disparate knowledge about food, as well as her unequal access to upscale supermarkets in the food desert that is Detroit, she tries to model her airs of sophistication on those of Mary. The theme of her meal, she proclaims, is "white trash, because I'm trying to own up to what I am these days, ha-ha, and anyway the Cheetos are always the first things to go at a party, right? Even when they're sitting right next to the Brie" (D'Amour 49). Similarly, in the buyout-scheme that is *Clybourne Park*, it is the racist white homeowner who appeals to the supposedly different tastes of the black couple intending to move in. Assuming the air of the underdog, Albert deadpans in response: "Do they *carry* collards and pig feet? […] Cuz I sho couldn't shop nowhere didn' sell no pig feet" (Norris 40).[5] Defiantly, he disputes the assumed difference in race and class by supposedly buying into the proposed assumption, and hence turns the notion of inequality upside down.

While the term inequality is generally thought along a vertical scale of economic and social differences, both in access to and distribution of resources, inequality in *Detroit* is redefined to happen across horizontal differences: the overstepping of class lines takes places between the yards of the middle- and the lower-class houses. But while Sharon and Ken might hope to align themselves with the middle-class values of the neighborhood they move into, the suburban homes presented in *Detroit* no longer serve as the kind of recognized middle-class neighborhood that could become "a badge of middle-class respectability" in which "daily interactions within a homogenous social milieu also serve to build up and reinforce both the substance and the boundaries of the middle class as a distinctive social group" (Blumin 1985: 332). In other words, rather than showing class boundaries as fluid, the play throws into question the idea of the middle class and the domestic spaces it traditionally occupied altogether. Significantly, both homes (as well the materials they are constructed of, its furniture, and its accessories) in *Detroit* are increasingly befallen by dilapidation as well as domestic accidents taking place in them. Both exemplify the fragility of a suburban life where owning property is more virtual than real. While Ben and Mary's middle-class home initially seems well put together (complete with propane grill and bourgeois tablecloth), their sliding glass door forever jams, the chairs from Patio Depot break under their weight, the umbrella collapses and hits Kenny on his head. Next door, Ben severely injures his leg when he crashes through Sharon and Kenny's half-finished deck with the sole fake plant. Speaking from the point of view of his own precarious financial standing, Kenny's first response to the crash is: "Do you have health insurance?" But without knowing it, he is also telling some truth about the couple's financial whereabouts that do not match their supposed middle class status. Eventually, a bacchanalian dance party spirals so out of control (furniture being smashed, neighbors making out with each other, sexual boundaries as well as married allegiances breaking down) that Ben and Mary initially do not even realize that Kenny is setting fire to a pile of shattered furniture. "Whoa. Isn't that kind of big?" asks a bewildered Ben – shortly before their house burns to the ground (D'Amour 88).

Thus, the play does not shift resources along a vertical scale, but rather infects both parties with diminishing resources along horizontal gradations. Prone to "injury, violence, poverty, indebtedness," the neighbors' lives are equally

[5] A precedent that negotiates racist discourses via food, can be found in the sitcom *All in the Family*, season 1, episode 8, titled "Lionel Moves Into the Neighborhood." Here, Archie asks his deliveryman Lionel to keep a black family from moving into the neighborhood – unbeknownst to Archie, Lionel's family. Lionel: "They'll be happier with their own kind" / Archie: "You took the words right out of my mouth. There's not a chicken shack of a rib joint within miles of here." / Lionel: "No *ribs*? Lawd Almighty, what is we gonna do?"

precarious (Butler and Athanasiou 20). In what Ben deems the "fucking financial wasteland of [...] day-to-day existence" (D'Amour 27), their condition of induced inequality and destitution relegates them – both materially and with their health – to a place that Butler and Athanasiou call the "proper place [of] non-being" (Butler and Athanasiou 19-20). Incidentally, a comic twist causes Ben, who had gotten laid off from his job as a loan officer, to sit home all day in order to get started on a financial counseling business. In his mind, teaching "other people how to clean up" the financial wasteland of their lives depends upon the ability to imagine economic security where there is none: "It's really all about envisioning your life as financially sound" (D'Amour 27, 14). Evaluating one's net worth as a human being who (virtually) owns property and oversteps class lines is thus presented as an act of the imagination, if one taken in vain.

Threatened by the financial downfall from belonging to the middle class, Ben is holding on to a discourse of class that is imagined as purely "economistic," that is "a discourse of money" which leaves considerations of "both the power and the pain of class relations" by the wayside (Ortner 170). To make the power and pain of class relations more palpable, then, is the role of Sharon and Kenny. To be sure, they are not "class-conscious" in the sense that Anthony Giddens notes as more typical for the working than the middle class – self-consciously recognizing the existence of classes generally, and their own class affiliation specifically (Giddens 1981: 112). They believe in the possibility of transcending class boundaries, up until their sudden and unexpected disappearance from their home and neighborhood. Following in the footsteps of the later Giddens, they experience class no longer

> as class, but as constraints (and opportunities) emanating from a variety of sources. Class becomes individualized and [...] is experienced less and less as a collective fate. [...] The individual relates to the class system not just as a producer but as a consumer. Lifestyle and taste [...] become as evident markers of social differentiation as position in the productive order. (Giddens 1994: 143)

Differentiating themselves socially via acts of consumption, however, is ultimately out of reach for Sharon and Kenny, who are not able to affiliate themselves with the consumerist lifestyle of their (supposedly) more affluent neighbors, say by gracefully serving and sophisticatedly consuming Whole Foods delicacies. That said, having to witness how powerless their next-door neighbors actually are in the face of their impending economic decline, the only way to assert any power in this unequal relationship is to rob Mary and Ben from the last thing they own – by burning down their house.

In contrast to *Detroit*, the logic of a scale of differences does not apply in *Clybourne Park*. As Ta-Nehisi Coates emphasizes in an *Atlantic* article on housing policies, black inequality must be considered different from other types of inequality: "It was the branding of black people as outside of American society, outside of American law, and outside of the American social contract. And this branding was done even as black people pledged fealty to the state, paid taxes to the state, and died for the state […]." To be sure, racialized housing policies such as redlining systemically kept African Americans from accumulating wealth through home ownership in the pre-Civil Rights Era. *Clybourne Park* plays with the possibility of a politics of redistribution that may, after all, shift resources along a scale that does not imagine African Americans as outside of the laws and social contract of US society. Repeated scenes in which African-American characters claim proprietary rights serve as "an act of resistance" (Butler and Athanasiou 21). This could be read as the beginning of re-working the "dream" Coates invokes over and again in *Between the World and Me,* his letter to his adolescent son. At one point, he defines the dream by locating it in a domestic environment: as "perfect houses with nice lawns […] driveways […] treehouses," built on the black body and marked as exclusively white. Rather than wanting "to fold his country over his head like a blanket" any longer, Coates asks the American public to acknowledge the fraught history of black and white relations instead by stating that "the Dream rests on our backs, the bedding made from our bodies" (Coates 2015: 11). That way, those who once produced property (made from cotton or other raw materials) while being property, would no longer be owned.

That said, as Walter Benjamin's angel of history already knew and Thomas Piketty repeats in *Capital in the Twenty-First Century*: "the past devours the future" (Piketty 571).[6] Coates, for one, makes a clear case for how our profoundly unequal racial present has been caused by past white supremacist systems. How inequities of race and class are a remnant of this very past is a discussion that contemporary real estate plays such as *Clybourne Park* and *Detroit* have only begun to bring to the forestage. They are not too optimistic. As Sharon suspects, today's opportunities may be based on luck rather than personal achievement: "to be honest I feel like the real opportunities are the ones that fall into your lap. Like winning the lottery or someone's rich uncle needing a personal assistant. That almost happened to me once, Mary. And everything would have been different" (D'Amour 60). Crucially, however, the scene in which *Detroit* culminates and in which Mary's and Ben's once solid home goes up in flames (in the tradition of Detroit's infamous Devil's Night, with its innumerable acts of arson) and their dream of the good middle-class suburban life up in smoke, demonstrates in a nutshell that the two plays show property in the form of real estate to have become

[6] Reading Paul Klee's painting "Angelus Novus" as the angel of history, Benjamin writes: "Where we perceive a chain of events, he sees one single catastrophe which keeps piling wreckage upon wreckage and hurls it in front of his feet. The angel would like to stay, awaken the dead, and make whole what has been smashed. But a storm is blowing from Paradise; it has got caught in his wings with such violence that the angel can no longer close them. This storm irresistibly propels him into the future to which his back is turned, while the pile of debris before him grows skyward. This storm is what we call progress" (257-58.)

a relative value. In times of financial precariousness and increasing housing inequality, real estate, now, refers to value in the form of family history and memories rather than economic stability, as the young African American Lena explains:

> That's just a part of my *history* and my *parents'* history – and honouring the *connection* to that history – and, *no one*, myself included, likes having to dictate what you can or can't do with your own home, but there's just a lot of *pride*, and a lot of *memories* in these houses, and for some of us, that connection still has *value*, if that makes any sense?" (Norris 79)

But *Detroit* calls the idea of home even as nostalgic memory into question. Here, an elderly Frank, while hoping that Ben and Mary will rebuild, sadly muses upon the troubled present (and past) of real estate by acknowledging that, as Charles Isherwood puts it poignantly in his review of the play, "perhaps even the past isn't what it used to be": "Such a perfect memory, sometimes I wonder if it was real at all" (cited in Isherwood). This memory, of course, is white. Either play re-evaluates real estate, and the necessity of waking up from the dream of homeownership, to audiences who, by and large, are comparatively well off and liberal. Incidentally, it is now members of these audiences who live through the fear of being priced out of housing markets and the promises of home (stability, shelter, ownership, and citizenship) due to rapid changes in classed (and all too slow changes in racial) configurations. As *Detroit* and *Clybourne Park* exemplify, moving in and out is becoming a reality for members of classes that previously had not equaled moving houses with moving down. That an increasing number of people from all kinds of classes grapple with housing inequality today renders the plays' underlying assumption that real estate, property, and homeownership are in need of reconstruction now more than ever only more salient.

Works Cited

Basso, Beatrice. "Bruce Norris in the Danger Zone." *Theatre Communications Group* October 2011. <www.tcg.org/publications/at/oct11/brucenorris.cfm>.

Benjamin, Walter. *Illuminations*. New York: Knopf, 1969.

Blumin, Stuart M. *The Emergence of the Middle Class: Social Experience in the American City, 1760-1900*. New York: Cambridge University Press, 1989.

---. "The Hypothesis of Middle-Class Formation in Nineteenth-Century America: A Critique and Some Proposals." *American Historical Review* 90 (1985): 299-338.

Butler, Judith, and Athena Athanasiou. *Dispossession: The Performative in the Political*. Cambridge, UK/Malden, MA: Polity Press, 2013.

Coates, Ta-Nehisi. *Between the World and Me*. Melbourne: The Text Publishing Company, 2015.

---. "So That's Just One of My Losses." *The Atlantic* 21 May 2014. <www.theatlantic.com/businescs/archive/2014/05/so-thats-just-one-of-my-losses/371396>.

D'Amour, Lisa. *Airline Highway: A Play*. Evanston, IL: Northwestern University Press, 2015.

---. *Detroit: A Play*. New York: Faber and Faber, 2011.

De Tocqueville, Alexis. *Democracy in America*. <http://xroads.virginia.edu/~hyper/detoc/toc_indx.html>.

Giddens, Anthony. *Beyond Left and Right: The Future of Radical Politics*. Cambridge, UK: Polity Press, 1994.

---. *The Class Structure of the Advanced Societies*. London: Hutchinson, 1981.

Hansberry, Lorraine. "A Raisin in the Sun" (1959). *The Norton Anthology of African American Literature*. New York/London: W.W. Norton & Company, 1997. 1728-89.

Isherwood, Charles. "Desperately Trying to Stay Stuck in the Middle." *The New York Times* 18 September 2012. <www.nytimes.com/2012/09/19/theater/reviews/detroit-with-amy-ryan-and-david-schwimmer.html>.

Jones, Gavin. *American Hungers: The Problem of Poverty in U.S. Literature, 1840-1945*. Princeton/Oxford: Princeton University Press, 2008.

Kaplan, Cora. "Millennial Class." *PMLA* 115.1. Special Topic: Rereading Class (January 2000): 9-19.

"Lionel Moves into the Neighborhood." *All in the Family*. CBS. 2 March 1971. <www.youtube.com/watch?v=TOc5O1ISgcY>.

Norris, Bruce. *Clybourne Park*. London: Nick Hern Books, 2011.

Ortner, Sherry B. "Reading America: Preliminary Notes on Class and Culture." *Recapturing Anthropology: Working in the Present*. Ed. Richard G. Fox. Santa Fe, NM: School of American Research Press, 1991. 163-89.

Peluso, Nancy Lee, and Michael Watts (eds.). *Violent Environments*. Ithaca: Cornell University Press, 2001.

Piepenburg, Erik. "Integration, Gentrification, Conversation." *The New York Times* 3 August 2011. <www.nytimes.com/2011/08/07/theater/clybourne-park-by-bruce-norris-a-gentrification-study.html>.

Piketty, Thomas. *Capital in the Twenty-First Century*. Cambridge: Harvard University Press, 2014.

"Real Estate." *Oxford English Dictionary*. <http://www.oed.com.oed.emedia1.bsb-muenchen.de/view/Entry/238664?redirectedFrom=real+estate#eid>.

Schrager Lang, Amy. *The Syntax of Class: Writing Inequality in Nineteenth Century America*. Ann Arbor: The University of Michigan Press, 2006.

Stoler, Ann Laura. *Imperial Debris: On Ruins and Ruination*. Durham, NC: Duke University Press, 2013.

Thompson, Edward Palmer. *The Making of the English Working Class*. London: Victor Gollancz Ltd, 1963.

Wiese, Andrew. "'The House I Live In:' Race, Class, and African American Suburban Dreams in the Postwar United States." *The New Suburban History*. Ed. Kevin M. Kruse and Thomas J. Sugrue. Chicago/London: The University of Chicago Press, 2006.

Making Black Lives Matter at the (New) Nadir: The Legacy of Charles Chesnutt for Black Activism in the New Millennium

Shirley Elizabeth Thompson

In the waning years of Barack Obama's presidency, the grassroots movement #BlackLivesMatter mobilized against police brutality and returned to first principles, insisting on the bodily integrity of black people and the precious value of their lives. Founded by activists Alicia Garza, Patrisse Cullors, and Opal Tometi in 2013 as a social media campaign after George Zimmerman was acquitted in the killing of Trayvon Martin, #BlackLivesMatter manifested in the streets in August of 2014 after Officer Darren Wilson killed teenager Michael Brown in Ferguson, Missouri (Garza). Since then, it has functioned as a 'platform' in both senses of the word: as a visible stage from which to project the predicament of blackness to the world and as a space for corralling witness testimony, cultural polemics, and scholarly criticism and refining this thought for political use. In a collectively authored "Vision for Black Lives," movement leaders have called for reparations for "past and continuing harms" inflicted by the government, corporate actors, and other institutions profiting from the racial vulnerability suffered by blacks "from colonialism to slavery through food and housing redlining, mass incarceration and surveillance" (The Movement for Black Lives). By illuminating intertwined and mutually reinforcing systems of racial and economic inequality, they have echoed and popularized the work of scholars who have diagnosed and worked to counter historically entrenched regimes of "racial capitalism" (Robinson 2000: 9; see also Robinson 1987). Athletes, actors, musicians, and artists in a wide variety of genres have lent their experience, notoriety, and creativity to the critical work of #BlackLivesMatter provoking a "golden age" of protest art and reinvigorating a black pubic sphere (Brooks).

In his acceptance speech for the 2016 Black Entertainment Television (BET) Humanitarian Award, actor Jesse Williams demonstrated his bona fides as a popular theorist of #BlackLivesMatter. Before a rapt crowd of celebrities and a television audience of over seven million viewers (and many more on social media), he painted a vibrant picture of the precariousness of black lives. Williams named a fundamental antagonism between a 'whiteness,' piratical in its plunder, and 'us': "This invention called whiteness uses and abuses us, burying black people out of sight and out of mind while extracting our culture, our dollars, our entertainment, like oil, black gold" (Williams). Williams deemed whiteness to be an "extractive" force, "ghettoizing and demeaning our creations then stealing […] [and] gentrifying our genius […]." It operates, he continued, within a market cavalier in its disregard for black lives, "trying us on like costumes before discarding our bodies like rinds of strange fruit." In hip-hop fashion, Williams' metaphors piled up and bled into one another in ways that mirrored the overlapping layers of economic, political, and social inequality impinging on black lives. Williams' urgent formulations figured blackness as an alternate subjectivity running counter to (and potentially constructively critical of) the normalized liberal subject most recognizable in the political sphere as the citizen and the economic sphere as the market agent.

Specifically, Williams signals the ongoing crisis of a liberal property regime, founded in a slave system that, in the language of Supreme Court Justice Roger B. Taney's opinion in *Dred Scott v. Sanford* (1857), rendered blacks as "an articles of merchandise" with "no rights a white man is bound to respect." Critical of those who would hew too closely to the demands and expectations of a system that readily collapses personhood into its marketable properties, Williams cautions against the pitfalls of pursuing blackness as a form of specially privileged status property that merely mimics the logics of whiteness (Harris 1734). In this vein, he chides his fellow entertainers for facilitating a culture of hyper-materialism and prioritizing their 'brands.' In his formulation, the celebrity body chases the brand only to evoke the yearning of enslaved bodies to break free of it: "We spent centuries praying with brands on our bodies. And now we pray to get paid for brands on our bodies" (Williams). For Williams, and other activists, attending to the material conditions and embodied struggles shaping black lives, the ongoing contestation over property in black genius centers black bodies as the fundamental battleground in the quest for "equal rights and justice" and an unconditional "freedom". It may also signal the emergence of more expansive expressions of rights, justice, and freedom (see also Smallwood; Johnson 2016).

The predicament of blackness and property taken up by these early twenty-first-century activists strongly echoes concerns rooted in the political economy of the dawn of the twentieth century, an era that historian Rayford Logan termed the "nadir" of African-American history (Logan xxi.). In this earlier period, the legal, political, economic, and disciplinary apparatus of slavery persisted and mutated in the wake of emancipation in such powerful institutional and legal "afterlives of slavery" as the convict-lease system, Jim Crow segregation, political disenfranchisement, and unpredictable regimes of terroristic violence (Hartman 2007: 6). Attempts to incorporate blacks as free laborers and free citizens provoked what W.E.B. Du Bois, in *Black Reconstruction*, called a "counterrevolution of property," a consolidation of property interests committed to the subjugation of black freedom dreams, united across regions and political affiliation and continuing to reverberate to this day (580-636). In a powerful sense, emancipation and the Reconstruction-era amendments had precipitated a valorization crisis. Enslaved people, valued at close to four billion dollars of the nation's wealth, could no longer be counted on or (counted as) a stable holder of value in a wildly speculative economy. When blacks could no longer be listed on a plantation ledger or a bill of conveyance next to an agreed upon sum of money, it was not clear how they would be counted. When freed from their status as property without compensation for the owners of that property, it is not clear that black people would even *count*. The specter of Black Americans as a "surplus population" (Gilmore 70-78) has resurfaced in recent decades in the era of post-industrialism and the expansion of global financial markets, forming a disturbing parallel to the early years of Jim Crow, a "new nadir," in the words of Sundiata Cha-Jua (38). Both periods have exhibited both a vehement backlash against mid-century strides in civil rights for African Americans and a consolidation of property interests heavily invested both in racialized (and gendered) social stratification and in increasingly convoluted and accelerated processes of capital accumulation. Both periods witnessed the emergence of a black leadership class – "black faces in high places" according to Keeanga-Yamahtta Taylor following Amiri Baraka – whose interests and inspirations countered those of the black masses and threatened to subvert the project of black liberation (Taylor 75-106).

Given these congruencies, I would like to turn to the late nineteenth-century fiction of the African-American writer, Charles Chesnutt, an especially cogent theorist of the dynamics of the counterrevolution of property and the difficult ethical and political conundrums facing black individuals and communities. Far from a natural, self-evident relation, property, in his schema, manifests as the cold-hearted and undeniable theft at the heart of capitalist endeavors. As many revisionist scholars have argued, Marx's notion of "primitive accumulation" does not accurately serve as capitalism's origin story nor does it solely refer to the enclosure of the English commons (873-76). Rather it encompasses the histories of the Atlantic slave trade and colonial conquest and hinges on the violent appropriation of black bodies, as a "new species of human capital," and indigenous land (Singh 30). Moreover, these regimes of violent domination have persisted over time, producing a set of laboring classes, in which differentiation by race, gender, and status, "provides the indispensable material and ideological support, prop, or pedestal on which capitalism's development depended and on which it continues to depend" (Singh 37). By dramatizing the ongoing and therefore not-so-primitive processes of plunder ravaging the bodies and lives of black people, Chesnutt's accounts depict un-redressed traumas of slavery. In his stories, pained and sardonic figures in black haunt the margins of the entrepreneurial spirit animating the American dream, forcing white and black would-be strivers to reckon with their legacies (Thompson 418-23).

The author of short stories published in *The Atlantic Monthly* and other magazines and in collected volumes, several novels, a play and a handful of essays, Chesnutt experienced his most productive period from the late 1880s to the early 1900s. This period ran parallel to the most dramatic reversals of Reconstruction-era civil rights gains, including *Plessy v. Ferguson* (1896), the implementation of voting restrictions, the escalation of lynching, and outbreak of race riots in several cities. Championed by the burgeoning literary establishment, Chesnutt balanced his concerns for black rights and black creativity with the demands of a mainstream readership growing more comfortable in its racial prejudice (Thompson 423-24). In careful characterization and plotting, Chesnutt exposes the anti-human logics at the heart of a system that would commoditize human beings and their essential qualities. He also attempts to articulate an ethical response for African Americans faced with building respect and posterity within a system of racial capitalism marked not only by economic inequalities but also by ontological disparities. In effect, he asks his readers to insist on the myriad ways that black lives and experience might matter. Although these are themes that permeate his oeuvre, I will focus on Chesnutt's critique of property amid slavery's afterlife in two short stories: "The Goophered Grapevine," his first published story (*The Atlantic* 1887) collected in *The Conjure Woman and Other Conjure Tales* (1899), and "The Wife of His Youth," collected in the 1899 volume *The Wife of His Youth and Other Stories of the Color Line*.

"The Goophered Grapevine" is one of Chesnutt's Uncle Julius stories and as such structured as a tale within a tale. The frame narration is in the voice of John (unnamed at this point), a white man who with his wife, Annie, has relocated from the North to the postbellum South. Motivated in part by Annie's fragile health, the pair is also looking for good investments in plantation land. The meat of these stories consists of old yarns spun by Julius, a formerly enslaved man who continues to reside on or near the plantation and performs odd jobs for the couple. Aware of the general public's voracious appetite for 'old Negro yarns,' Julius leverages their affective power to gain some kind of material benefit. The stories function as currency and allow him to access valuable goods. Parodies of the popular Uncle Remus tales published by Joel Chandler Harris, the stories seem benign on only the most superficial level of dialect and folksiness. A vehicle for Julius's truth telling, they are actually grim accounts of the ravages of enslavement and a master's brutal struggle for domination over his slaves. In Julius' internal tale, Mars MacAdoo seeks to deter his slaves from 'stealing' his grapes and contracts with a local conjure woman, a free black woman named Aunt Peggy, to 'goopher,' or put a hex on, the grapevine so that anyone attempting to steal the fruit would wither and die. When Henry, an unsuspecting recently purchased slave, eats from the vine and begins to fall ill, his fellow slaves and the overseer convince Aunt Peggy to release him from the goopher. In more accurate terms, she alters it, causing his appearance and health to wax and wane over the seasons in alignment with the vine's growth cycle. His fate becomes organically linked to the vine in ways that are of economic and material benefit to master and slave alike. After a few years of trading on Henry's special predicament, MacAdoo engages in a raw deal that ultimately kills both the vine and the slave, a transaction that, according to Julius, continues to haunt the vineyard to the present day. Julius, it must be noted, has built a cabin on the land in question and has been deriving income from his own cultivation of grapes (Chesnutt 2000: 1-13).

Beneath this folksy yarn, Chesnutt distills some of the key predicaments of property relations under slavery. In legal terms, it is commonplace to claim that property does not consist of "things" but rather a set of social relations and obligations (a "bundle of sticks or rights") in reference to tangible or intangible things (Baron 62-67). Legal theorists have enumerated rights and liabilities – "standard incidents" – attaching to the ownership of property, including the right to possess, the right to use, the right to manage, and the right to security, among others (Honoré 370-75). Even so, the things themselves are not insignificant. As fields of or stages for contestation, they bring to light struggles over such rights, relations, and obligations. By crafting layered narratives of ownership claims and their dynamics, Chesnutt disrupts and challenges more straightforward legalistic accounts of ownership, grounded in assumptions of secure self-possession and just appropriation favored by contract theorists (Stanley 1-59; Macpherson 194-220). Deriving from John Locke, such accounts distinguish a self from nature by its capacity for reason and reflection and its consistent self-consciousness (Locke 1996: 137-50). Property is justly appropriated when one, having exclusive claim to one's body and hands, mixes one's labor with nature and transforms it (Locke 1980: 19). Chesnutt delves underneath such "labor-desert" theories of property to reveal instead that property depends on contestations over occupancy that in turn depends on the messy, morally arbitrary, and mutually destructive workings of the will (Radin 973-74). American practitioners of contract point to the U.S. Declaration of Independence which transposes Locke's first order rights to property in "life, liberty, and estate" (Locke 157) into the phrase "life, liberty, and the pursuit of happiness. Instead, the terrain of contestation undergirding will-based theories of property exhibits something more akin to Jefferson's description, in "Query 18" of *Notes on the State of Virginia*, of the planter's household as "a perpetual exercise of the most boisterous passions, the most unremitting despotism on the one part, and degrading submissions on the other" (Jefferson 162).

In Chesnutt's "The Goophered Grapevine" the Lockean vision pervades John's narration in the frame tale. To make up for years of "shiftless cultivation" that "had well-nigh exhausted the soil" (2), John would – by applying his careful, rational attention – transform the vineyard into a "striking illustration of the opportunities open to Northern capital in the development of Southern industries" (13). However, John's fantasies of just appropriation barely conceal the war of wills animating his deeper quest for wealth and status. His concern for 'industry' aside, what John really aspires to is not really to labor on the land, but for property in what James Madison described as "repose," that "remnant of time" that takes him out of a dependence on nature, qualifies him to be a responsible citizen of the republic, and distinguishes him as a master among mere men (Madison 266-68). In this vein, John appears to be one of the victors in what Du Bois characterized as the "fierce fight for mastery" among the old planter regime, new Northern investors, and a fractured laboring class made up of poor whites and disenfranchised blacks (610). When we parse the meat of the stories, the internal tales narrated by Julius, this notion of property as a working of one's will through the ownership of things becomes even more apparent as an afterlife of mastery and slavery. In his stories, those 'things' are, in fact, people owned as slaves, who might critique the nefarious logics and practices governing the property relation and develop subversive alternatives to liberal proprietorship.[1]

In destabilizing the liberal account of just appropriation, the interior tales that Julius relates dismantle the self-possessed agent of contract. In the process, he troubles the integrity of the boundaries that distinguish human selves from the natural world, that distinguish human selves from one another, and that help to constitute the categories governing social and political relations. In the "Goophered Grapevine," Mars Dougal MacAdoo has not gained property by virtue of his own labor but because he has violated the personal integrity of others. He has turned them into instruments, extending his own will and intent into their bodies. His proprietorship depends on a regime of constant surveillance and the arbitrary and disproportionate application of violence. He metes out, for example, the wildly disproportionate sentence of death for the 'theft' of scuppernong grapes on persons he claims to own. By enacting his will on the world through his property, he creates the conditions for his own personhood, compelling recognition in the marketplace, and respect and cooperation from his neighbors.[2] By managing and profiting from nature's bounty, MacAdoo seeks to insulate himself the risks associated with nature's unpredictability.

As someone who is not in possession of himself, Henry, the slave, is in no position to distinguish himself from nature. Rather than transforming nature into property, as a Lockean theorist would have it, his labor is subsumed within both nature and the property of others. In his too-intimate connection to the grapevine, the "noo nigger" Henry literally embodies the processes by which the material stuff of sinews and soil come together to produce the abstract surplus value that constitute his master's profit (Chestnut 2000: 7). Moreover, for an annual return of \$1,000, Mars Dougal routinely sells Henry for \$1,500 in the spring, when the scuppernong sap is rising, and buys him back in the winter for \$500, during his and the vine's dormant period. Henry's body is such a proficient conduit for these processes that he isn't even made to labor in the fields, but is allowed to spend most of his time on the plantation resting and eating. Henry is a model of productivity and a model of fungibility, sheer efficiency, and sheer value.

The social space between MacAdoo and Henry, the owner and the thing owned, is intimately proximate in the sense that slaves, as chattels personal, move through

1 Recent studies of property from the perspective of the enslaved include Dylan Penningroth, *Claims of Kinfolk*; Anthony Kaye, *Joining Places*; and Stephen Best, *Fugitive's Properties*.

2 My sense of how masters constitute themselves in their social worlds through and in reference to slaves is informed by Walter Johnson, *Soul By Soul* and *River of Dark Dreams* and Ariela Gross, *Double Character* among other important histories. Johnson's *River of Dark Dreams* is in keeping with Karl Marx's description of capital's harnessing of nature, human capacity, and technology.

legal space with the body of the master. However, in terms of their claim to rights that society is "bound to respect," the difference between the two could not be more vast. MacAdoo, the "master," is the proper subject of property, one who has successfully established, in James Madison's formulation, both a "right to his property" and "a property in his rights" (Madison 266-68). The sublime balance he strikes hinges on the unspoken assumption of his bodily integrity, the undisputed fact that his material body forms a clear boundary between the interior of the self and the external world. MacAdoo exhibits a "privileged form of embodiment," whereby an inviolate body housed a secure subject, a "generalized existential norm" characterizing late nineteenth-century US markets, political culture, and social life (Cherniavsky xiv-xvi). After the demise of the Reconstruction-era experiment in political and social equality and the end of federally sanctioned civil rights, the expectation and experience of bodily integrity constituted a chief aspect of the property accumulating in 'whiteness' (Harris 1729-31).

On the postbellum plantation, John best exemplifies this norm of bodily integrity, unimpeded mobility, and free agency. In contrast, Julius and his cohort, are tied to the plantation by a regime of perpetual indebtedness and constant public surveillance (Hartman 1997: 125-63). Their franchise stripped from them, they witnessed their numbers further bolster the political representation of their white overlords, including new transplants such as John and Annie (Woods 88-89). Amid an atmosphere of ever-present terroristic violence and a "racial data revolution" that produced statistical evidence of black criminality (Muhammad 15-34), the formerly enslaved and their children disciplined their bodies and public attitudes in the high-stakes performance of accommodation and deference exemplified in these stories. In their highly regimented "Jim Crow etiquette," the storytelling practices Julius employs have registered in the public imagination as subservience, but they also protected lives and safeguarded black property from the appetites and whims of old and new would-be masters (Ritterhouse 22-54). Within the strictures of Jim Crow, black writers and other cultural workers sought to restore and defend the value of black lives and developed a rich tradition of creative expression, including the blues and other tragicomic art forms marked by double entendre, "signifyin'" and a deeply serious sense of play (Woods 25-39; Gates; Thompson 425-26).

In "The Wife of His Youth," Chesnutt seeks to expose and destroy the inflated value ascribed to the illusion of white skin. If whiteness was the property saving persons from the second-class citizenship of Jim Crow, then near-whiteness operated as a kind of test of white privilege, a condition that alternatively challenged and affirmed it. With *Plessy v. Ferguson* (1896), Homer Plessy generously but futilely undermined the integrity of his white appearance to demonstrate the logical inconsistency undergirding its higher social value. However, African Americans might also contribute to the overvaluation of near-white skin when held up as a leading visual indicator of 'respectability,' a basis for, if not the chief substance of, intra-racial class animosities. Charles Chesnutt takes aim at the colorism of the black 'talented tenth' and the limited notions of proprietorship governing their sense of worth. Also set on the terrain of the post-bellum United States, this story unfolds among a set of African-American social strivers in a "certain Northern city," a group that came to be known widely as the "Blue Veins" after the (assuredly unproven) notion that "no one was eligible for membership who was not white enough to show blue veins" (Chesnutt 1968: 1). Keenly aware of the ambivalence of near-whiteness, Mr. Ryder and his cohort hang in the balance of "absorption by the white race and extinction in the black" (7). They pursued 'self-preservation' in the effort to maintain a skin complexion that fell within the acceptable boundaries of near-whiteness. In doing so, they asserted and maintained their social status if not their bodily integrity.

In the "Goophered Grapevine" and the other conjure tales, the narrator John's unconscious comportment and unquestioned mastery of language affirm his self-proprietorship and his membership in the propertied class. In the "Wife of His Youth," Mr. Ryder is consumed by the attempt to emulate what the Johns of the world enjoy as a matter of course. His successful proprietorship depends on his physical appearance: "His features were of a refined type, his hair was almost straight" (Chestnutt 2000: 4). It is bolstered by his comportment: "he was always neatly dressed; his manners were irreproachable, and his morals above suspicion" (4). It manifests in his diction and his refined pursuits: "Poetry was his passion. He could repeat whole pages of the great English poets; and if his pronunciation was sometimes faulty, his eye, his voice, his gestures, would respond to the changing sentiment with a precision that revealed a poetic soul and disarmed criticism" (4). It could even be detected in the qualities of his various possessions: "He was economical, and had saved money; he owned and occupied a very comfortable house on a respectable street. His residence was handsomely furnished, containing among other things a good library, especially rich in poetry, a piano, and some choice engravings" (4-5). However, the unassailable virtue of Ryder's wife or fiancée and her reputation for sexual modesty and delicacy would be the real markers of his propriety. In the Uncle Julius stories, John's wife, Annie, is the exemplar in this regard, with her secure whiteness, her weak constitution, and her gullible nature. As the curtain opens upon the action of Chesnutt's story, Mr. Ryder has almost settled on the choice of a bride, a certain Mrs. Dixon, a widow of refinement, education, and acceptably light skin. Of "rather ruddy complexion, and of lively disposition and buxom build" Mrs. Dixon was no "sweet pale Margaret, [...] rare pale Margaret". Nevertheless, she would be "the palest lady he expected at the ball" (8-9).

In the course of Mr. Ryder's preparation for the event, a mysterious stranger appears at his door. A small woman of black skin, grey tufts of hair and blue gums, dressed in the brilliant red and blue hues of slave superstition, she was "a little bit of the old plantation life, summoned up from the past by the wave of a magician's wand" (10). In thick dialect, she inquires about her long lost husband, "a mulatter man" by the name of Sam Taylor who had been a freeborn black man, apprenticed to work on the same plantation. To make a short story even shorter: it turns out that

Ryder and Taylor are one and the same, and the dilemma becomes clear. Should Ryder disavow the "wife of his youth," marry Mrs. Dixon, and continue his upward climb into the "uplift" class (see Gaines's book title)? Or should he acknowledge the bond he entered into under bondage, even though "Eliza Jane's" appearance and manner would defy the ethos and the aesthetics of the Blue Veins? Might he find a way to honor all of his social expectations, contradictory though they may be? In his careful recounting of the perils of their courtship and married life under slavery – including a harrowing escape, the sale of souls down the river, and the distancing effects of time and skin color – Ryder challenges the Blue Veins' commitment to a "politics of respectability" that tended to reproduce and project the values, manners, and aesthetics of middle-class whiteness (Higginbotham 185-230). He turns their sympathies toward the formerly enslaved woman of rare "devotion and confidence," and, anticipating the radical work of the queer woman of color who founded #BlackLivesMatter, he centers the experience and commitments of the most vulnerable and socially maligned subjects as a basis for reconstructing the ethics of black liberation (Chestnutt 2000: 20). "To thine own self be true," Ryder quotes, seconds before formally presenting the wife of his youth to his society friends (22).

Chesnutt's complicated and multilayered narrative technique creates a dense and dramatic field of shape-shifting characters, fluid moralities, and competing property claims. On the kind of stage constructed by his storytelling, property interests can be understood in terms of their props. If property reverberates on that line between a concrete thing and an abstract relation, between the internal realm of self-conscious proprietorship and the external material world, and between human beings in just political relation and the state of nature, then the 'props' or 'thingy-ness' of property enable this shifting back and forth and facilitate a critical engagement with the norms of proprietorship, citizenship, and market activity. Chesnutt's stories contest the notion of property as "a fundamental natural right" rather than a powerful engine of racial stratification and economic inequality (Harris; Darity and Myers). The conjure at the center of Chesnutt's stories – and Aunt Peggy herself is just the most literal practitioner of conjure – is Chesnutt's means of achieving the sleight of hand allowing readers to witness property's many iterations and contradictions. Conjure facilitates the 'big reveal' that transforms the little blue-gum woman into the wife of Mr. Ryder's youth, turns Mr. Ryder the Dean of the Blue Veins into Sam Taylor, the former slave, and provokes the Blue Veins to delve beneath the translucent properties of their skin to confront their African bloodlines and all that blackness signifies. When accessed through its props, the property relation performs spectacular feats of conjure, making 'Henry' (if that is indeed his name) into a thing to be bought and sold, a man that fears death, a grapevine, and the holder of sheer value.

There is power in this magic. Considered in terms of their market function, black bodies and black imagination, as props of property, have emitted an exciting, transferable energy fueling the various drives – envy, anxiety, inadequacy, lust –

that create economic value. However maligned black people have been, black skin and black culture have always been objects of "love" and targets of "theft" (Lott). Much like the twenty-first-century activists who proclaim that "Black Lives Matter," Chesnutt, speaking through Uncle Julius and Mr. Ryder, subverts the fungibility of blackness, the lucrative slippages among various fantastical forms and abstractions. He highlights instead the material and embodied realities of black life in the post-Reconstruction period. In Julius' telling, the fact of Henry's subjugation becomes as visible on the post-slavery plantation landscape as the fact of Michael Brown's violent, state-sanctioned death on the streets of a latter-day Missouri suburb. Following Ryder's bidding, the Blue Veins have no other choice than to look upon the former slave, Eliza Jane, and – as we do of Rekia Boyd, Sandra Bland, or Aiyanna Stanley-Jones – "#SayHerName" (AAPF). By giving space and tangible shape to the testimony of the enslaved in an age of public repudiation of African-American memory, Chesnutt presages Jesse Williams' pointed assertion: "Just because we're magic, doesn't mean we're not real" (Blight 2, 300-38).

Works Cited

African American Policy Forum (AAPF). "Say Her Name." <www.aapf.org/sayhername>.

Baron, Jane B. "Rescuing the Bundle of Rights Metaphor in Property Law." *University of Cincinnati Law Review* 82.1 (2014): 57-101.

Best, Stephen M. *The Fugitive's Properties: Law and the Poetics of Possession.* Chicago: University of Chicago Press, 2004.

Blight, David W., and American Council of Learned Societies. *Race and Reunion: The Civil War in American Memory*. Cambridge: Belknap Press of Harvard University Press, 2001.

Brooks, Daphne. "How #BlackLivesMatter Started a Musical Revolution." *The Guardian* 13 March 2016. <www.theguardian.com/us-news/2016/mar/13/black-lives-matter-beyonce-kendrick-lamar-protest>.

Cha-Jua, Sundiata Keita. "The New Nadir: Contemporary Black Racial Formation." *The Black Scholar* 40.1 (Spring 2010): 38-58.

Cherniavsky, Eva. *Incorporations: Race, Nation, and the Body Politics of Capital.* Minneapolis: University of Minnesota Press, 2006.

Chesnutt, Charles. "The Goophered Grapevine." *Conjure Tales and Stories of the Color Line.* Ed. William L. Andrews. New York: Penguin, 2000.

---. "The Wife of His Youth." *The Wife of His Youth and Other Stories of the Color Line.* Ann Arbor: University of Michigan Press, 1968.

Darity, William A., and Samuel L. Myers. *Persistent Disparity: Race and Economic Inequality in the United States since 1945*. Cheltenham, UK: Edward Elgar, 1998.

Du Bois, W.E.B. *Black Reconstruction in America: Toward a History of the Part Which Black Folk Played in the Attempt to Reconstruct Democracy in America, 1860-1880*. Vol. M170. Cleveland: World Pub, 1964.

Ely, James W. *The Guardian of Every Other Right: The Constitutional History of Property Rights*. New York: Oxford University Press, 1992.

Gates, Henry L., Jr. *The Signifying Monkey: A Theory of African-American Literary Criticism* (1988). Oxford: Oxford University Press, 2014.

Garza, Alicia. "A Herstory of the #BlackLivesMatter Movement." *The Feminist Wire* 7 October 2014. <www.thefeministwire.com/2014/10/blacklivesmatter-2/>.

Gaines, Kevin K. *Uplifting the Race: Black Leadership, Politics, and Culture in the Twentieth Century*. Chapel Hill: University of North Carolina Press, 1996.

Gilmore, Ruth W. *Golden Gulag: Prisons, Surplus, Crisis, and Opposition in Globalizing California*. Berkeley: University of California Press, 2007.

Gross, Ariela J. *Double Character: Slavery and Mastery in the Antebellum Southern Courtroom*. Princeton: Princeton University Press, 2000.

Harris, Cheryl I. "Whiteness as Property." *Harvard Law Review* 106.8 (1993): 1707-91.

Hartman, Saidiya V. *Lose Your Mother: A Journey Along the Atlantic Slave Route*. New York: Farrar, Straus and Giroux, 2007.

---. *Scenes of Subjection: Terror, Slavery, and Self-Making in Nineteenth-Century America*. New York: Oxford University Press, 1997.

Higginbotham, Evelyn B. *Righteous Discontent: The Women's Movement in the Black Baptist Church, 1880-1920*. Cambridge: Harvard University Press, 1993.

Hohfeld, Wesley Newcomb. "Fundamental Legal Conceptions as Applied in Judicial Reasoning." *The Yale Law Journal* 26.8 (1917): 710-70.

Honoré, A.M. "Ownership." *Oxford Essays in Jurisprudence*. Ed. Anthony G. Guest. Oxford: Oxford University Press, 1961. 370-75.

Jefferson, Thomas. *Notes on the State of Virginia.* Ed William Peden. Chapel Hill: The University of North Carolina Press, 1996.

---. *Writings: Autobiography/ Notes on the State of Virginia/ Public and Private Papers/ Addresses/ Letters*. Ed. Merrill D. Peterson. New York: Library of America, 1984.

Johnson, Walter. "To Remake the World: Slavery, Racial Capitalism, and Justice." *Boston Review* 19 October 2016. <http://bostonreview.net/race/walter-johnson-slavery-human-rights-racial-capitalism>.

---. *River of Dark Dreams: Slavery and Empire in the Cotton Kingdom*. Cambridge: Belknap Press of Harvard University Press, 2013.

---. *Soul by Soul: Life inside the Antebellum Slave Market*. Cambridge: Harvard University Press, 1999.

Kaye, Anthony E. *Joining Places: Slave Neighborhoods in the Old South*. Chapel Hill: University of North Carolina Press, 2007.

Locke, John. *Two Treatises of Government.* N.p.: Everyman, 1993.

---, and Kenneth Winkler. *An Essay Concerning Human Understanding: Abridged and Edited, with an Introduction and Notes*. Indianapolis: Hackett Publishing Company, 1996.

---, and C.B. Macpherson. *Second Treatise of Government*. Indianapolis: Hackett Publishing Company, 1980.

Logan, Rayford W. *The Negro in American Life and Thought: The Nadir, 1877-1901*. New York: Dial Press, 1954.

Lott, Eric. *Love & Theft: Blackface Minstrelsy and the American Working Class*. Oxford: Oxford University Press, 2013.

Macpherson, C.B. *The Political Theory of Possessive Individualism: Hobbes to Locke*. Vol. 84. Oxford: Clarendon Press, 1964.

Madison, James. "On Property." *National Gazette* 27 March 1792. Papers 14: 266-68. <http://press-pubs.uchicago.edu/founders/documents/v1ch16s23.html>.

Marx, Karl. *Capital: A Critique of Political Economy Volume 1*. London: Penguin Books, 1990.

The Movement for Black Lives. "A Vision for Black Lives: Policy Demands for Black Power, Freedom, and Justice – Platform." <https://policy.m4bl.org/>.

Muhammad, Khalil G. *The Condemnation of Blackness: Race, Crime, and the Making of Modern Urban America*. Cambridge: Harvard University Press, 2010.

Penningroth, Dylan C. *The Claims of Kinfolk: African American Property and Community in the Nineteenth-Century South*. Chapel Hill: University of North Carolina Press, 2003.

Radin, Margaret Jane. "Property and Personhood." *Stanford Law Review* 34.5 (1982): 957-1015. <www.jstor.org/stable/1228541>.

Ritterhouse, Jennifer L. *Growing Up Jim Crow: How Black and White Southern Children Learned Race*. Chapel Hill: University of North Carolina Press, 2006.

Robinson, Cedric J. *Black Marxism: The Making of the Black Radical Tradition*. Chapel Hill: University of North Carolina Press, 2000.

---. "Capitalism, Slavery and Bourgeois Historiography." *History Workshop Journal* 23.1 (1987): 122-40.

Singh, Nikhil P. "On Race, Violence, and so-Called Primitive Accumulation." *Social Text* 34.3 (2016): 27-50.

Smallwood, Stephanie. "Commodified Freedom: Interrogating the Limits of Anti-Slavery Ideology in the Early Republic." *Journal of the Early Republic* 24.2 (2004): 289-98.

Stanley, Amy D. *From Bondage to Contract: Wage Labor, Marriage, and the Market in the Age of Slave Emancipation*. Cambridge: Cambridge University Press, 1998.

Taylor, Keeanga-Yamahtta. *From #BlackLivesMatter to Black Liberation*. Chicago: Haymarket Books, 2016.

Thompson, Shirley E. "The Hard Work of Black Play: Charles Chesnutt's Conjure Tales and a Counterculture of Incorporation." *Leisure Studies* 27.4 (2008): 411-26.

Williams, Jesse. "2016 BET Humanitarian Awards Speech." <http://genius.com/Jesse-williams-2016-bet-humanitarian-award-speech-annotated>.

Woods, Clyde A. *Development Arrested: The Blues and Plantation Power in the Mississippi Delta*. London/New York: Verso, 1998.

After *Black Lives Matter*: Black Death, Capitalism, and Unfreedom

Rinaldo Walcott

Introduction: When Black Lives Do Not Matter

The cultural scene in Canada, especially its literary and art institutions, exhibit all the qualities of global anti-blackness that in this moment of *Black Lives Matter* we might notice if we so care to. I begin this short essay about the culture industries broadly construed, with the invoking of the ongoing murders of Black people in North America, because I believe that such murders are neither mere coincidence nor are they about to come to an end anytime soon. Indeed, if any single thing characterizes contemporary Black life in Canada, it is the way in which Black lives seem not to matter at all, especially in the nation's major institutions – museums, art galleries, universities, government, and so on. Indeed, if there ever was a time in the recent past when making such a claim would have been seen as entirely cynical or even wrong and out of place, that time has now passed.

Even the much vaunted and celebrated Canadian state policy of multiculturalism has not been able to stem the foundation and ongoing tide of anti-blackness in Canada. Everywhere you look, Black life is in dire straights in Canada. Whether we are looking at poverty, prisons, joblessness, under-employment, housing, education and the list could go on, Black life is mostly stuck somewhere at the bottom of every marker, along with Indigenous or Aboriginal and First Nation's peoples. What is particularly striking is that no level of government or any other major institution in the nation ever seems to find it necessary to speak directly to Black people about their collective well-being, and thus the pain that Black people are collectively living with and under remains mostly out of view to others.

I will therefore address the ways in which contemporary protests concerning the deaths of Black people in North America have cast new light on thinking about the ways in which capitalism and its multiple forms of unfreedom are the foundation of those deaths. Significantly, it is important to note that the history of political activism by Black Canadians has often focused on police shootings and other forms of police misconduct as well as other moments of cultural inequality. Working with the long and sustained Black critique of capitalism by Black intellectuals,[1] I suggest that Black death cannot be delinked from the ways in which cultural institutions operate. Here I argue that Black life is and will always

[1] Here I think of the body of work of W.E.B. Du Bois, Eric Williams, Walter Rodney, Cedric Robinson, and Ruthie Gilmore Wilson.

be shaped by forms of inequality, given that current capitalist foundations are premised on the historical foundation of the exploitation of Black unfree labour and simultaneously the excision of Black life from institutions and institutional power in part derived from that very labour. In this essay I suggest new forms of collective belonging and ways of life beyond capitalist organization and late modern articulations of the human as homoeconomicus.

The Politics of Compromise is Anti-black

The history of Black collective pain and exclusion is rather long, but I will locate my discussion of it from the 1980s onward herein. Indeed in 1971 the late Pierre Elliott Trudeau introduced his multicultural policy to the Canadian parliament stating clearly that it would not change the character of the nation as consisting of two founding peoples – English and French. In 1988, the then Prime Minister Brian Mulroney made multiculturalism an Act of the Canadian Charter of Rights and Freedoms which is an Act of the Constitution. Between the move from Policy to Act, political and cultural organizing among and by Black people, along with many others, achieved significant gains that mostly bears fruit in the late 1980s and throughout the 1990s.

In the late 1980s and 1990s activists' protests attempted to open up the possibilities for art-making by people of color across a wide range of disciplines and the results of this work cannot and should not be easily discounted in Canada. In publishing, for example, a range of small presses as well as major presses began to publish the works of non-white Canadians, producing a robust list of writers working in novels and in poetry. Indeed, in a certain register the cultural work was quite successful drawing on the discourse of multiculturalism to both contest representation and to produce forms of state and other kinds of recognition. In a different register the work was also tremendously personally and collectively painful and difficult and some individuals paid a significant personal and professional price for challenging the system as it was then. The challenge to institutional power at that time still bares its scars today. The silence on one of Canada's best living poets, NourbeSe Phillip, is a case in point. It appears that she has yet not been forgiven for her significant critiques of numerous Canadian cultural institutions and their racist programming as well as their structural racist exclusion.

What is quite profound about the art activism of that period is that activists already understood the problem to be a problem of structure. But in that moment, they understood the practice of exclusion and misrecognition to be structural and therefore alterable; I will return to structure later, but suffice it to say now, it is extremely clear that the structure was indeed not fixable and only malleable. The malleability of the structure allowed for a whole new set of structures to emerge to manage and buttress the inclusion of people of color into the existing institutions.

Those new institutional arrangements going under the names and functions of equity offices and equity officers came with well conceived and written policies meant to produce change. The newly established offices bearing the names of equity and diversity and sometimes anti-racism were in part conceived, developed, and implemented by cultural activists, many of whom were invited back by the institutions to sit on committees to spearhead institutional change. In fact, in the aftermath of such committee work many artists found themselves drawn into institutions to implement and run such offices. However, in the aftermath of 1980s/90s art activism, it is quite clear that equity offices, equity officers, and the most fantastic equity policies do not and cannot change structures that are fundamentally anti-black.

In her study *"Where Outreach Meets Outrage": Racial Equity at The Canada Council for the Arts (1989-1999)*, Andrea Fatona has documented this period of arts activism in Canada by concentrating on the Canada Council for the Arts (CC). The CC is a national body that funds professional artists across a range of disciplines. Its main method of assessment is the peer-review or juried method. Fatona documents the period between 1989 and 1999, a period that I have already claimed was the most fertile period of non-white artists' contestations of exclusion, their simultaneous piecemeal inclusion and a creative output that has since dwindled. In her study she interviews all of the major players, artists, and professionals who worked inside the CC, including its senior directors in the transformation of the CC's engagement with non-white artists. Fatona finds that Black artists-activists played a significant and leading role in organizing and challenging the institution, but also in leading and working with the institution to effect meaningful change. Indeed, meaningful change, if it could be called that, was fleeting and one might argue it was not achieved at all. In the aftermath of the heroic efforts of many cultural workers NorbeSe Phillip's critique remains important still. She wrote: "Multiculturalism as we know it, has no answers for the problem of racism or white supremacy – unless it is combined with a clearly articulated policy of anti-racism, directed at rooting out the effects of racist and white supremacist thinking" (Phillip 1992 qtd. in Fatona 2011: 119). Fatona writes that the CC eventually acknowledged institutional racism unlike other institutions, but such an acknowledgement did not and does not support a sustained level of engagement for Black artists across Canada (193). So why is this so?

Indeed, it is my contention that what became clearer post-2000 are the ways in which anti-blackness at the structural level has worked and continues to work to make Black art and Black art-makers disappear and/or only occupy a tangential relation to national institutions. Importantly, there is nothing like a crisis to demonstrate the ways in which racial capitalism shapes Black life. The repeated crises of the neoliberal economy alongside the security and surveillance of the post-9/11 state made this clear to many if it was not clear before. Fatona writes: "The issue of racial hierarchies amongst people of color was mentioned in relation to the First Advisory Committee for Racial Equality at the Canada Council for the

Arts. The issue also arose in my conversations with Black artists regarding multi-racial activist formations in the communities" (2011: 190). Racial hierarches work to produce 'the black' as the "dysselected" other, as Sylvia Wynter terms it, meaning the furthest away from whiteness and thus the most impossible to incorporate structurally (2003: 310). However, my argument is that incorporation is fundamentally impossible for 'the black.' Furthermore, the conditions under which incorporation is understood are so deeply freighted with the detritus of racial capital and white supremacist logics that incorporation can and only does occur at the symbolic level, leaving all other Black beings or Black life forms marked for poverty and death as a repetition of modern life (see Walcott).

The starkness of my claims is positioned alongside the accounting for how neoliberal changes in full effect produced an abundance of what Zymunt Bauman has termed "wasted lives." When one takes such an insight to the artworld and its institutions – art galleries, printing houses, museums, festivals, and so on –, one can see how these practices and conditions are linked to larger phenomena like Black death. The unsustainability of the project of incorporation is revealed in the moment in which what looks like change meets its demise in the moment of economic claims or a crisis of economy. I make this case because one could see a significant change in the Canadian artworld at the moment of art activism in the 1980s and 90s but once that long decade came to a close, the kinds of activities that had been previously present and made possible by activism disappeared in the 2000s. Why was it not sustained? The 2000s mark the full onslaught of the neoliberal project in Canada. Thus part of the story is the way in which the neoliberal reordering of the economics of the cultural sphere impacted how policies for equitably sharing resources were interrupted by a logics of efficiencies, radical individualism, managerialism, audit culture, etc. However, when neoliberalism and anti-blackness combine, the impact on Black art and Black art makers produced a profound context of disappearance and, one might say, remade the landscape in a manner that now calls for renewed forms of activism.

The world of writing is a case in point. The same writers who made the move from small presses to larger national and international presses exist today as they did two decades ago: Austin Clarke, Dionne Brand, Lawrence Hill, Cecil Foster, Andre Alexis, and so on. A few younger writers, such as Esi Adugyan or David Chariandy, have made it into the realm of publishing, but by and large Black writers remained locked out of significant forms of circulation and their work is mostly published by small, not well circulating presses. This inability to sustain ongoing incorporation in fact points to how fundamentally the structural underpinnings remain in place and are indeed anti-black. Incorporation only works temporally and temporarily at the moment of contestation and confrontation, but retaining its routinization it reverts back to exclusion and diminution. So I argue that the unsustainability of incorporation is not merely anti-black but that its anti-blackness is foundational to capitalism and its asymmetrical and disjunctive practices – what we call inequality.

Racial Capitalism Cannot be Reformed

We might want to ask why these failures exist despite what one might characterize, if being generous, as the good intentions of attempted social change? The reality is that the history of most contemporary anti-racism struggles has been fraught with the problem of attempting to repair or renovate a system that cannot be repaired. In fact, one might make the claim that if a politics of destruction is not central to contemporary political organizing and resistance then such actions find themselves in a repetitive cycle. That cycle will merely continually delay, to put it mildly, desires for freedom and liberation by compromise, interruption and the undermining of more radical actions through incorporation into late modern capital. The point I am making here is not new, but has been articulated by Frantz Fanon, Sylvia Wynter, and a host of intellectuals and scholars working in what we call the Black radical tradition.

The cultural industries are a particularly pernicious and difficult problem for racial capitalism. In the contemporary era when culture is invoked it is so often taken to be simply within the realm of representation – that is often understood as presence and recognition minus labour and compensation. The question of labour is often suspended or not acknowledged at all because the myth of art as something special and deeply personal still pervades how we tend to relate to it. Seldom are we forced to think of art as a form of labour, as requiring much more than the personal to animate its contributions to cultural life. So if in general understandings of art, the labour of art remains ephemeral, then for Black art-makers this problem is significantly compounded if not altogether not acknowledged as such. Since Black people hold a problematic relation to capitalism in general, it is further compounded for Black cultural workers, I would argue.

In what follows I am guided by Cedric Robinson's insights in *Black Marxism* to articulate an understanding of racial capitalism that underpins our contemporary moment and our logics of economy and aesthetics. By racial capital, I mean to signal the co-constitutive coupling of the history of unfree African labour (racial/African enslavement) and ongoing white supremacy and eurocentrism as producing the conditions through which Black life is conditioned, experienced, and made known. To account for racial capitalism as a significant and ongoing force we must acknowledge that transatlantic slavery is the foundation of modern capitalism both in practice and in its ideas. Edward Said's *Culture and Imperialism* remains one of the most significant excavations of the relationship between racial slavery, imperialism, and the emergence of the modern. However, Du Bois, Eric Williams, and Robinson have also contributed significantly to our understanding of the development of racial capitalism and how it underpins the world as we presently know and experience it. Indeed, their contributions point to how the modern world could not be as it presently is without the vast wealth acquired from African enslavement, plantation economy, and continental African colonial exploitation.

My assertion of racial capitalism is meant to make the link or provide the foundation for how 'discredited' cultural knowledges and practices that constitute anti-blackness, and the ways in which premature Black death shapes contemporary Black life, exist on the same continuum. The argument is that racial capitalism has embedded in it all the elements necessary for the comingling of economy and social and cultural death as well as physical death. From C.L.R. James's *The Black Jacobins* to Du Bois's *The Suppression of the Atlantic Slave Trade* and from *Black Reconstruction* to Williams's *Capitalism and Slavery*, these founding texts of racial capitalism offer us an analysis of modern capital that is indivisible from white supremacist and Eurocentric logics of the post-Columbus world. It is my argument, then, that strategies of inclusion framed as multiculturalism, equity, social justice, and so on cannot and do not work towards Black freedom and liberation, but instead retrench inequality and brutalities of all kinds. The last two decades have shown us that reforming the existing state does not ameliorate Black suffering, but instead works to uphold logics that already cast blackness aside, to put it mildly. What is at stake then, is a radical accounting of the underpinnings of contemporary life and how those underpinnings require Black waste and disposability as their very calculable logics.

Fred Moten, in his discussion of both Douglass and Marx, has been an astute analyst of the historical and contemporary relationship between Black unfreedom, labour and capitalism. Pinpointing how slavery makes 'the black' both commodity and labour, Moten argues that both capitalism and its critics, as in Marx, failed to account for the commodity that speaks. The inability to make such an accounting means that Black life remains perpetually unacknowledged as always complicating capital in ways that we have yet to fully grapple with beyond those of the Black radical tradition. Moten has argued that Black people are "laborers who were commodities before, as it were, the abstraction of labour power from their bodies and who continue to pass on this material heritage across the divide that separates slavery and 'freedom'" (6). To be clear, the enslaved is a commodity even before the arrival in the Americas as labourer and indeed the enslaved is never ever just labourer. It is the hybrid condition of labourer and its excess that complicated our historical present. Indeed to come to terms with it will require new forms of being together that neoliberalism prohibits us from thinking at this present time. Suffice it to say that we must now begin to imagine new modes of living lives that exceed capital as the foundational element of 'human' organization. By making such a claim I call modernist logics of capitalism into disrepute given that those logics underpin capitalism's brutal calculus that everywhere marks Black life for death from the ghettos of North America to the Strait of Gibraltar.

Let me return to the deadly outcomes of such anti-black logics and their cultural impact in the realm of the culture industries. Indeed, in Canada current debates concerning the proposed "Memorial to the Victims of Communism – Canada, a land of Refuge" in Ottawa championed by Prime Minister Stephen Harper; and similarly the proposed 'privately funded' Mother Canada monument on the East Coast (in a environmentally sensitive national park); alongside the now up and running Human Rights Museum in Winnipeg, all in my view represent significant outcomes and losses for a more radical collective possibility in Canada. The current conservative government and its neoliberal wealthy backers (in the case of the Canadian Museum of Immigration at Pier 21, the Human Rights Museum, and the Mother Canada monument [the Asper family]) have attempted to re-narrate Canadian history in a number of ways. Chief among those is to unproblematically forge identifications with a singular European past, as the outstretched arms of the proposed Mother Canada monument suggest, especially during and after the First and Second World Wars. This move works in a number of ways to project an image of Canada that the historical record actually does not support. But the institutions also function as sites for a liberal and corporate multiculturalism that reproduces racial hierarchies in numerous ways. For example the Black presence in all these institutions is extremely limited and largely framed only through twentieth-century migrations. Indeed to do otherwise would call attention of the history of slavery in Canada and even more so to a multicultural policy and rhetoric that obscures a pre-confederation Black presence and its attendant structural racisms, in favour of a more recent discourse of Canadian benevolence and multicultural inclusion. A benevolence and inclusion that requires forgetting late nineteenth-century racist migration legislation and enforcement that 'deemed unsuitable' Black peoples. It is my argument that the very logics and foundations of these institutions draw from historical and contemporary forms of anti-blackness that are so pervasive and diffuse that the logics of their very structure cannot comprehend what is at play and what then is at stake for Black subjecthood and Black lives.

The story of Africville and its destruction is another case in point. Let me briefly recount it here. Africville was a community settled by Black loyalists and their descendants in what later became the city of Halifax. In the 1960s the community was raised to the ground and its residents relocated. The community had been long neglected for city services and the neglect was a significant part of the excuse to demolition Africville. The Africville Seaview Baptist Church was the center of the Black community. Parks and Recreation Canada, which manages 'heritage sites,' is now responsible for managing the "memorial and museum" park that Africville has become with a replica Seaview church serving as the central piece. The city of Halifax in 2010 apologized for the destruction of Africville, but unlike other groups, Black Canadians have never received any form of apology from any federal government for slavery and ongoing anti-black discrimination. I retell the Africville story as an example of how incorporation works: it works to reproduce the status quo, as a finished and perfected modernity, not as an outcome of that which the modern must deny but also one from which the modern itself derives. Perfectibility is accorded to white logics of the world, while the terror of that perfectibility is shrouded in apologies that do not require the shape of the world to change. Such logics, as in the logic of apology and reconciliation, asks that those on whom the foundations of modernity where constructed take this world as it is.

When such logics are extended into the artworld similar dynamics are at play. I am suggesting that Black Canadian art-making relies on an infrastructure that was not designed to make Black art possible in the first instance, because it was fundamentally not structured to make Black life possible either. I think this is made clear to any of us who wish to see it now. Nonetheless if we can be clear about the contexts within which Black life and Black art-making happens and is produced we must contend with the late modern capitalist structural anti-blackness that continually seeks to make blackness disappear from anything called Canadian despite claiming otherwise. Therefore what we might call the reformist (and I don't use that word as a bad word) efforts of the 1980s and 1990s which meant to produce modes or practices to make Black artists intelligible and recognizable to various art institutions have significantly run their course and might be marked as failure. Reform is not always and everywhere useless though, reform can be read as a compromise on to something altogether more promising. Indeed, many cultural institutions could well point to individuals and for sure to policies and practices coming from that period as sources of learning from the historical past. However, on further investigation something more troubling comes into sight.

Across the cultural industries in Canada Black work gets some engagement, but truth be told, often that engagement is for reasons that produce liberal and corporate multiculturalism to benefit the narrative of a benevolent state and its institutions. Indeed, many an institution believes, for example, that if they show one Black artist that they have done their share of work, as one noted curator at a university gallery has reportedly said. Similarly, institutions refuse to acknowledge that the scholarly and intellectual apparatus necessary for the intellectual project of Black art-making is crucial to its reception. Therefore universities in Canada are deeply implicated in the problem I am narrating here as well. The limited numbers of Black academics is a significant problem, but as well the demands that their work address certain areas also produce forms of performative engagement that buttresses the status quo keeping things just as they already are.

Conclusion

Indeed Canada's Black population tends to mirror Black Briton in a number of ways ranging from art to education. The literary scene, mentioned above, mirrors that of Britain. Why the similarity? Recently, the Black British writer Bernadine Evaristo (ALA conference 2015 in Bayreuth, Germany) gave an account of the same time period in Britain in which a similar dynamic was at play. She, too, recalled the activism of the 1980s, the burgeoning of work in the 1990s, and its disappearance in the 2000s. She spoke of multiple efforts currently to rebuild and to sustain the public presentation and sustenance of Black artistic contributions in

Britain. Evaristo's account is important in that it further indexes how racial capitalism works across the globe and especially in so-called western metropolises. The Native American artist Jimmie Durham has pointed out that the contemporary museum practices what he calls "vampirical activities" (20). His critique means to alert us to the ways the museum has come to learn to work with its past in the aftermath of the 'culture wars' without actually changing its foundations. Vampires only expire when they are totally destroyed, given that the very foundation of capital both in its economic and ideological underpinnings are structurally anti-black, we have no choice left to us but to imagine and put into practice a different world, one in which having to claim Black lives matter is greeted with puzzlement.

Works Cited

Bauman, Zymunt. *Wasted Lives: Modernity and Its Outcasts*. Cambridge: Polity Press, 2004.

Durham, Jimmie. "Cowboys and…." *Third Text* 12.4 (1990): 5-20.

Fatona, Andrea. "Arts Funding, the State and Canadian Nation-Making." *Critical Inquiries: A Reader in Studies of Canada*. Ed. Lynn Caldwell, Carrianne Leung, and Darryl Leroux. Halifax: Fernwood Publishing, 2013. 33-50.

---. *"Where Outreach Meets Outrage": Racial Equity at The Canada Council for the Arts (1989-1999)*. Dissertation. University of Toronto, 2011. <https://tspace.library.utoronto.ca/handle/1807/31747>.

Moten, Fred. *In The Break: The Aesthetics of the Black Radical Tradition*. Minneapolis: University of Minnesota Press, 2003.

Robinson, Cedric J. *Black Marxism: The Making of the Black Radical Tradition*. (1983). Chapel Hill: University of North Carolina Press, 2000.

Said, Edward. *Culture and Imperialism*. New York: Vintage, 1993.

Walcott, Rinaldo. "The Problem of the Human: Black Ontologies and 'the Coloniality of Our Being.'" *Postcoloniality – Decoloniality – Black Critique: Joints and Fissures*. Ed. Sabine Broeck and Carsten Junker. Frankfurt a. M./ New York: Campus Verlag, 2014. 93-108.

Wynter, Sylvia. "Unsettling the Coloniality of Being/Power/Truth/Freedom: Towards the Human, After Man, Its Overrepresentation – An Argument." *CR: The New Centennial Review* 3.3 (2003): 257-337.

---. "1492: A New World View." *Race, Discourse, and the Origin of the Americas*. Ed. Vera Lawrence Hyatt and Rex Nettleford. Washington: Smithsonian Institution Press, 1995. 5-57.

Exhibiting Inequality at the Canadian Museum for Human Rights

Jodi Giesbrecht

Introduction

Over the past several decades, museums around the world have increasingly focused on a wide array of social and political issues in their exhibitions and related programming. Constituting a profound shift in conventional museological practice, this effort to grapple with subjects not previously included in sites of public history – subjects related to race, gender, class, sexual orientation and gender identity, disability, human rights and social justice, and similar issues, for instance – has also required museums to address the myriad ways in which inequality has shaped both historical and contemporary experiences across a number of social, cultural, economic, and political spheres. Because inequality affects such diverse sites of experience, museological efforts to examine such issues must embrace a wide range of methodological, theoretical, and curatorial frameworks, and examine a host of distinct subjects including state and institutional practices, social norms and cultural beliefs, legal discourse, and economic structures.

This paper will discuss the subject of inequality in the context of current museological practice, using the recently opened Canadian Museum for Human Rights (CMHR) as a case study to examine the ways in which museums are grappling with questions of equality and inequality, justice and injustice. After providing an overview of recent trends in museological practice and a discussion of the CMHR's exhibition content and curatorial approach, I consider some of the challenges and opportunities in treating inequality as the subject matter of public institutions like museums. In particular, I emphasize the difficulties in curating exhibitions on subjects like inequality, which have both abstract and concrete dimensions and must be examined through an intersectional lens. Curatorial practice that takes seriously the subject of inequality and that seeks to contribute positively to human rights and social justice, then, must adopt a self-reflexive approach that acknowledges the ways in which museums themselves, as institutions of power and privilege, are embedded in discourses of hierarchy and exclusion.

Museological Practice

History – Museums

Museums, particularly in the West, have a long history of perpetuating inequality. Founded during the height of Western imperialism, many museums were built to house vast collections of curios, specimens, and appropriated or stolen material culture from Indigenous and other populations of colonial territories. Displaying such items in ways that emphasized themes of Anglo-Saxon superiority, racial hierarchies, human mastery over nature, and imperial might, museums produced and reproduced a host of exclusions and marginalizations based on Victorian notions of race, gender, ability, class, species, and related categories. In Canada, a settler colony of Great Britain, late nineteenth and early twentieth-century museums' collection and exhibition of local natural history specimens and Indigenous material culture symbolized the supposed success of white Anglo settlers in mastering what was perceived to be a wild and dangerous frontier (Sheets-Pyenson 5). Emblems of colonialism and racist, patriarchal ideas about progress and civilization, then, museums have been deeply implicated in the production of inequality and injustice across a wide number of spheres.

New Museology and Engaged Subject Matter

The history of museums as sites of appropriation and exclusion is key to understanding the profound changes that occurred in the mission and mandate of many such institutions during the last quarter of the twentieth century and continuing to the present day. Some scholars and museologists have dated this shift as beginning in the 1960s and 70s, when individuals and organizations more broadly challenged the status quo and demanded greater rights and equality (Message 28). Beginning at that time, museums changed the focus of their collecting and exhibitions programs and re-evaluated their educational roles to address and engage with pressing social and political issues, to repatriate appropriated, stolen, or otherwise ill-acquired artefacts to their owners and communities, and to include the stories of peoples such as women, minorities, racialized communities, persons with disabilities, and others whose experiences were conventionally misrepresented, stereotyped, or excluded altogether from conventional museum exhibitions. Growing more and more aware of their capacity of museums to effect issues of equality, justice, and respect, then, museums have come to recognize this form of engagement as a social responsibility, seeking to exert their cultural authority in ways that challenge narratives of power and exclusion (Sandell 4-5). Museologist Stephen Weil has described this as a movement from an inward to an outward focus, "from being *about* something to being *for* somebody," describing the supposedly 'new' museum as "a transformed and redirected institution that can, through its public-service orientation, use its very special competencies in dealing with objects to contribute positively to the quality of individual human lives and to enhance the well-being of human communities" (231).

The efforts of many museums to rectify practices of exclusion and to address important social and political issues has also entailed a profoundly self-reflexive awareness of the myriad ways their cultural capital mediates broader societal relations. Influenced by postmodernist and poststructuralist challenges to the concepts of progress, objectivity, and authenticity or truth, recent museological theory and practice has become attuned to the ways in which the collection and presentation of artefacts or other forms of exhibitions are neither neutral nor value-free activities but are laden with relations of power to shape and frame narratives and meaning more broadly. Efforts to develop exhibitions and programming in conversation with communities, to enhance awareness of issues like cultural appropriation, to seek visitor engagement and user-generated content, and to promote education and participation have been essential means of moving toward a museological practice that challenges dominant narratives, represents histories of conventionally marginalized people, examines issues of difference and equality, critiques stereotypes, and fosters equality, justice, and respect (Sandell 9; Fleming 213).

Canadian Museum for Human Rights

Overview of Galleries and Curatorial Approach

The Canadian Museum for Human Rights (CMHR) opened in September 2014. Located in Winnipeg, Manitoba, Canada, the CMHR's mandate is "to explore the subject of human rights, with special but not exclusive reference to Canada, in order to enhance the public's understanding of human rights, to promote respect for others and to encourage reflection and dialogue" (Canada section 15.2). The CMHR was first envisioned by Winnipeg businessman Israel Asper as a centre for Holocaust and human rights education, and in 2008 was established as a national museum, the first to have been built ground-up since 1967, and is located outside Canada's national capital region of Ottawa Ontario. Guided by five core principles related to dialogue, commitment, integrity, architecture, and accessibility, the CMHR aspires to create meaningful and relevant encounters with core human rights principles.

Exhibition content at the CMHR was developed through a participatory and collaborative process, beginning in 2009 with a series of public engagement sessions that were held in each of Canada's thirteen provinces and territories. Museum representatives were joined by a Content Advisory Committee that consisted of a group of human rights scholars, lawyers, activists, and experts, and met with thousands of Canadians to listen to their perspectives regarding the kinds of issues and stories they wished to see included in a human rights museum. This public engagement process resulted in a 2010 report published by the Content Advisory Committee, to convey the first-hand stories, experiences, and perspectives of Canadians. As noted by the CAC,

> asking the public to contribute their stories and ideas was not only a sure way to provide the Museum with a wealth of stories, it was also an important act for an organization that is premised on inclusion: to practise what it preached and to reach out to begin a conversation with people across the vast and diverse country of Canada. (2)

The Museum's in-house subject matter experts used a variety of methodologies in further identifying, developing, and refining exhibition content, including archival, oral history, community-based, and digital research tactics. A variety of peer reviewers, advisory councils, designers, media producers, interpretive specialists, and others collaborated in bringing exhibition ideas to reality.

Content within the Canadian Museum for Human Rights is grounded in ideas as opposed to objects. As opposed to curating displays around a collection of material artefacts, the CMHR begins first with the subject matter and ideological approach and identifies various assets, whether physical or digital, to tell the story through a variety of means, including passive, active, participatory, and immersive. The Museum's collection is comprised not of digital assets and not three-dimensional objects, most notably its collection of oral history interviews with those whose lives have been affected by human rights issues or who have dedicated their lives to such activism. With ten permanent and two temporary galleries, the CMHR's exhibition includes over 100 hours of video, five feature films, an immersive multimedia experience, a 360 degree film, 26 small format films, 27 large scale linear media projections, 512 video clips, 2543 images, 18 mixed media story niches, 19 digital interactives, and over 100,000 words of original text in Canada's two official languages, French and English.

The CMHR's ten core galleries are framed thematically rather than chronologically. Beginning in the gallery entitled *What Are Human Rights?*, visitors are first introduced to the concept of human rights from a variety of perspectives, including legal, cultural, philosophical, political, and historical. The subsequent gallery, *Indigenous Perspectives*, contains exhibitions that examine rights and responsibilities from the points of view of Inuit, First Nations, and Métis and includes an outdoor space for smudging and ceremony. The following two galleries, *Canadian Journeys* and *Protecting Rights in Canada*, provide stories in historical and legal contexts on the key issues, events, milestones, and struggles that have animated Canada's human rights history. Visitors then encounter a suite of galleries that contain a greater amount of international content: *Examining the Holocaust*, which looks at the Holocaust through key human rights themes including the abuse of state power, war and genocide, and persecution, including an effort to understand how individuals become complicit in such atrocities, *Turning Points for Humanity*, which examines the Universal Declaration of Human Rights and related declarations and covenants as well as grassroots movements from around the world that have sought to put the ideals of the UDHR into practice, and *Breaking the Silence*, which uses primary documentary evidence – oral histories, documents, photographs, archival materials – presented in an interactive digital study table to examine a number of mass atrocities and genocides with a focus on individual and community efforts to expose such violations and bring perpetrators to justice. Two subsequent galleries examine subjects geared toward children and adolescents such as cyberbullying, media literacy, youth activism, education, and children's rights, while a gallery called *Rights Today* focuses on contemporary global affairs with an effort to draw connections between Canadian and international issues and between different areas of human rights activism. In addition, two temporary galleries allow the Museum to bring in a number of externally produced exhibitions on a rotating schedule.

In developing content for these galleries, the CMHR employed a number of strategies to align its methodological practice with its subject matter – in other words, to ensure that principles tied to human rights and social justice grounded not just exhibition content, but also research and curatorial practices. Striving toward processes that are inclusive, participatory, accessible, and relevant, the Museum desires to present stories that give back to communities and individuals whose stories are being shared, that create space for dialogue, and that fight back against discrimination, marginalization, and inequality. An important means of doing so is through the presentation of multiple voices and multiple perspectives on difficult subjects, and the privileging of direct testimony over museological interpretation, facilitated through digital means of exhibiting personal stories. Emphasizing non-linearity, user-generated content, personal storytelling, interactivity, and diverse voices, exhibits seek to challenge the singularity of narratives and experiences typical of earlier historiographical and museological practice. Of course, there exists a gap between such ideals of inclusion and equality and the reality of museums' collections and exhibitions that are inevitably shaped by issues of power, privilege, exclusion, and hierarchy, to which I will return subsequently.

Accessibility is an important means through which the CMHR addresses inequality with regard to methodology and practice. Setting world standards for inclusive design, the Museum has worked closely with an Inclusive Design Advisory Council, which has been integral in ensuring accessibility is foundational to all programs and projects at the Museum. Given the CMHR's emphasis on new media, technology, and digital platforms as means of storytelling, the need for accessible interfaces and installations was early on identified as a key priority to ensure visitors with mobility, visual, auditory, and other forms of disability could access content. Inclusive design as such became "not a design style, but an orientation to design" (Wyman et al.). Inclusive standards were applied across all facets of the Museum's operational and museological functions, from exhibitions, collections, and programs, to human resource practice, architecture, and procurement. Within the exhibition, captions, ASL/LSQ, described video, transcriptions, universal keypads, Universal Access Points or UAPs consisting of tactile floor strips for cane detection, Braille markers, and Bluetooth beacons that activate text-to-speech audio descriptions, and an approach to graphic design grounded in inclusiveness are some of the ways in which inclusiveness is integrated in all aspects of the CMHR's practice. Given the dynamic and rapidly evolving nature of both technological platforms and inclusive design, these tactics will necessarily continue to evolve (Wyman et al.).

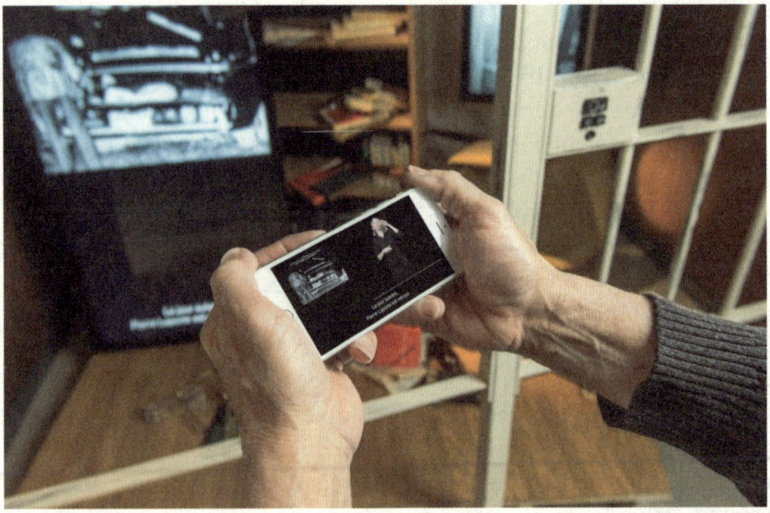

Fig. 1: Canadian Museum for Human Rights' mobile app. The Museum's mobile app contains accessibility features such as described audio and ALS/LSQ interpretation. Photo: Canadian Museum for Human Rights/Ian McCausland

Exhibits on Inequality at the CMHR

The subject of inequality is both abstract in its theoretical articulations, and concrete in its lived experience; as scholars have noted, equality is "one of the most cherished and controversial rights" in that it is primarily redistributive in nature, challenges systemic inequalities and the injustices embedded in relational and institutional practices, and critiques the ways in which rights and freedoms, power and privilege, and material resources are distributed throughout society (Faraday et al. 10). Concepts of equality and inequality, then, are central to human rights discourse across a number of areas of study.

As such, the subject of inequality runs across all ten of the CMHR's core galleries and is examined in exhibitions focused on historical, legal, and contemporary issues. Given the Museum's thematic approach to storytelling, there is no single exhibit or gallery on the topic of inequality; rather, it is interwoven throughout each of the galleries to demonstrate the diverse ways equality and inequality intersect with a number of issues related to human rights and social justice. These exhibits address topics including race, gender, class, sexual orientation and gender identity, disability, age, religion, and related categories of identity and experience, interrogating the myriad ways inequality is produced and reproduced within these broader matrices of power.

Fig. 2: The *What Are Human Rights?* gallery. Exhibits within this gallery combine personal storytelling, artefact displays, and other mixed-media installations to convey the multiple ways in which human rights can be understood. Photo: Canadian Museum for Human Rights/Ian McCauslan

Within the *What Are Human Rights?* gallery, visitors encounter a series of exhibits that connect abstract human rights concepts including equality and inequality, justice and injustice, dignity, respect, and the violation of dignity and respect, with concrete lived experiences. A large immersive multimedia experience features six individual Canadians who speak candidly about their lived experiences, including an Iraqi-Canadian artist who uses art as a means of freedom of expression to speak out against oppression, a young woman who challenged discrimination by advocating for a gay-straight alliance to be established in her conservative religious school, and a Paralympic swimmer who speaks to the challenges of inclusion and equality for persons with disabilities within sports. In drawing parallels between everyday experience and broader efforts at codifying protections against discrimination and related forms of rights abuses, such exhibits strive toward helping visitors understand the relevance of human rights and social justice in their everyday lives and connect their own struggles to those of others, past and present, within Canada and abroad. By introducing the public to such spheres of lived experience in addition to human rights conventions and declarations, the museum hopes to foster greater understanding of concepts that can otherwise seem disconnected from everyday life.

A variety of exhibits within the *Canadian Journeys* gallery address inequality in historical and contemporary contexts and across a wide range of issues. Eschewing a teleological or chronological framework, this particular gallery presents content in an eclectic, non-linear way through distinct mixed-media and digital approaches, intended to convey the complexity and multiplicity of human rights discourse and to challenge singular narratives. Here visitors encounter exhibits on the forced relocation and dispossession of Japanese-Canadians during the Second World War and related episodes of civilian internment, the efforts of Viola Desmond, a Black businesswoman who lived in Nova Scotia and challenged racial segregation in the mid-twentieth century, the head tax and immigration exclusions leveled against Chinese Canadians throughout the nineteenth and twentieth centuries, the appalling rates of missing and murdered Indigenous women in contemporary Canada, the history and continued impact of the system of Indian Residential Schools funded by the Canadian government and carried out by a number of churches that forcibly removed over 150,000 children from their homes and communities, the experiences of temporary agricultural workers from Latin-American countries who work in Canada's fruit and vegetable agro-industries, and a large number of other stories. Relying heavily on oral histories and first-hand testimonies, these exhibits seek to build a sense of empathy with those whose stories are being told and to draw connections between the number of sites and categories of experience through which inequality is made manifest.

Income inequality is examined in this gallery through a number of exhibits focused on the historical evolution of social policy in twentieth-century Canada. Addressing specific elements of social policy such as old age pensions, unemployment insurance, medicare, maternity leave, pay equity, and related issues, these exhibits point to the profound transformation of ideas regarding rights and responsibilities to security and welfare that occurred during the first half of the twentieth century in Canada, when many came to see issues of poverty and unemployment not as individual moral failings as had been the dominant perspective in the past, but as structural consequences of industrial capitalism and, in response, increasingly mobilized into alternative political parties or concerned citizens' groups to demand greater social security from the federal state. The postwar establishment of a welfare state along universalist principles, as well as the negative consequences of social policy in perpetuating many forms of hierarchies and exclusions – the colonial interventions into the ways of life of Indigenous communities, the regulation of women's bodies and sexualities, or the forced sterilization of persons with disabilities, all in the name of health, science, and progress, for instance – as well as the recent retrenchment of social security are also examined.

The subject of inequality is examined in a number of additional exhibits and galleries. In the "Protecting Rights in Canada" gallery, for instance, a gallery focused on human rights in a legal and constitutional context, a series of exhibits approach the subject through a legal framework, demonstrating the ways in which legal instruments such as the *Canadian Charter of Rights and Freedoms* defines matters of equality as grounds for legal protection. The right to equality is enshrined in s.15 of the *Charter*, which states that "every individual is equal before and under the law and has the right to equal protection and equal benefit of the law without discrimination and, in particular, without discrimination based on race, national or ethnic origin, colour, religion, sex, age or mental or physical disability." The intersectionality of inequality with discrimination points as well to the means through which categories of difference are expressed in and through the law and therefore must be challenged through legal as well as social and political means (Sheppard 35). Given that s.15 equality rights have been interpreted by Canadian legal authorities as substantive rather than merely formal (Greene 264; Porter 25-26), exhibits also address a series of court cases through which laws perpetuating inequality have been overturned, often through popular mobilization culminating in litigation. An interactive debate table in this gallery uses multimedia content to explore ten landmark court cases in recent Canadian history in which visitors are encouraged to participate, express their views, and debate with others. Thus, this gallery also focuses on the grassroots efforts of individuals and organizations to mobilize against discriminatory laws that reproduce rather than mitigate inequality, using interactive and participatory multimedia installations to foster increased engagement. The effort to combine recognition of both top-down or state-led initiatives and bottom-up or grassroots-led initiatives seeks to indicate the many ways in which the law has itself been a site through which inequality and injustice have been contested and negotiated by state and civilian actors alike.

Such issues are also addressed in subsequent galleries focused on international content; in the Turning Points for Humanity gallery, for instance, the Universal Declaration of Human Rights is examined as a well-intentioned beginning of a more expansive effort to articulate, define, and codify human rights and fundamental freedoms, including the Convention on the Elimination of Discrimination Against Women (CEDAW), the United Nations Declaration on the Rights of Indigenous Peoples (UNDRIP), and a variety of others. Here too, exploration of legal norms and formal declarations is balanced by exhibits that challenge the essentializing logic and Western bias of such instruments and that examine the agency and activism of ordinary people around the world who have struggled against inequality, who have struggled to make the abstract ideals espoused by human rights discourse into lived realities. Running throughout these exhibits is recognition of the many violations and challenges that persist despite the codification of rights, and problematization of the efficacy of formal instruments to combat structural abuses such as inequality.

Fig. 3: The *Turning Points for Humanity* gallery. Material on the articles of the Universal Declaration of Human Rights and related covenants is juxtaposed with stories about grassroots forms of activism and mobilization from around the world. Photo: Canadian Museum for Human Rights

Other exhibits similarly strive to examine the ways in which inequality is experienced and contested outside the sphere of litigation or codification and is reinforced by deeply held ideologies, stereotypes, and values that structure everyday life. Issues that visitors can readily identify with, including gender equity, sexual orientation, poverty, race and ethnicity, employment and income, ability, age, and related topics encourage understanding of the ways in which daily experiences intersect with structural issues, from capitalism to colonialism to patriarchy, in shaping the forces of equality and inequality. Given the large numbers of schoolchildren and youth who visit the Museum, stories featuring young people who have taken action against discrimination or other injustices are particularly valuable in promoting learning on this subject. The gallery entitled *Inspiring Change*, for example, contains a large artefact case that examines several issues including the activism of students for affordable tuition in Quebec, the use of graffiti art as a form of protest in Egypt, and the efforts of youth in Georgia to organize their school's first racially integrated prom in 2014. The *Actions Count* gallery similarly features initiatives against bullying and related youth-established projects that have targeted inequality in spheres of life relevant to young audiences.

On a global level, the *Rights Today* gallery combines a number of mixed media installations to draw connections between diverse human rights struggles in all parts of the world. An interactive map organizes content within five major themes – women's rights, children's rights, Indigenous rights, labour rights, and the right to health – through a digital map that integrates twitter and RSS feeds alongside data visualizations. An installation featuring the activism of Canadian and international human rights defenders emphasizes the significance of individual agency in challenging oppression, while an exhibit called *Everyday Objects* interrogates the abuses and violations that often shape commodity chains behind popular consumer goods. In this gallery, similar to those already described, inequality is a theme that runs across the exhibition in order to demonstrate the intersectionality of human rights issues with those of social justice.

Exhibiting Inequality – Challenges and Opportunities

While not exhaustive, this high level overview of the Canadian Museum for Human Rights' mission, mandate, curatorial approach, and subject matter highlights some of the opportunities and challenges in studying issues like inequality through the medium of collections and exhibitions. Given the fairly recent shift in museological focus to matters of human rights and social justice within museums, the kinds of methodologies, strategies, and approaches best suited to examine these subjects are only beginning to be developed (Orange and Carter 111). As such, a host of theoretical and practical challenges remain. These questions include the means through which museums might represent difficult subjects and abstract concepts in publically accessible ways, the role of balance and perspective in museological practice, and the need to engage in continuous self-reflection on the social responsibility of museums as institutions of power.

Intersectionality and Ideology

In providing an overview of museum content, it's evident that the multifaceted ways in which inequality intersects with myriad forms of discrimination, marginalization, and exclusion, and the dialogic relation between inequality and processes of racialization, colonialism, patriarchy, and capitalist exploitation cannot be treated in its totality in any one particular exhibition but must be interwoven throughout diverse exhibitions dealing with human rights and social justice broadly. Further, these concepts must be rendered accessible and understandable, and connected to visitors' lived experiences if they are to have meaning. Digital and other forms of storytelling provide one mechanism through which difficult subject matter is rendered relevant and accessible; oral history as well as other non-textual means can provide space for creative engagement with non-traditional forms of learning.

Yet, in interpreting abstract subject matter in easily understandable and accessible ways, an additional and related difficulty becomes the need to take caution against teleology or oversimplified narratives that reduce the complexity of human rights discourse to a kind of gradual unfolding of universalization and social betterment. As academics such as Samuel Moyn have noted, the propensity toward whiggishness is particularly acute in human rights scholarship, which often revises history as a kind of staging ground for the gradual but inevitable realization of rights and freedoms (6). With regard to the subject of inequality, museums must be cautious not to suggest that the codification of rights or growing acceptance of the concept of human rights has reduced inequality or ameliorated injustice. Here the need to recognize continued violations of rights despite legal protections, as well as the use of rights as rhetoric to mask such abuses, is imperative in mitigating against the tendency toward teleology that museological exhibitions often inadvertently convey, as well as against the tendency toward abstraction that scholarly writing typically embodies.

Two examples from the CMHR illustrate these points. The *Human Rights through Time* exhibit that comprises a key element in the Museum's introductory *What Are Human Rights?* gallery presents 100 events, ideas, and measures related to the evolution of concepts of justice, equality, liberty, and dignity from ancient history to the present day, in a global context. The basic conceptualization of this exhibit, then, is inherently teleological; although the timeline represents abuses of rights, mass atrocities and genocides, and related violations alongside progressive measures such as the establishment of international covenants and human rights monitoring bodies, a timeline of human rights history in and of itself cannot avoid the kinds of reductionist analyses cautioned against by Moyn and others. The theoretical and conceptual organization of the CMHR's *Canadian Journeys* gallery represents an alternative approach. The deliberate eschewing of a chronological framework in favour of a thematic approach that emphasizes multiple voices, complexity, and incomplete or open-ended narratives is better able to challenge whiggish or progressive narratives.

Balance and Perspective

The CMHR, similar to other public institutions with an educational mandate, must also be careful to maintain balance and multiple perspectives throughout its exhibition and program offerings. Accordingly, we cannot solely provide a cavalcade of human rights abuses and violations but must also tell stories of courage, resilience, agency, and struggle, and offer tools through which visitors may feel empowered to take action against injustice and inequality in their own lives. The representation of differing points of view and multiple perspectives is similarly critical in providing space for the accommodation of diversity and freedom of expression and in ensuring the voices of conventionally marginalized communities are heard. In practice, this need for balance and multiple points of view can be difficult to achieve.

In telling the stories of temporary agricultural migrant workers who labour in Canada's fruit and vegetable, meatpacking, and related industries, for instance, we used an approach that conveys workers' experiences in their own words and from their own perspectives. This exhibit, located in the *Canadian Journeys* gallery, features the stories of four such workers, told through four individual screens that play first-hand interview footage. The films do not include narration and seek to convey the workers' points of view rather than the Museum's. While this approach does much to convey the personal nature of human rights issues and encourage empathy from visitors, we cannot escape the fact that all content presented is still curated, organized, and framed in ways that reflect institutional objectives. The role of museums and related organizations in shaping and controlling knowledge, in this sense, cannot be avoided despite the effort to present experience from personal points of view.

Fig. 4: *An Uncertain Harvest*, 2014. An exhibition on the experiences of agricultural migrant workers at the Canadian Museum for Human Rights uses digital storytelling to convey migrants' perspectives in their own words. Photo: Canadian Museum for Human Rights/Aaron Cohen

Museums, generally speaking, have much work to do in building trust with individuals and communities whose culture and ways of life have been misrepresented and misappropriated, the museological shift toward greater engagement and sensitivity in recent decades notwithstanding. Such processes must necessarily be ongoing.

Self-Reflexiveness

Finally, museums must, in addressing matters of social and political concern such as inequality, engage in continuous self-reflection with regard to the social responsibility and political capacity as public institutions. In seeking greater public engagement and involvement of wide publics in participating in exhibition development and related programming, museums continue to reach toward mandates that are increasingly activist in nature. While there is much to laud in such efforts, we might also evaluate our expectations of museums and consider their capacity to realize social betterment (Conn 15-17). The line between social engagement and political engagement, for instance, is often fuzzy; to be effective in their role as educational institutions and in dealing seriously with questions such as inequality or injustice, museums must be free from corporate or political interference. Ongoing evaluation of strategies, motivations, and influences is integral in truly serving the public interest.

A related concern is for museums to recognize the tension inherent in the effort to promote progressive social agendas, on the one hand, and the many ways in which museums remain institutions of power and privilege, on the other hand. Despite efforts to engage communities, share curatorial authority, embrace multiple perspectives, include those conventionally excluded from museological representations, and related strategies designed to combat inequality, museums inevitably continue to privilege some stories over others and organize knowledge. The question is thus how museums might challenge hierarchies and exclusions while recognizing their own implication in those structures of knowledge (Sandell and Nightengale 42; Hallam and Street 1-9). Who holds the power to represent what stories, and for what purposes, remains a fundamental problematic of museological and curatorial practice (Young 209).

The decolonizing curatorial and museological approaches the CMHR has taken to representing content on Indigenous rights reflect some of these concerns. Locating Indigenous content across all of the Museum's core galleries, representing stories from individual and community points of view, integrating exhibits curated by Indigenous artists and scholars, and including exhibits on the history of colonialism and violation of Indigenous rights within the narrative of Canadian history are some of the ways in which the Museum has recognized its responsibility to confront issues of colonial injustice and the history of museums in perpetrating such injustice; still, as a Crown corporation, the capacity of the CMHR to enact processes and practices that are wholly decolonial is questionable. Until a nation-to-nation relationship is established between the Canadian state and Indigenous nations, such efforts remain incomplete.

Fig. 5: The *Indigenous Perspectives* gallery. An installation features the perspectives and writings of three Indigenous authors and activists in their own words. Photo: Canadian Museum for Human Rights/Ian McCausland

In addressing social and political issues with critical perspectives, then, museums must be prepared to continuously negotiate a series of contradictions. They must provide space for sharing personal stories, including trauma, without indulging in a pornography of violence or a fetishization of personal or historical wounds, move toward decolonization and reconciliation while acknowledging the involvement of museums within processes of settler colonialism, engage broad publics while maintaining curatorial and research independence, and seek to effect progressive social change while understanding the capacity of museums to organize knowledge in regressive ways. Given that the turn toward social engagement and activism is still, relatively speaking, a recent phenomenon, the evolution of museological practices geared toward the amelioration of inequality must necessarily continue to evolve in the coming years.

Works Cited

Canada. House of Commons. *Bill C-42: An Act to Amend the Museums Act and to Make Consequential Amendments to Other Acts*. Library of Parliament 22 February 2008.

Canadian Charter of Rights and Freedoms. Part I of the *Constitution Act 1982*, being Schedule B to the *Canada Act 1982* (UK). 1982: c11.

Conn, Steven. *Do Museums Still Need Objects?* Philadelphia: University of Pennsylvania Press, 2010.

Content Advisory Committee. *Content Advisory Committee Final Report to the Canadian Museum for Human Rights*. Winnipeg: Canadian Museum for Human Rights, 2010.

Faraday, Fay, Margaret Denike, and M. Kate Stephenson (eds.). *Making Equality Rights Real: Securing Substantive Equality under the Charter*. Toronto: Irwin Law, 2006.

Fleming, David. "Positioning the Museum for Social Inclusion." *Museums, Society, Inequality*. Ed. Richard Sandell. London and New York: Routledge, 2002. 213-24.

Greene, Ian. *The Charter of Rights and Freedoms: 30+ Years of Decisions that Shape Canadian Life*. Toronto: James Lorimer & Company Ltd. Publishers, 2014.

Hallam, Elizabeth, and Brian V. Street. *Cultural Encounters: Representing 'Otherness.'* London/New York: Routledge, 2000.

Message, Kylie. *Museums and Social Activism: Engaged Protest*. London/New York: Routledge, 2014.

Moyn, Samuel. *The Last Utopia: Human Rights in History*. Cambridge: Belknap Press of Harvard University Press, 2010.

Orange, Jennifer A., and Jennifer J. Carter. "It's Time to Pause and Reflect: Museums and Human Rights." *Curator: The Museum Journal* 55.3 (2012): 259-66.

Porter, Bruce. "Expectations of Equality." *Diminishing Returns Inequality and the Canadian Charter of Rights and Freedoms*. Ed. Sheila McIntyre and Sanda Rodgers. Markham: LexisNexis Canada Inc., 2006. 25-39.

Sandell, Richard (ed.). *Museums, Society, Inequality*. London/New York: Routledge, 2002.

---, and Eithne Nightengale (eds.). *Museums, Equality, and Social Justice*. London/New York: Routledge, 2012.

Sheets-Pyenson, Susan. *Cathedrals of Science: The Development of Colonial Natural History Museums during the Late Nineteenth Century*. Kingston/Montreal: McGill-Queen's University Press, 1988.

Sheppard, Colleen. *Inclusive Equality: The Relational Dimensions of Systemic Discrimination in Canada*. Montreal/Kingston: McGill-Queen's University Press, 2010.

Weil, Stephen. "From Being About Something to Being for Somebody: The Ongoing Transformation of the American Museum." *Daedalus* 128.3 (1999): 229-58.

Wyman, Bruce, Corey Timpson, Scott Gillam, and Sina Bahram. "Inclusive Design: From Approach to Execution." *MW2016: Museums and the Web 2016*. 24 February 2016. <mw2016.museumsandtheweb.com/paper/inclusive-design-from-approach-to-execution/>.

Young, Lola. "Rethinking Heritage: Cultural Policy and Inclusion." *Museums, Society, Inequality*. Ed. Richard Sandell. London/New York: Routledge, 2002. 203-12.

Notes on Contributors

Julia Faisst is assistant professor of American Studies at the Catholic University of Eichstätt-Ingolstadt. Her fields of interest include American and US ethnic literatures and visual cultures, space and architecture, and class and poverty studies.

Jodi Giesbrecht is Manager of Research & Curation at the Canadian Museum for Human Rights (CMHR) in Winnipeg, Manitoba. The CMHR is the first museum solely dedicated to the study of human rights in a Canadian and international context.

Colin Gordon is F. Wendell Miller Professor in the Department of History at the University of Iowa. He is also a senior research consultant at the Iowa Policy Project, for which he has written or co-written reports on health coverage, economic development, and wages and working conditions.

Barbara Hahn is professor and chair of Economic Geography at the University of Würzburg. Her research interest is on urban geography, geographical trade, German Business in the United States, and retail globalization.

Lisa Keister is Gilhuly Family Professor in the Department of Sociology and director of Student Programs, Duke Network Analysis Center, at Duke University. Her research areas are economic sociology, organizations and management, and social networks as well as wealth accumulation and the factors that contribute to wealth disparities, including social networks, religion, and inheritance.

Susanne Pickel is professor of Political Science (Comparative Studies) at the University of Duisburg-Essen. Her research examines European political behavior, political culture, political participation, responsibility, transitional justice, and survey methodology.

Eberhard Rothfuß holds the chair of Social and Population Geography at the Geographical Institute of the University of Bayreuth. His research interests are pastoralism and ethnic tourism in Southern Africa, Afro-Brazilian identity, socio-spatial urban inequality (Favelas), collective governance, critical (Southern) theory, and intercultural hermeneutics.

Axel R. Schäfer is professor of American Studies at Johannes-Gutenberg-University Mainz. His research focuses on nineteenth- and twentieth-century US intellectual and cultural history, with a particular emphasis on religion and politics, transatlantic social thought, and public policy.

Kerstin Schmidt is professor of English and chair of American Studies at the Catholic University of Eichstätt-Ingolstadt and a board member of the Bavarian American Academy. Her research focuses on nineteenth- and twentieth-century North American literature and culture, with a particular emphasis on modern/postmodern drama and theater, ethnic writing in the United States and Canada, race and diaspora studies, media studies and radio culture as well as theories of space/place in American literature, photography, and architecture.

Shirley Thompson is associate professor of American Studies and African and African Diaspora Studies at the University of Texas at Austin. Her current work uses the lenses of law, economics, literature, and history to explore legacies of slavery for African-American encounters with property and ownership.

Rinaldo Walcott is associate professor and director of the Women and Gender Studies Institute at the University of Toronto. His research is centered in Black diaspora politics, gender and sexuality, and decolonial politics.

David Wilson is professor of Geography, Urban Planning, and the Unit for Criticism and Interpretive Theory at the University of Illinois at Urbana-Champaign. His research areas are urban political processes in cities of the global west, contemporary urban restructuring in North American cities, and the dynamics of change in America's Rust Belt urban centers.